The Libertarian Party

The Libertarian Party
and Other Minor Political Parties
in the United States

by

Joseph M. Hazlett II

McFarland & Company, Inc., Publishers
Jefferson, North Carolina, and London

British Library Cataloguing-in-Publication data are available

Library of Congress Cataloguing-in-Publication Data

Hazlett, Joseph M., 1958–
    The Libertarian Party and other minor political parties in the
United States / by Joseph M. Hazlett II.
        p.   cm.
    Includes bibliographical references and index.
    ISBN 0-89950-693-3 (lib. bdg. : 50# alk. paper) ∞
    1. Libertarian Party.   2. Third parties (United States politics)
3. Democracy—United States.   I. Title.
JK2391.L9H39   1992
324.273′8—dc20   91-50942
                                                                         CIP

Manufactured in the United States of America

McFarland & Company, Inc., Publishers
    Box 611, Jefferson, North Carolina 28640

To my children,
Emilee and Aimee,
this book is lovingly dedicated.
Allow your curiosity to grow,
for you will have to provide
the answers.

Acknowledgments

I would like to thank MMA for all her support, help, and most of all, patience while I was working on this endeavor.

Contents

1

Introduction

*Next to the Holy Trinity, the two-party system is the most
sacred concept in town.*

— Ed Clark, 1978

According to political scientist Clinton Rossiter:

> One of the most momentous facts about the pattern of American
> politics is that we live under a persistent, obdurate, one might say almost
> tyrannical, two-party system. We have the Republicans and we have the
> Democrats, and we have almost no one else. The extent of this tyranny
> of the two parties is most dramatically revealed in the sorry conditions
> of third parties in the U.S. today.[1]

Despite what Rossiter claims to be the sorry conditions of third parties,
they do exist and aspire to fill elected offices at all levels of government.
Third, alternative, or minor parties in the United States have offered candidates in just about every presidential election since the early 1800s. It is
obvious that most of their electoral success has been limited to the local,
state, and congressional offices since they have never captured the
presidency.[2]

The notion of a third party has never really been precisely defined.[3]
However, the term, third, or minor political party, has been applied to those
parties since the Civil War that have opposed the two major parties.[4] Minor
parties are an important feature of the U.S. electoral process and although
their rate of electoral success is minimal, they persistently appear on the
political landscape. As William Hesseltine notes:

> Although the number of separate "parties" in state and cities have run
> into the hundreds, their careers have been brief, their impact transitory,
> and their very names lost from memory. Few third parties have conducted
> national campaigns, and only a bare half-dozen can truthfully be said to
> have influenced national elections. Yet, by voicing grievances and by pro-
> posing panaceas, third parties have exerted significant influence upon the
> policies and programs of the major parties. In a curiously anomalous man-
> ner, third parties have bolstered the traditional two-party system.[5]

1

Nonetheless, minor parties have accomplished more in American politics than simply helping to maintain the survival of the two-party system.

In addition to influencing the ideas and policies of the two established parties, minor parties in the United States perform several functions. One function is to serve as a means for the expression of certain issues or reforms. In other words, "the high-jinks of third party activities have called attention to new ideas to be examined for future promises rather than feared as radical dangers."[6] Some scholars claim that minor parties are even more successful at formulating issues and reforms than the major parties.[7] This may be due to the fact that minor parties do not fear alienating a section of the electorate as much as the two major parties, and thus are more likely to experiment with new issue and reform ideas in their campaigns. Minor parties do not always realize their political limitations in building winning majorities as much as the major parties, and because of this they have sometimes been far in advance of the major parties as issue formulators.[8] Minor parties hope to convert voters to their views, but tend to do this in a manner that is markedly different from the major parties. Some are willing to challenge accepted norms, principles, and institutions of society while remaining rigidly dedicated to their ideological foundations, even if it means that they will suffer in terms of voter support. If they do propose a new idea or policy that is accepted by the public, then it may be adopted by one of the two major parties.[9]

A second function of minor political parties is to provide an avenue of protest for those minority groups discontented with prevailing majority views.[10] By serving as a vehicle of expression for the politically discontented or alienated, minor parties again force many issues onto the political agenda. They also provide a legitimate electoral alternative to those voters who believe themselves to be slighted or ignored by the major parties. Voters may view a minor party as a means of registering protest against the candidates and or issues backed by the major parties.[11] This feature of minor party dynamics may help to increase the level of participation in an election.

Some political scientists believe that minor parties serve as indicators of electoral realignment. For example, Walter Dean Burnham states that minor party protests can be called "protorealignment phenomena" in that a pattern emerges between these protests and electoral realignments.[12] In realigning elections, minor parties may serve as a bridge for voters to switch from one major party to the other.[13] The level of minor party activities may indicate a gap between the expectations of the electorate and the abilities of the major parties to satisfy these demands. When this takes place, an electoral realignment is possible, spurred on by the minor parties and their stress of the voter's needs, and the limits and realities of the political process.[14]

The level of minor party efforts can also indicate major party failures to satisfy the demands of the electorate.[15] Pendleton Herring concluded that "the rise of a third party to any position of influence would be a portent of serious rigidities in our political system. It would not indicate a movement to be frowned upon but would suggest that our [major] party leaders had failed in their task of harmonizing and adjusting the economic and social forces in their communities."[16] The electoral success of a minor party can signify that the two major parties have not performed according to the expectations and wishes of the electorate. This would imply that voters turn toward a minor party as a vehicle of representation and promotion for their particular issue preferences.[17]

The past few decades of American politics have witnessed the rise and fall of numerous minor political parties of varying significance. However, as Frederick Haynes has commented: "The utopian character of minor party demands, as they appear to the practical American, has aroused his sense of humor. His amusement has not always allowed him to see the real nature of the organization beneath the apparent absurdity."[18]

Some of the more recently formed minor parties, such as George Wallace's American Independent Party of 1968, have demonstrated a significant electoral impact.[19] With an increase in the percentage of independent voters, the minor party idea is not as hopeless of it once was.[20] It is possible that minor parties can appeal to independent voters for a variety of reasons, and thus may grow in size and electoral influence.

However, minor parties in the United States face a wide range of social, economic, and legal barriers that inhibit their growth, influence, and success. These barriers are discussed in detail later, but at this point it should be noted that, even with these substantial and numerous disadvantages, many minor parties have been able to achieve some electoral successes and therefore they cannot simply be dismissed as an occasional artifact in the body politic. Besides the two major parties, over thirty different minor party candidates have been supported in the electoral college at some time. Since 1824 only three times has no popular vote for a minor party been recorded in a presidential election.[21] As John Hicks noted in 1933:

> To the superficial observer the history of American third party movements might appear to be only a long succession of jeremiads. It is true enough that the successes of these parties at the polls have been ephemeral and their hopes of endurance unfounded. But their chronic reappearance is a fact in American history that cannot be overlooked. To dismiss third parties lightly under these circumstances is to show a lamentable disregard for the facts.[22]

Hicks is suggesting that minor parties should not be solely addressed in terms of electoral successes, but must also be considered for the many functions that they perform within the American political system.

study of 158 political parties in 53 nations.[31] Janda's study had the primary goal of imposing some intellectual order upon the mass of facts concerning political parties, and therefore present a conceptual framework for future analysis.[32] By organizing and interpreting factual materials and concepts drawn from the existing literature, Janda created a framework with value in its theoretical capacity.[33] In other words, the framework is "pretheoretical" in that it provides a basis for developing and testing hypotheses regarding party dynamics at some point in the future.[34]

None of these research efforts has given any significant attention to minor political parties in the United States. As has been previously argued, there is an absence of a strong conceptual or explanatory framework for the analysis and understanding of minor parties, as well as a need to develop hypotheses for further research. Accordingly, the purpose of this study is twofold. First, the literature on minor parties will be reviewed. This review should yield a more orderly presentation which can in turn serve as a basis for the design of an explanatory framework for the study of American minor political parties. This framework will seek explanations of three basic elements: (1) the formation, or origins of minor parties; (2) the functions, organizational structure, influence, performance, and barriers that minor parties meet in the electoral system; and (3) the reasons that a minor party succeeds or fails in the political system.

A second purpose of this study is to apply this explanatory framework to a case study of a contemporary minor party, the Libertarian Party. The examination of the Libertarian Party will be informed by the framework's explanations relative to the formation of minor parties; the extent of its functions, influence, organization, and performance in the political system; and what may indicate that the party will succeed or fail in the future. McDonald states that "any time is a good time to reexamine what is known in order to see it in a new perspective and see if the old notions will stand up under fresh challenges.[35] This study seeks to classify the old notions into a more coherent framework and to examine them through the Libertarian Party. As such, this study is a first step in the long process of developing useful generalizations and hypotheses regarding minor political parties in the United States.[36] A framework developed from the many explanations found in the literature provides at least a beginning tool for future analysis of minor party operations and dynamics as they challenge the American political status quo.

It is important to clarify the scope and limitations of this research. This study is not intended to test hypotheses regarding any particular phase of a minor party's operations or performance. It will offer a review of the existing literature regarding minor parties as a means of developing a more coherent and suggestive framework for the evaluation of the alternative explanations concerning the formation, performance, and success or failure of minor parties. The case study involving the Libertarian Party will be utilized to illustrate this explanatory framework.

Most minor party studies have been descriptive and historical in nature. Works of this type shy away from speculation about the various phases of minor parties in general. There have been studies dedicated to the Populist, Socialist, Communist, and various right-wing parties, but none to the Libertarian Party.[37] However, a case study may be explanatory in its purpose. In other words, a single case study can be used to revise or clarify existing hypotheses or theories.[38] A case study can also be used to develop and suggest general explanations and hypotheses of behavior that can then be systematically tested at some future time.[39] In this instance, the case study of the Libertarian Party will be related and systematically compared to the three-part explanatory framework in order to observe which minor party explanations were adequate in elucidating the various dynamics of the Libertarian Party. Any deviations between the explanations found in the framework and the case study can be noted as an indication of possible explanatory inadequacies and the need for further analysis. The Libertarian Party is analyzed utilizing the explanatory framework as a manner of demonstrating how such a framework can provide a greater degree of clarity and coherence in the research of American minor political parties.

Interpretive research, such as this study, is a mode of inquiry that enhances the understanding of a particular social or political event, as opposed to positive research which attempts to empirically construct theories about events, or critical research which seeks to philosophically modify a person's beliefs or values.[40] Through a comparison of the case study with the explanatory framework, this study will utilize a "referential process in which something is understood by comparing it to something already known."[41] In other words, the Libertarian Party will be better understood by comparing it to those minor party explanations found in the framework.

The Libertarian Party

Since its formation in 1971, the Libertarian Party has steadily increased its membership and has challenged more and more seats at all levels of government. Its unique ideological perspective attracts a variety of diverse groups to its banner. Because of this wide doctrinal foundation, the Libertarian Party defies the usual right- or left-wing labels. One advantage of this ideological breadth has been to increase the party's appeal and draw adherents from liberal, conservative, and sometimes, radical ranks.[42] Such a broad doctrinal base has attracted members who ascribe to such diverse ideological orientations as anarchism, anarcho-capitalism, minarchism, classical liberalism, utilitarianism, objectivism, and of course, libertarianism.

Membership and electoral strength of the Libertarian Party have both increased to the point where the party appeared on all 50 state ballots and received 881,612 popular votes in 1980. Despite the fact that in the 1984 presidential election its vote dropped to 228,796 and it appeared on only 38 ballots, the party remained the strongest of all minor parties in terms of ballot access and votes cast. In the 1988 race the party received 432,116 votes, a slight improvement. Yet, even in the face of electoral disappointments, the Libertarian Party appears to be more durable and capable of offering a serious challenge than many other minor parties which have disappeared after a single electoral defeat.

The Libertarian Party is associated with several publications, study and educational programs, and libertarian "think tanks," such as the Cato Institute and Reason Foundation, that has enabled the party to build a support-base in the electorate. One observer of the party has noted that these varied programs and activities are not necessarily aimed at recruitment, but are more concerned with the refinement of the party's philosophical foundation.[43] The party hopes that by teaching, explaining, and exploring the philosophical and theoretical bases of its brand of libertarianism, it can "convert the ideologically wavering across the line into the party."[44]

As an ideological position, libertarianism can be defined in a variety of ways. The purpose here is not to explore the many definitions of libertarianism, but to examine a minor party which has labeled and characterized itself as "libertarian." As Friedman and McDowell have aptly noted, libertarianism in the United States can be characterized as "a political movement which is an odd, amorphous sort of phenomenon; but however difficult it may be to pin down a single definition of libertarianism, one fact is clear: since its founding in 1971, the Libertarian Party has made rather steady progress in American politics."[45] In fact, by 1978 the Libertarian Party had become the third largest party in America in terms of votes received. It is, therefore, a significant representative of contemporary minor political parties in the United States and deserves further analysis.

Utility, Scope and Limitations of the Study

The utility of this study is directly related to its purpose. Through an extensive literature review, the field of research will be clarified. There is a definite need for a better tool of analysis through a synthesis of the several explanations into a single framework.

Secondly, the framework itself will provide a useful tool of analysis. The explanatory framework is the equivalent of Braybrooke's axiomatic system, or what Wasby calls a propositional inventory. As Wasby states, it is useful to develop propositional inventories because it permits the development of general theories.[46] Wasby continues and claims that "a propositional inventory is not the equivalent of a theory, mainly because the propositions are not fully related to each other."[47]

Braybrooke asserts that political science requires active efforts to seek out explanations, not merely assessing their value, and develop a system to coordinate investigative efforts.[48] The framework will serve to enhance comparative analyses of minor parties. Although its utility can be initially judged by how well its organization permits analysis of a minor party, the ultimate value of the framework can be best demonstrated when, as Kenneth Janda suggests, valid and fruitful party theories are developed from it.[49]

This study stops short of proposing any new theories. It simply hopes that through the use of a case study, the newly formed framework will provide an insight into the other political parties operating in the United States. As Wasby notes, this is a legitimate use of a case study for, although case studies were initially descriptive in nature and purpose, "they can be utilized to test a theory or to develop hypotheses for further testing."[50] The analysis of the Libertarian Party will allow an exemplification of the explanations contained in the framework. Thus, while the case study is descriptive, it is also explanatory in that it attempts to clarify and revise existing ideas about minor political parties.

It is important to delineate the scope and limitations of this research. This study does not use quantitative methods to test any of the explanations. No claim of causality or linkage is made, for this is up to the reader to decide. As such, the evidence is presented for personal judgment. A single case study cannot provide the data necessary to fully evaluate the framework due to limited validity and reliability.

Chapter Summary

In this introductory chapter it was explained that the field of minor party research is somewhat lacking and in explanatory disarray. The need for a framework of analysis is evident. The purpose of this study is to develop an explanatory framework, and then utilize a case study to illustrate the framework. Since the Libertarian Party appears to be the most viable, serious, and currently popular minor party, it serves as an excellent subject for a case study analysis. The method of comparing the framework to the case study was described.

In Chapter 2 the nature and definition of a minor party will be developed in more detail. The several types of minor parties will be reviewed, as well as the general differences between a minor party and the major parties, and pressure groups will be explained. From this conceptual foundation, the three-part framework can be developed from a review of the literature.

Chapter 3 introduces the analysis of the Libertarian Party. Because the party stresses its philosophical base in both its goals and platforms, a brief review of some of the more influential libertarian thinkers will be done. The chapter will then turn its focus to the party itself. Its history, organizational structure, and performance will be examined in direct relation to the explanatory framework developed earlier.

In the concluding chapter, a final evaluation of the Libertarian Party will be undertaken. The chapter will begin by analyzing America's "status quo democracy" and what this means for minor political parties. Finally, some predictions for the 1992 presidential election will be made, based upon the explanatory framework.

2

The Nature and Definitions of Minor Political Parties

When I see all of the trouble that the Italians and some of our other European friends have in forming a government, I am darned glad we have a two-party system in this country. I am not going to sit here quietly and listen to you denigrate the two-party system. It has served our country well for the last two hundred years.
— John B. Anderson, in a debate
with Eugene J. McCarthy 1980

The hallowed two-party system has become a hollowed system and is in reality, a shell.
— John B. Anderson 1983

In this chapter, a foundation is developed for the systematic analysis of minor political parties in the United States. Following a discussion of the relationship between democracy and political parties, a statement of what constitutes a political party and more specifically what constitutes a minor party is developed.

Subsequently, several types of minor parties are examined. The second part of this chapter reviews the literature concerning minor parties and develops the three-part explanatory framework discussed briefly in Chapter 1.

Democracy and Political Parties

One of the most important characteristics of a democratic system of government is the parallel evolution of political parties within the system. A democratic government rests on the rights to organize and compete for the control of the government by peacefully appealing to the electorate, combining these varied interests into a legitimate majority, and then offering candidates for decisionmaking positions through reliable and legitimate processes that reflect the electorates' issue preferences.[1] In support of the integral relationship between parties and democratic political systems, John Crittenden has noted that

> In democratic nations, the concepts of freedom and equality have required that the people be regarded as sovereign, and contested elections have become the primary method of insuring that government will be accountable to the people. Since parties are almost certain to emerge whenever elections are held, and since parties dominate election outcomes, it is easy to understand the close relation between democracy and competing parties.[2]

It is obvious that political parties have come into existence in a democracy to perform certain critical functions within the political system. They are distinguished from other groups by their primary function, that of competing with similar groups to fill electoral offices.[3]

E. E. Schattschneider has stated that modern democracy is but a by-product of political party competition and concluded that "since parties operate in a legal no man's land they are able to produce startling effects: in effect they may empty an office of its contents, transfer the authority of one magistrate to another magistrate or to persons unknown to the constitution and laws of the land."[4] Since parties are essential for a democratic system to operate, these groups must be defined in more detail. The following section sets out to determine what is meant by the concept political party.

Definitions

Political parties are usually defined in terms of the many functions that they perform in a democratic system. The key function which aids in the conceptualization of a political party is that of competing with similar groups for the purpose of controlling governmental power through the election system. Most definitions found in the literature agree that a political party is a group of individuals who are clustered around a set of interests whose furtherance they make an issue and whose value they generalize into ideals.[5] In other words, a political party is an organization whose members are sufficiently homogeneous to band together for the primary goal of winning elections, which in turn will entitle them to exercise governmental power and enjoy the influence, perquisites, and advantages of authority in the system.[6] Therefore, the concept of political party is defined in terms of self-promoting electoral functions.

As Kay Lawson states, a political party can be conceptualized as a group that simply calls itself a party, and seeks power for the purposes of determining public policy in accordance with its members' directives.[7] This group, or party, performs many functions that include formulating public issues— and thus increasing public awareness—nominating candidates for various offices, securing the election of these candidates through the mobilization and molding of public support, and enforce the adherence of the candidate to the group's programs after the election.[8] There are several secondary functions that parties perform other than seeking electoral victory, although these may be interrelated with the primary goal of electoral success. Among the secondary functions are the generation of symbols of identification and loyalty; the aggregation and eventual articulation of interests; political socialization of the voters to maintain popular support; organizing opposition to those in authority; overriding the dangers of sectionalism in favor of promoting a single national interest; fostering governmental stability; reducing and simplifying the choice of candidates at all levels of government; and legitimizing the decisions of government.[9] However, the primary focus of a political party remains the goal of gaining and maintaining governmental power through the election system.

Therefore, one can define a political party as an "organization consisting of office holders, or aspirants to, elective officers."[10] Primacy is given to the winning of elections through a coalition of interests in order to form a majority of voter support. In the process of seeking power, a party will manage group conflicts and at the same time mobilize and compete ideologically for mass support.

As mentioned earlier, the concept of a third, or a minor political party has never really been defined in exact terms. The minor party label has been applied to any organization that seldom finishes better than third place behind the two major parties.[11] There are, of course, other definitions of a minor party. Legislation has produced legal definitions of what constitutes a minor party primarily in terms of its strength at the polls.[12] This determination varies from state to state. Even though citizens have the right to organize a political party, state legislatures have the right to regulate them by requiring a minimum number of members and votes in order to ensure an uncluttered ballot.[13] Many states define a political party according to the results of a statewide election for a specific office. For example, New York defines any group as a party that has acquired 50,000 votes for a gubernatorial candidate; whereas Colorado requires 10 percent and Massachusetts 3 percent of the last gubernatorial vote for any group to be defined as a party.[14] Kentucky uses 2 percent of the state's presidential vote for a minor party and 10 percent to be considered as a major party.[15] While Pennsylvania requires 2 percent in at least ten counties for the highest statewide vote to be considered a party, Ohio has three levels of political parties. In Ohio a major party is one with 20 percent of the gubernatorial vote, an intermediate party is one with 10 percent and a minor party, 5 percent.[16] Some states require a secondary criteria for definition of a minor party such as the nomination of candidates through a statewide or national convention, as is the case in Iowa, Oregon, and Washington. [17]

The Federal Election Commission (FEC), which regulates presidential elections, defines a minor party solely in terms of voter strength. A minor party is any party that has received 5 percent or more, but less than 25 percent, of the popular vote in the preceding presidential election.[18]

A minor party in the United States can be defined in the same general terms as a political party, except that its size and rate of electoral success is less substantial than the two major parties. Just like their major party counterparts, minor parties attempt to fulfill all of the functions prescribed earlier. It is obvious from an examination of history that they are not always successful at all functions. Just because they do not always succeed at the polls like the two established parties, this *should not* disqualify them from being labeled as real, or true political parties.

In sum, a minor party is any group of individuals, other than Democrats and Republicans, that are united by some common interest, who raise money, offer candidates, and actively campaign for some office or offices under a party label, regardless of their rate of success. A minor party is not the same as an independent. An independent is simply a nonparty candidate.[19] They do not have the benefits of a party label or symbol, its recognition, or its resource base. Nor is a minor party the equivalent of a pressure group. The primary distinction is that a minor party seeks to place a candidate in office, while a pressure group actively supports and attempts to influence one of the major parties as a method of propagating its goals.[20] Pressure groups tend to be concerned with policy outputs and their attitudes toward these are somewhat fixed. On the other hand, political parties, including minor parties, are more concerned with governmental personnel and are not governed by such a rigid determination of policy attitudes as are pressure groups.[21] Pressure groups may support a candidate, but seldom do they sponsor one in an election like a party does.

Other than the criteria of size and electoral success, a minor party differs from the two major parties in several aspects. In general, minor parties tend to be more ideologically focused than the two major ones. Unlike the major parties, which at times suffer a gap between ideology and programs, minor parties seem to revolve around a particular ideology, sometimes to the point of alienating any possible support from the electorate. The major parties devote themselves almost entirely to election functions, while giving little attention to ideological questions.[22] In the hopes of not alienating any segment of the population, the major parties tend to be ideologically ambiguous, and they have never been ideological, being more issue oriented in order to build an election winning coalition. [23] Clinton Rossiter has stated that minor parties are simply deviations from the political norm in the American two-party system whose main function is to apparently preserve the norm (i.e., status quo democracy).[24]

Due to the general lack of electoral success, minor parties are usually viewed as insignificant. This has led many political scientists to dismiss minor parties as unimportant and claim they are not really political parties at all. Schattschneider states that a political party can be defined in terms of its purpose— that of gaining control of government through the election process.[25] Since minor parties, in Schattschneider's opinion, only use elections as points of departure for other agitation, they are not real political parties.[26] Another point that Schattschneider argues is that a true political party wishes to attract a majority of support by representing and compromising among a mass of varied interests. Minor parties, on the other hand, deal in principles divorced from power. In other words, minor parties revolve around such precise, symmetrical, and consistent sets of principles and programs to implement these that they cannot, or will not, compromise in order to attempt a reconciliation of a number of incompatible interests needed for a majority since it is not seriously trying to win an election.[27] Minor parties deal in ideological nuances and principles and not in actual power seeking through the electoral process.

William Goodman echoes Schattschneider's assessment that minor parties are not true or real political parties. Goodman states that with a few exceptions at the local level, minor parties are not in the full sense political parties at all.[28] Since they fail to meet many of the definitional criteria of a party, they are better labeled as agitational associations, debating societies, or educational organizations.[29]

Regardless of the view, or opinion, of minor parties in the United States, they are "true" political parties. They do seek to mobilize interests in society and represent these in government through electoral victories. Just because they may not be as successful as the two established parties should not discount their qualifying status as political parties. They do provide a viable alternative to the usual Republican-Democrat dichotomy and offer a range of issue choices not normally found in the two major parties.

Minor parties are not, as the popular view sometimes holds, full of cranks, reformers, and discredited leaders that have no consequences for the American political system. It is true that some candidates run for frivolous reasons, but they are not classifiable as minor party candidates. True minor parties seek to capture electoral offices at the national, state, and local levels. Some spend millions of dollars in these efforts. Although the rate of success is minimal, this should not discount these parties. Therefore, minor parties do sufficiently fulfill the functionary definition of a political party and thus do not deserve the scholarly dismissal that they have received.

Unlike the two major parties that tend to be somewhat similar in structure, organization, and platform stances, there are many types of minor political parties. The next section will examine the several kinds of minor parties in the United States.

Minor Party Types

There are many types of minor parties in the United States. However, minor parties can be classified in several ways. One way is to classify them as those that are doctrinal and those which are nondoctrinal in their platform base. Doctrinal parties function in the realm of ideological principles and moral augmentation.[30] Parties of this type range from socialist to capitalist, conservative to liberal.[31] Minor parties which are nondoctrinal are those based on socioeconomic, nationality, or religious foundations such as the Know-Nothing Party, the 1936 Union Party, and the Christian Nationalist Party.[32]

Rossiter has developed a more elaborate classification scheme of minor parties consisting of six types. These types are the one-issue obsessionists, the one-state party, personality parties, major party factions, left-wing splinter groups, and the true minor political parties.[33]

The first type of minor political party, the one-issue obsessionist, concentrates its campaign around a particular issue that its members believe salient for society. As V. 0. Key states, issue parties are "founded to promote a principle to which neither of the major parties would respond with alacrity."[34] Issue parties primarily serve as a means of agitation in American politics.[35] A prime example of a one-issue obsessionist minor party is the Prohibitionist Party (now called the National Statesmen Party) and more recently, the Right-to-Life Party.

The Prohibition party has nominated candidates for every presidential election since 1872. Formed in 1868, its primary goal was prohibition, but its platform was eventually broadened to include several other issues such as women's suffrage, direct election of the U.S. Senate, and civil service reform. Primarily a medium of agitation, it has not polled a very impressive vote.[36] Yet the party has continued to exist and has, to some extent, kept the prohibition issue alive. The Right-to-Life Party focuses its efforts on opposing abortion and, through its agitation, has tried to keep the issue in the mainstream of political debate.

The second type are the one-state parties. This type of minor party focuses its efforts only at the state and local levels. In New York the Liberal Party and Conservative Party are examples of one-state parties. In order to exert its influence in national affairs, a one state party will often fuse with one of the major parties, sometimes being permanently swallowed up in the process.[37] The New York Conservative Party's support is often sought by the Republican Party in order to ensure local election successes.[38]

In presidential elections, state minor parties usually seek to align themselves with one or the other of the major parties that may cause their absorption into the major party. In New York, however, the Conservative Party is an exception to this method of general decline of state minor parties.

The New York Conservative Party acts partly as a political party and partly as a lobby group.[39] It can sponsor and endorse its own candidates as would any party, or, due to New York law allowing joint endorsements, it can shift its support to another party's candidate.[40] In this manner it acts as an interest group, hoping to influence a major party by bargaining with its offer of support.

John Gargan has utilized aggregate data analysis to examine the support base of a state minor party, New York's Conservative Party. The Conservative Party was formed in 1962 by a small group of New York City Republicans who were dissatisfied with the influence of liberals in the party.[41] It has been on the ballot as a minor party and has endorsed candidates in both major parties when they are deemed acceptable. "Candidates supported by the party have taken positions which, though conservative in comparison with the views of the major parties, are certainly well within the broad mainstream of national and New York State politics."[42]

According to Gargan, support for the party tends to be drawn from the urban areas in the state.[43] Despite this regional appeal, the party "has achieved an established position within the state in a relatively brief period of time."[44] In fact, the strength of the Conservative Party was apparent enough for the Republican Party to actively seek its endorsement in the 1972 and 1974 presidential elections. New York State election law permitting minor parties to endorse major party candidates has given the Conservative Party an enhanced bargaining power. In 1970 the party achieved a notable measure of success as a minor party by having its own candidate, John Buckley, elected to the U.S. Senate. It was also the margin of victory or defeat for many candidates in local and state legislative elections.[45] Therefore, this state minor party has performed many functions resulting in some electoral successes.

Another example of a significant one-state minor party with some electoral success was the Farmer-Labor Party of Minnesota. Originally organized in 1917 from Bull-Moose Republicans as the Nonpartisan League, it was renamed the Farmer-Labor Party in 1922. It offered candidates for governor and the U.S. Senate in every election through 1942, and succeeded in electing governors in 1930, 1932, 1934, and 1936.[46] The Farmer-Labor Party eventually united with the Democratic Party in 1944 under the leadership of Hubert Humphrey.[47]

Some minor parties are personality or candidate oriented. These parties follow a dissident hero, such as the Bull-Moose Party of 1912 that formed in support of Theodore Roosevelt.[48] Usually, these parties fade and disband when the candidate reenters one of the major parties, or when and if he entirely withdraws from the political scene.

Under Rossiter's fourth category, minor parties may result from dissidence and factionalism in one of the two major parties. This type of minor party can be exemplified by Strom Thurmond's States' Rights Democratic Party of 1948, commonly known as the Dixiecrats, and George Wallace's 1968 American Independent Party (AIP). Both parties represented a split over issues in the Democratic Party which was large enough to cause support for a minor party effort.[49] Parties of this category usually cease to operate after one election and its members usually return to one of the major parties.[50]

Left-wing splinter groups make up the fifth minor party category. The Socialist Party, under the leadership of Eugene Debs, split from the Socialist Labor Party in 1901 and serves as an example of this type.[51]

Finally, the sixth category in Rossiter's classification scheme consists of "true minor parties." Parties in this category are those "with the ingredients of a potential major party, of which the Populists of the late nineteenth century are the classic and perhaps only genuine example in American history."[52] As will be observed, the Libertarian Party can also be placed in this "true minor party" category.

The Explanatory Framework

The field of minor party research is somewhat lacking in its attempts to systematically develop an analytical model or framework for the examination of a minor party. As already mentioned, there are explanations, generalizations, and hypotheses about the origins, functions, and causes for the decline of minor parties spread throughout general party literature. Although many political scientists have argued in favor of propositional inventories or explanatory frameworks of analysis, their concern was focused on the two major political parties. No one has stressed the need for such a framework that concerns minor parties, nor has anyone attempted to develop such an analytical tool. One of the purposes of this work is to categorize and examine the many explanations found in the literature so that a framework of analysis can be developed.

An explanatory framework can be helpful in elaborating present and enhancing future research. This study's three-part framework of explanations is similar to a three-part propositional inventory where several unrelated and diverse statements that describe, explain, or evaluate a subject—in this instance minor parties—are categorized and listed so that a clearer understanding of the subject can be gained and a guide for future research is provided. As in a propositional inventory, the explanations in this framework are not necessarily interrelated or even cumulative in their power to describe or explain minor party behavior.

In order to better enhance the analysis of a minor political party, the relevant explanations, or propositions, were categorized according to the phase of a party's history with which they were concerned. Three phases have been identified: those related to a minor party's formation; the functions of minor parties within the political system during the period of its existence; and the failure or success of a minor party.

The first phase deals with those explanations that concern themselves with the various reasons for the formation of a minor party in the American political system. This explanatory category can be divided into four main areas that, in turn, can be further subdivided.

The four main formation explanations concern crises, voter disillusionment, celebrity candidates, and factionalism. The crisis explanation can be divided by the type of crisis: political, social, and economic. Whereas celebrity candidates and voter disillusionment are single explanations, factionalism is not. It can be divided into major party or minor party splintering.

The second category, or phase two of the framework, involves the explanations of what a minor party does within the political system. In other words, what functions are performed by a minor party. Not all of these functions are done on purpose. Minor parties are unaware that they perform some functions until a researcher analyzes their past and discovers some relationship or association between a minor party and a particular political phenomenon. For example, although some political scientists believe minor parties indicate electoral realignment, it is plausible to venture that minor parties do not form with the expectations of performing this function.

Phase two explanations include the functions of issue or reform innovator; major party platform idea provider; issue educator; a safety or pressure valve for the discontented; an avenue of protest; election spoiler; and electoral realignment indicator. As will be observed, some of these are overlapping and can occur simultaneously.

The final category of explanations, phase three of the framework, is probably the most complex. This phase concerns itself with those explanations for the decline, or failure of American minor political parties. Whereas these explanations can be subdivided as external or internal causes, the subcategories of institutional, social, and organizational causes of failure best typify the many explanations.

Institutional causes include state and federal ballot access laws; the single-member district/plurality election system; the electoral college; federal campaign finance laws; and the amount and type of media exposure. Social cause explanations include the wasted vote idea; the political socialization process in America; and the American social consensus and dualism explanation. Finally, the third subcategory of explanations consists of the following: low resource base; the lack of committed workers; high or demanding membership criteria and low incentives to join; regional or sectional support base; ideological extremism; party factionalism; and fusion

Chart 1
The Explanatory Framework

Category 1: Phase 1—Formation Explanations

Crisis:
  Political
  Social
  Economic
Voter Disillusionment
Celebrity Candidate
Factionalism:
  Major Party
  Minor Party

Category 2: Phase 2—Functions

Issue and Reform Innovator
Major Party Platform Ideas
Issue Educator
Pressure or Safety Valve for Discontented Avenue of Legitimate Protest
Election Spoiler
Electoral Realignment Indicator

Category 3: Phase 3—Decline and Failure Explanations

Institutional:
  Ballot Access Laws
  Single Member/Plurality Elections Electoral College System
  Federal Campaign Finance Laws
  Media Exposure
Social:
  Waster Vote Idea
  Political Socialization Process
  Social Consensus and Dualism
Organizational:
  Low Resource Base
  Lack of Committed Workers
  Membership Criteria
  Membership Incentives
  Regional/Sectional Support Base
  Ideological Extremism
  Fission Within the Minor Party
  Fusion with or Cooptation by a Major Party

with, or cooptation by one of the two major parties. This subcategory involves the structure and organization of the minor party itself.

Chart 1, on page 20, summarizes the three categories of explanations. It should be noted that each category of explanations can have a cumulative effect in expressing the history of a minor party. For example, in phase 1 a crisis of some sort can spur on voter disillusionment and eventually produce party factionalism. In phase 2, the minor party performing as issue or reform innovator may also be an issue educator, while serving as an avenue of protest for some discontented minority. In phase 3, failure to get media attention may be the cause, or the result, of failing to gain ballot access which in turn leads to the wasted vote argument, the lack of members and workers, and a low resource base for the party. It is obvious, then, that a minor party's history can be explained by several of these explanations at the same time. The explanations may build upon each other in helping to understand minor political parties in the United States.

As should be evident from the discussion thus far, there may be many explanations related to an understanding of even one phase of a minor party's history. In sum, the framework is a manner of organizing the numerous explanations about minor political parties into three easily readable and comparable categories. Consequently, a case study of one minor party is a useful tool to illustrate the utility and explanatory power of the typologies of minor parties offered by political scientists. The following discussion examines in detail the first of the three categories of explanations contained in the framework.

Phase 1—The Formation of Minor Parties

Numerous explanations have been offered in the literature as to why minor political parties form. These can be placed into four categories: (1) the crisis explanations; (2) voter dissatisfaction explanations; (3) candidate explanations; and (4) major or minor party factionalism explanations. The first group of formation explanations, that a crisis spurs minor party efforts, identifies various types of crisis: political, social, and economic.

According to Daniel Mazmanian, political crisis is probably the most crucial factor in encouraging the formation of minor parties. He states that the "leading precondition for a significant third-party vote is severe political crisis."[53] Political crisis can be defined as an episode of extraordinary division in the public's opinion over one or more relevant issues. In other words, a political crisis occurs when there is a high level of conflict over a few very salient issues. The emergence of significant minor parties apparently coincides with these periods of intense issue conflict or political crisis, and as Mazmanian concludes, can also be dependent upon a "division of the electorate on one or more of these issues into at least one intense and estranged minority and a broad majority; rejection or avoidance of the minority position by the major parties that causes alienation of the minority; and a politician or political group willing to exploit the situation by initiating a new party."[54] These conditions are cumulative and each is necessary for the next phase to begin.[55]

A prime example of a minor party developing out of a political crisis was the American Independent Party (AIP) of 1968. By the mid–1960s, two important issues, Vietnam and civil rights, were causing conflicts and division within the electorate that, in turn, created an estranged minority consisting of segregationists and "hawks."[56] This issue conflict created the political crisis which attributed to the formation of the AIP.

The AIP appealed to this intense minority of segregationists and hawks because their views were perceived as not well represented in either major party.[57] The legitimate avenue of expression for these views was therefore missing and the AIP was able to fill the vacuum. Although at the beginning of 1968 Alabama Governor George Wallace had toyed with the idea of a coalition with any major party candidate that supported his positions, by the summer of 1968 polls showed that Wallace might be able to win an independent attempt at the presidency.[58]

In sum, political crisis spurred on the formation of the AIP. The cumulative conditions of political crisis were present. There was severe national conflict over a few salient issues, in this instance Vietnam and civil rights; these divided the electorate into an estranged and intense minority; the avoidance and rejection of the minority's position by the major parties took place; and a political leader, George Wallace, was willing to exploit the situation and lead the alienated minority through a new political party.[59] Wallace was able to lead a group of voters who were issue oriented, hawks, and segregationists. Since both major parties rejected these positions as extreme, the only legitimate avenue for their expression was through a minor party.

As mentioned previously, there are other crisis explanations for the formation of minor parties. Besides political crisis, some scholars believe that social crisis contributes to minor party efforts. Indeed, Frederick Haynes has stated that "social and economic problems are the real forces behind third parties."[60] The social crisis explanation is similar to the political crisis explanation and in fact may be inseparable from it. A social crisis consists of a social rather than a political issue, which leads to division in the electorate, and which the major parties ignore or refuse to represent. A social crisis is, in other words, an issue oriented phenomena that has emerged from tensions present in society.[61]

Several minor political parties arose to further a particular stance on an issue during a period of social crisis. The Liberty and Free-Soil parties of the mid–1800s are salient examples of minor parties that developed out of social crisis. Their platforms were focused almost entirely on the abolition of slavery.[62]

The Liberty Party was formed in 1840 for the main purpose of agitating the abolitionist cause. By the 1844 presidential election the Liberty Party was able to garnish a total of 2.3 percent or 62,300 votes.[63] The Liberty Party eventually joined in 1848 with another antislavery party, the Free-Soil Party. In the 1848 presidential election the newly formed Free-Soil Party achieved a significant 10.12 percent of the popular vote.[64] Both the Liberty and Free-Soil parties were dissatisfied with the Whig and Democrat's handling of the slavery issue. Before forming a minor party, the members of the Liberty and Free-Soil parties had attempted to persuade the major parties, the Democrats and Whigs, to commit themselves to opposing slavery.[65] Failing to do this, the minor party route was chosen in order to agitate for the abolitionist cause. Eventually, these minor parties and other factions of the Whigs and Democrats fused in 1854 to form the Republican Party.[66] In sum, some "third party movements spring from an issue which takes over from major party loyalty."[67]

Minor parties may also develop out of times of economic crisis, although this explanation can be disqualified. Agricultural and industrial adversity has caused several farmer and labor parties to be formed.[68] Economic performance, if it is poor, may make the voters turn away from the party in office. A failing economy can make voters abandon the major parties and seek new alternatives in the form of a minor party, thus turning to these parties out of hope and or due to the perceived or real failures on the part of the major parties to keep the national economy healthy.[69] Minor parties that formed due to economic crisis have been numerous and their performance varied. In fact, one of the first minor parties to achieve any measure of electoral influence, the Greenback Party, was a "farmers' movement" made up of several Granger parties in the 1870s, and developed in time of economic stress.[70] "In many presidential elections before 1900 it was mathematically possible for farmer and labor parties to hold a balance of power in terms of popular votes."[71] For example, the Greenback Party, in the 1880 election received 308,578 votes, while the difference between the winning Republican and defeated Democrats was only a marginal 9,464 votes. In terms of popular votes, the Greenbackers held the balance of power.[72] Although the parties that have formed in periods of economic crisis have never won the presidency, they have had some success at the local, state, and congressional levels.

The Minnesota Farmer-Labor Party serves as a prime example to demonstrate the electoral impact of this type of party. In gubernatorial contests between 1922 and 1944, the Farmer-Labor Party was the leading opponent of the Republican Party while the Democrats ran a disappointing third.[73]

Farmer-Labor gubernatorial candidates were successful in 1930, 1932, 1934, and 1936; U.S. senatorial wins occurred in 1922, 1928, 1934, and 1936; and twenty–four seats in the U.S. House of Representatives were gained during the same period.[74]

Elections in which the Farmer-Labor parties made a considerable showing coincided with periods of agricultural adversity in which farm prices declined significantly.[75] These periods demonstrate eras of economic protest voting but cannot be said to include all parties formed out of economic crisis, or out of financial stress. By the 1870s, one minor party did come into prominence over the debate regarding the use of government-issued greenbacks. A business depression lasting from 1873 to 1879 had produced the usual unrest and discontent, and this, compounded with the lack of currency, meant the time seemed appropriate for a new party to form and challenge the two major parties.

This minor party, the Greenback Party, was formed with the firm intentions of remaining in business indefinitely, and with the confident expectation of quickly capturing control of the government.[76] After the Civil War farmers demanded a further issuance of paper money, or greenbacks, in order to inflate agricultural prices and alleviate the growing farm debt crisis. Meanwhile, labor interests were not faring much better due to falling wages and strikes. In 1876 many supporters of greenbacks realized that in order to press their cause, and because the major parties were ignoring their demands, an independent political party had to be formed and, consequently, a national convention was held. The result was a national independent party, commonly known as the Greenbacks. The main focus of the Greenback Party was to keep and increase the greenbacks in circulation in order to stabilize farm prices and to prevent the Treasury Department from revoking their use.[77] The party also sought to reduce interest rates, and supported labor reform legislation.

Drawing upon agrarian discontent in the West and labor unrest in the East, the Greenbacks reached their peak in 1878, receiving 12.7 percent of the total votes cast in state elections.[78] In the 1880 presidential election the Greenback candidate, General James B. Weaver, waged an aggressive campaign but failed to continue the expectations of party growth after 1878. Weaver achieved only 308,000 votes, or 3.32 percent of the total. By 1888 the party had passed into political history.

Another minor party in the late 1880s, the Populist Party, was able to gain national status through "economic discontent, hard times, voter dissatisfaction; a feeling that unjust burdens were being borne especially by Southern and Western farmers, and [the belief] that wealth was being siphoned from the West to accumulate in the East."[79] The Populist Party was formed in 1890 around the three main political grievances of money, land, and transportation.

The Populists opposed the generous government aid that railroad corporations were receiving which in turn monopolized and charged unfair freight rates. They were also upset about western land speculation by eastern investors; and they supported an increase in the money supply much as the Greenbacks had and for similar purposes.[80] Populists viewed the two major parties as mere oligarchies, controlled and managed by the wealthy who ignored the needs of the working masses. These were the views carried forth in the Populists' first national campaign in 1892. The former Greenback candidate, James B. Weaver, was nominated as the party's presidential candidate. Weaver polled 1,040,866 votes out of a national total of 12,052,000 votes and, more impressive still, got 22 electoral votes.[81] Once the Democratic Party had adopted many of the Populist campaign issues for its own platform in 1896, the Populist party began to decline. It never recovered from the defeat in the 1896 election and formally disbanded in 1912.

Although the Farmer-Labor, Greenback, and Populist parties apparently developed out of economic crisis, one drawback to this formation explanation should be noted. Two periods of severe economic crisis in U.S. history have failed to produce a minor party, the Reconstruction era and the period of the Great Depression.[82] If the economic crisis explanation was totally reliable, some minor party should have arisen during these times to express various interests in electoral politics. Mazmanian speculates that the solution to this discrepancy was that the Democrats were able to provide a somewhat adequate representation of dissident interests until 1876, and that the Depression of the 1930s was too sudden for any minor party to take an advantage in order to form an adequate opposition to the major parties.[83] Finally, during the Depression the two major parties offered views contrasting enough to offset any other political opposition. Mazmanian, therefore, concludes that "the economic protest thesis is of limited use in the understanding third parties that have emerged out of intense social, racial, or foreign policy controversies."[84]

Each of these crisis explanations revolve around a salient and intense issue conflict. When voters perceive the major parties as failing to adequately represent their interests, they may turn either to an established minor party or form a new party in order to have their interests expressed in the political system. Obviously, the categories of issues will be economic, political, or social in nature. Therefore, the three crisis explanations are essentially issue conflict explanations. Each type of crisis can be boiled down to the idea that when there is a high level of conflict, this will contribute to voter disillusionment with the major parties, and the end result will possibly be the development of minor parties.

This leads to the next major type of formation explanation, that of voter dissatisfaction with the major parties. Dissatisfaction with the major parties can be for several reasons and can be expressed through the formation and the support of a minor party. When the major parties are perceived as deteriorating, the voters may lose faith in one or both major parties. Voters in turn, will either abstain from voting or support an alternative political party.[85] This loss of faith may be due to neglected issue preferences within the major parties, a perceived fruitlessness in continued support of the major parties, or what the voters deem as unacceptable candidates being nominated by the parties.[86] When one or a combination of these factors are present, the voters will become dissatisfied with the major parties. Therefore, an alternative is sought by the voters through the auspices of a minor party. Key's review of minor party formation notes that "the leaders of dissident groups usually had no special desire to form a minor party, and did so only when it seemed impossible to convert the dominant elements in one of the major parties to their views."[87] Given such circumstances, a portion of the electorate will vote against the major parties by voting for a minor party, and if no minor party exists to adequately reflect the interests of the estranged voters, one may be formed. A prime example is the previously mentioned American Independent Party of 1968.

In 1970 Senator Eugene McCarthy predicted that there would be a liberal minor party by the 1972 election because the level of overall dissatisfaction with the major parties was widespread, not just regional or narrowed to one group.[88] Supporting this contention, Gargan notes that "throughout American history, the emergence of national or state-level minor party movements has been a manifestation of discontent with the existing political order on the part of a segment of the electorate."[89] William Riker states that there is good empirical evidence to support the explanation that disillusioned voters will reduce the size of a major party and will generate votes for a minor party.[90]

In a recent study, Rosenstone, Behr, and Lazarus, found that voter estrangement causing minor party voting only takes place when there is a substantial distance between the voters and the major party candidates.[91] This distance can be a result of disappointment with the ambivalent or moderate stance of the party on a specific and prominent issue.[92] Therefore, scholars concur that voter dissatisfaction does cause new minor party efforts in the political system.

A minor party may also form around a celebrity candidate. Most of the minor parties in the twentieth century have tended to be personality or candidate oriented.[93] "When well-known national leaders for example, have headed third-party tickets, their support has been quite high."[94] Teddy Roosevelt running on the Bull-Moose Progressive ticket in the 1912 election received 28 percent of the popular vote. He was the life of the Progressive Party. The party was, in essence, a personality-oriented movement revolving around him, and could be argued as amounting to idolatry.[95] One can hypothesize that a celebrity, or prominent candidate, is more apt to run on a minor party ticket during times of crisis or dissatisfaction with the major parties.[96] As such, specific candidates of special attractiveness may, under certain circumstances, sway voters to leave a major party and vote for them and a minor party.[97] Rosenstone, Behr, and Lazarus's work concludes that a nationally prestigious candidate made it much easier for a voter to defect from a major party and vote for a minor one. In fact, one finding of the study found that minor party voting is 1.14 times higher when a prestigious minor party candidate is qualified on each state ballot.[98]

The last formation explanation examined is that of party factionalism. A party's objective is to win elections, and to do this several factions and interests must be coalesced into a majority. Sometimes, the factions in the party are so apart on issue stances and policy goals that one may "bolt the ticket" and form its own party. There have been at least four instances of a faction splintering from one of the major parties and running its candidate through the formation of a minor party.[99] The minor parties resulting from major party factionalism were the Liberal Republicans of 1872, the Gold Democrats of 1896, the Progressives in 1912, and the Dixiecrats of 1948. The major party factions usually maintain a separate identity for a single election and afterward drift back into one of the major parties.[100] Whereas a minor party may be the result of a major party splintering, several parties have resulted from minor party factionalism.

Minor parties are not immune to many of the same problems of internal conflict that have at times plagued the major ones. Minor parties that are the result of minor party factionalism tend to be much more enduring than their counterparts from the major parties. While a major party faction usually rejoins the party after the election, minor party factions may last several decades. For example, the Socialist Labor Party was formed in the late 1870s. Under the leadership of Daniel De Leon, it had become increasingly radical and militant in its doctrinal positions. This led to a split with the more moderate members in 1901, who formed the Socialist Party with Eugene Debs and Morris Hillquit as its leaders.[101] Both the Socialist and Socialist Labor parties are still politically active at this date.

The explanations offered for the formation of minor parties in the United States are therefore numerous and diverse. In sum, there are four main categories of formation explanations: those dealing with crisis, whether political, social, or economic; the voter dissatisfaction explanation; the visible, or celebrity candidate explanation; and the explanation that minor parties are created through major or minor party splintering or factionalism.

In the evaluation of these explanations it can be said that they are cumulative in their explanatory power. In other words, a crisis of some proportion may take place, causing voter dissatisfaction toward and within the major parties. The major parties splinter with a faction following a highly visible celebrity candidate willing to exploit and take advantage of the situation.

Of the crisis explanations, it is most important to remember that they revolve around an issue conflict. Issue conflict appears to be an inseparable and integral part of any crisis, whether it be political, economic, or social in nature. As can be observed in Chart 2, Mazmanian has defined periods of crisis in terms of intense issue conflict.[102] If, in fact, political, economic, or social crises do cause minor parties to form, these crises are synonymous with issue conflicts. The type of issue which is prevalent would determine the type of crisis. Many of the minor parties that developed out of a crisis, as mentioned previously, formed around one or two salient issues. Even splinter parties usually separated with the primary party over some issue conflict.

Regardless of how a minor party has developed, it performs may functions within the American political system. This leads into the second phase of a minor party's history and the second category of explanations, those dealing with the functions of minor parties.

Phase 2 — The Functions of Minor Parties

The many explanations regarding the diverse functions that minor parties perform can be divided into four main categories. These categories concern the issue and or reform innovator explanations; the election explanations; access and protest avenue explanations; and those explanations that propose minor parties as portraying the function of a social and power criticizer within the political system.

Probably the foremost function of minor parties in the United States is that of providing issue and reform ideas for the electorate, government, and the major parties. Some scholars argue that the feeding of new ideas, including those that are unpopular and controversial into the policymaking process is the chief function of minor political parties.[103] Rossiter suggests that several amendments to the U.S. Constitution, among them the twelfth, sixteenth, seventeenth, eighteenth and nineteenth, bear the imprint of many years of minor party agitation.[104] Charles Merriam and Harold Gosnell state, "As formulators of issues, the minor parties have often been more successful than the major parties; and as advance guards of new issues, these newcomers have been bolder than the established organizations."[105]

In fact, many ideas of minor parties were eventually enacted into policy or accepted as platform goals of the major parties. Examples are women's suffrage, prohibition, and the end of slavery in the United

propagandist in purpose, [they] serve to bring to the attention of the American public proposals that are too much in the nature of innovation, and therefore too radical, for either of the major parties to sponsor. Minor parties are the experimentalists of the American party system. They bear and nurture their progeny. Those who survive infancy and adolescence are induced by one or both of the great parties to bring their parents to a more pretentious domicile. Fundamental alterations of the major-party platforms result from this adaptation of minor-party policies.[116]

Yet, for each significant idea that minor parties may have proposed, there are just as many ideas that were advocated that are best forgotten as being too radical or inappropriate.

Some examples of these ideas are almost careless in content. In 1892 the Socialist Labor platform included the complete abolition of the U.S. Senate, the vice presidency and the presidency in favor of an executive board elected by the House of Representatives, the only true legislative body.[117] The Workers Party (Communist) of 1928 proposed a graduated income tax with all income over $25,000 confiscated and redistributed.[118] The Union Party in 1936 proposed a limit on personal income along with a guaranteed annual income.[119] Finally, the 1948 platform of the Christian Nationalist Party contained such extremist ideas as charging Jews with controlling all political power in the United States and supporting communism; proposing an amendment to the Constitution requiring racial segregation; offering money for Negroes to migrate to Africa; and the deportation of all communists and any aliens suspected of supporting communism.[120] It is obvious that these are only a few of the many platform ideas that men or parties have expressed, but these may be the ones best forgotten.

This issue formulator function is not without its critics. Much criticism is aimed at the argument on the grounds that it entails nothing but a series of unconnected and unproved propositions.[121] The fact that a minor party advocated an issue in its platform before a major party did is not a reliable indicator that the latter supported the idea because the former did so first.[122] To be sure, many minor party ideas have eventually appeared as policy or in major party platforms, but as Mazmanian has stated, the evidence is lacking to support this hypothesis.[123] One could state that these policy changes and reforms are common to all industrial nations and are a result of large events, such as war or depression, and not due to the agitation and propagandization of minor parties.[124] In conclusion, the manner in which public policy is formulated is extremely complex, and statements claiming that minor parties are the pioneers of policy have not been adequately researched.[125] Despite this, the fact remains that minor parties have proposed many important and accepted issues and reforms in their platforms and campaigns before any of the major parties.

A secondary function to that of issue formulator is that of serving as an agitational and educational service.[126] Of course, this is a function that any political party, major or minor, will perform in a democratic system. A political party serves as an educational institution in that it provides information and stimulates debates in the public forum. Minor parties, although limited, have scored real successes as educating agencies.[127] Fred Haynes concluded that the real value of minor parties is that they stir the political waters through their agitation, thus preventing political stagnation, and they achieve this by calling attention to social and economic issues that need to be addressed.[128]

As a means of education and agitation, minor parties enable a considerable body of political opinions to be expressed at the ballot box.[129] Therefore, they are sometimes consigned to the dual role of issue innovator and pressure valves for those voters lacking an outlet in one of the major parties.[130] This leads into another function of minor parties, that of serving as an avenue of protest or expression for discontented groups.

Minor parties, as many scholars agree, serve as a safety valve for the discontented or politically oppressed by offering an alternative to the major parties.[131] By serving as an avenue of protest, many groups have been able to express their dissent with various policies and processes through a legitimate route rather than through some illegal or unacceptable manner. As Key aptly noted:

> Even when the minor parties have no perceptible effect on the policy of government, they may serve a useful social function. They operate as a channel for the expression of discontent, which is often dissipated and rendered harmless by the exertions of verbalization and electoral activity. Now and then a minor party serves a significant function by publicizing an issue that a major party has the temerity to raise.[132]

Recruitment of candidates for office, especially for the president, is a function of the two major parties. However, groups that are dissatisfied with these choices have possessed the legal right to begin a minor party. James Ceaser claims that "an electoral process open to minor parties provides a fair chance for any excluded group, even if one concedes that the major parties enjoy considerable advantages by virtues of their established organizations and the loyalty of their followers."[133]

By providing an avenue of access to the system for discontented groups, minor parties exert some influence upon the major parties. If this expression of views is widely accepted, then the major parties may move to absorb this support. Thus, the net result is to strengthen the support of the major parties and not to weaken them.[134] Even with the many obstacles facing them, minor parties may force a major party to make important policy or issue changes through absorption of the new support and to avoid the threat of being supplanted by the minor party.[135]

Finally, by providing an escape or safety valve, minor parties have innocuously supported the two-party system. Those pressures that might have otherwise split open a major party have been able to find expression via a minor party.[136] Having minor parties which represent the left and right wings of the political spectrum have had the effect of reinforcing the major parties by reducing their ideological breadth, narrowing their membership bases, and generally making them much more homogeneous, durable, and representative.[137]

As Kay Lawson has concluded in regard to this purpose of minor parties, the general impact of these groups is in their influence upon the major parties. According to Lawson:

> The role of such parties has been to take up the cudgels for causes inadequately championed by the major parties, raise sufficient hue and cry to attract the attention of a major party whose electoral appeal will be more enhanced by the inclusion of a modified version of the new issues, and then to disappear as its fickle members abandon the purity of total commitment for the immediate satisfactions of partial victories and secure enfoldment in a major party. The result seems always to be that the ideological alignment of the major parties will have been shifted slightly. If such reshuffling of party programs and memberships has indeed been the chief accomplishment of minor parties, we must not blink at the conclusion that third parties have seldom seriously threatened the stability of the two-party system. On the contrary, they appear to have performed the crucial service of providing temporary accommodations for disenchanted major party members whenever the two powers have found it necessary to put their affairs in an order more consonant with changing public opinion. The net result of third party movements may well have been not to weaken but to strengthen the two-party system in American political life.[138]

In conclusion, it can be seen that minor parties are best regarded as a safety valve for letting off the steam generated by possible revolutionary, or at least discontented, groups, and for allowing these groups to discover just how much steam they can actually generate.[139] The number and strength of minor parties can therefore be a measure of how much discontent and dissatisfaction exists within the system, or how poorly the major parties are representing the varied interests of the political community.[140] By being an outlet of frustration, minor parties can be viewed as a check on the effectiveness of the major parties. Minor parties are on the outskirts, waiting and wanting to capitalize on any sign of weakness in the major parties.[141] When and if a major party neglects an issue and alienates a segment of the populace, a minor party remains ready to exploit the situation and cater to the support of these voters. In this manner, minor parties function as a critic of the major parties, and according to some scholars, may be a destabilizing force in American politics.[142]

The next function of minor parties in the United States may be that of an election spoiler, and or an indicator of electoral tension and realignment. Minor parties can prevent a majority of votes from going to any one of the major party candidates in an election. This is especially true at the state level. Minor parties may draw support from the voting public and thereby reduce the size of the major party polls.[143] Therefore, "despite popular misconception, minor parties have also on many occasions, by drawing support from one or the other of the major parties, determined the winner of a presidential contest."[144]

In the American system the election of the president is actually two contests, one for the popular votes and one in the electoral college. Although minor parties have had an impact on many popular elections, never has one either played the role of kingmaker in the electoral college by throwing its votes to one of the major parties, or forced a contingent election in the House of Representatives.[145] There have been a number of occasions where minor parties have played the anomalous role of taking votes away from one of the major parties, leaving victory to the other.

According to John Hicks, "In possibly half a dozen instances the third party vote has snatched victory from one major party ticket to give it to the other."[146] Minor party leaders believe that if their party can capture a high enough percentage of the popular vote in order to hold the balance of power, "they can gain greater concessions on questions of policy from the leaders of the major parties."[147]

The most recent example of a minor party thwarting a clear majority rule took place in the 1968 election. Mazmanian states that if Wallace's name had not been on the ballot, the gap between the victorious Nixon and his opponent, Humphrey, would have widened to an appreciable amount.[148] There are other earlier examples of this minor party role. The election of 1844 was won by James Polk. Ewing contends that if the Liberty party had not gathered 15,000 votes in New York at the expense of the Whigs, then most likely Henry Clay would have won the election.[149] The Liberty Party had polled enough votes in one important state, New York, to determine the national winner.

Another example of a minor party influencing an election outcome was in the 1848 election. Zachary Taylor's victory on the Whig ticket depended on the Free Soil Party, with Martin Van Buren taking votes away from Lewis Cass and the Democratic Party.[150] Ewing believes that the Greenback Party vote of 16,994 in New York gave that state to the 1884 Democratic candidate, Grover Cleveland.[151] There are other elections, namely those of 1860, 1892, and 1912 in which one could speculate that without minor parties on the ballot, the election outcome may have been altered.

The 1912 presidential election offers a further example of a minor party, in this case Theodore Roosevelt's Bull-Moose Progressives, operating as an election spoiler. Roosevelt's party split the support for the Republicans and gave the victory to Woodrow Wilson and the Democrats. However, as Key claims, the Progressives in essence really won since Wilson adopted and enacted many acts in accord with the progressive movement.[152]

Although national minor parties may thwart majority rule in presidential elections, state minor parties can also be election spoilers. New York's Conservative Party is willing to play the spoiler role and thus their threats are enhanced.[153] Their endorsement is often sought by the major parties in order to avoid electoral defeat.

In Wisconsin and Minnesota, minor parties have capitalized on voter discontent and have taken votes away from the Democrats, allowing the Republicans to win. In fact, the impact of minor parties was so great that from "1900 to 1932 Wisconsin politics were fought largely within the Republican party."[154] In 1934, with the formation of the Progressive Party, the Democrats and even the Republicans were threatened. The Progressive Party won three out of the five gubernatorial races between 1934 and 1942, while the Democrats finished third in all five.[155]

Finally, minor parties may be an indicator of election realignment and tension. Obviously, this is not a chosen or self-appointed function, but one that scholars believe minor parties perform within the system. Critical electoral realignments are not random, but have appeared with what Burnham terms, "a remarkable uniform periodicity."[156]

If minor parties do indicate critical electoral realignments, it is necessary to define just what is meant by a realigning election. Burnham has offered a two-part definition of this type of election. First, as Burnham notes, "A critical realignment is characteristically associated with short-lived but very intense disruptions of traditional patterns of voting behavior, and large blocks of the active electorate shift their partisan allegiance."[157] Secondly, critical elections show a high level of intensity that is "associated with a considerable increase in ideological polarizations, at first within one or more of the major parties and then between them."[158] An increase in issue distances results in the election being centered around very important issue clusters, "often with strongly emotional and symbolic overtones, far more than is customary in American electoral politics."[159] Therefore, critical realignments are emergent from societal tensions, usually over salient issues, and can be characterized as "issue-oriented phenomena, centrally associated with these tensions."[160]

Critical realignments are often preceded by significant minor party revolts that indicate the inability of the two established parties to integrate, or aggregate the emerging issue demands from the electorate. In this case, a minor party "may serve as a bridge for the movement of people from party to party and in the process lose its dissident elements to the other."[161]

Mazmanian explains that bridging occurs because dissatisfied groups, when withdrawing their support from the major parties, hesitate to change from one major party to the other, and therefore respond to the campaign appeals of minor parties.[162] Therefore, during a period of high tension, voters may utilize a minor party to switch their votes from support of the major parties.

These "protorealignment phenomenon," as Burnham calls those minor parties that precede realigning eras, are usually those parties that exceed 5 percent of the total popular vote.[163] The Anti-Masonic Party of 1832 can be correlated to the emergence of the second party system in the northern states; the Free Soil Party of 1848 and the demise of this second system; the growth of the Populists (1892) and the realignments of the late nineteenth century; and lastly, between the Progressives (1924, 1928) and the reorganization of American politics that began in 1928, are all examples of proto-realignment parties.[164] Most of these parties had a "leftist" orientation and represented groups who were against what they believed to be an elitist, corrupt, and unfair political system.[165] Burnham concludes that these parties offered, or predicted the issues that would become prevalent in the next election.[166] Thus, significant minor parties can be observed as the forerunners of critical electoral realignments.

John F. Freie further examined this role of minor parties in relation to the realignment process in order to discover if an association existed between the strength of the minor party and the sharpness of the realignment. Minor parties were considered independent variables in the realignment process. Two minor parties, the Populist Party of 1892 and the Progressive Party of 1924, were examined in relation to the realigning eras of 1884 to 1900, and 1916 to 1932. In addition, a more recent third party, the AIP, was examined in relation to evidence of a realignment of the 1960s and 1970s. Utilizing a data base composed of aggregate voting statistics at the county level, Freie hoped to discover if, in fact, the three minor parties did indicate a sharp realignment of voters.[167] Freie controlled for the effect of regionalism since each of these parties obtained a very high percentage of their votes from one specific area.[168]

Freie's conclusions support Burnham's explanation that minor parties are protorealignment phenomena. There were strong associations between the strength of the minor parties and the sharpness of the electoral realignment.[169] Therefore, the function of minor parties in the realignment process is indeed significant, whether it be as a bridging mechanism, an activation mechanism, or some other function. What is more, "the strength of the minor party's support can be positively associated with the sharpness of the realignment."[170]

However, Freie found a lack of evidence to classify the 1968 AIP as a protorealignment party similar to the earlier Populists and Progressives.[171]

Freie recommends more examination of the nature and role of minor parties as protorealignment phenomena; such as why are some more salient in this role than others, and what is the extent of the causality between a minor party and electoral realignments. Whatever their function in an electoral realignment, whether as a bridging mechanism or as a catalyst to realignment, minor parties may indicate a restructuring of party loyalties in the electorate.

The discussion has shown that minor parties frequently serve one or more of the following functions: (1) as issue and reform formulator; (2) a platform ideas for the major parties; (3) in education of voters; (4) an avenue of protest, or a safety valve for discontented groups; (5) a potential election spoiler; and finally, (6) an indicator of tension and electoral realignment. Rossiter notes that even though minor parties have done their part in keeping American politics honest, principled, lively, and progressive, their situation is nevertheless almost hopeless.[172] Unfortunately, "whatever glories they may have known in the past, they have been faced for a generation by an almost complete monopoly of votes, attention, money, influence and power by the two great parties."[173]

Minor parties decline and disappear from the political landscape due to many and varied barriers that they must face within the system. In the following section, the numerous explanations regarding the decline of minor parties in the American political system are offered.

Phase 3 — The Decline and Failure of Minor Parties

Although minor political parties have been present in almost every presidential election, they have met numerous obstacles in their electoral paths. Among these obstacles, and probably the foremost, are the several institutional causes or barriers that include ballot access laws, the single member district/plurality electoral system, the electoral college, and campaign finance laws.

Utilizing the concepts of decline and failure may be deemed harsh in describing the last phase of a minor party's history. Parties, including minor parties, have the primary goal of seeking and gaining control of elected offices. Whereas the two major parties perform this function at all levels, minor parties may only focus their efforts at one level of government at a time. Due to the many barriers that exist in the American political system, the success rate of minor parties is minimal. Thus, they do indeed fail in their electoral goals and efforts. If a minor party fails in capturing office too often, it will decline due to a lack of support, resources, and numerous other reasons. Therefore, not fulfilling the primary function of getting its candidates elected will have a detrimental effect upon the party and cause it to decline, and eventually fail. The first obstacle faced by American minor political parties is that of getting on the ballot, and this proves to be the key to a minor party's decline.

Problems of ballot access are really a twentieth-century phenomenon. Up until the adoption of the secret Australian ballot between 1888 and 1916, each party provided its own ballot and thus access was no problem as long as a party could muster candidates, a printing press, and votes it could seek electoral office.[174] Due to cluttered ballots, and possibly due to the two major parties' fears of being challenged, new ballot and stringent access laws were passed in almost all fifty states. According to Blackman, "Third party campaigns spurred a further tightening of ballot-access laws during the 1920s and 1930s; restrictions aimed primarily at subversive parties were added in the 1940s."[175] The increased number of elected offices forced state legislatures to attempt to place a limit on the number of candidates, giving the major parties preferential status while making it difficult for minor parties to get on the ballot.[176] Many of the present ballot laws have been established to protect the major party status quo.[177] The major parties can eliminate and curtail minor party competition by simply limiting their ballot access.[178] Key states that "public control of the ballot is used to exclude minor parties from the ballot or to make it difficult for them to meet the requirements to place their candidates on the ballot."[179] The maze of cumbersome regulations and procedures that the Democrats and Republicans have constructed have limited the effectiveness of minor political parties.[180] If a party cannot gain a place on the ballot, it obviously cannot get votes and will decline due to a lack of electoral support.

Each state imposes its own requirements for inclusion on the ballot for local, state, and federal elections, and this means that every minor party will not be on all ballots nationwide since they must face fifty-one sets of requirements with regard to getting on the ballot.[181] These requirements include filing petitions, deadlines, anti–Communist oaths, and past electoral performances with certain voting percentages. The lack of a uniform petition period and filing deadline means that minor parties cannot mount a single, unified, nationwide ballot drive, but must attempt fifty-one different efforts at various times with various requirements.[182]

First, a minor party seeking ballot status must file a petition of eligible voter signatures with the appropriate state election official. The number of required signatures to participate in the primary and or election varies in each state. Even the details and type of petition varies from state to state. Some states, such as Michigan, New York, California and Texas give specific instructions as to the paper size, binding, signatures only in ink, and notarization of the petition.[183] Other states, as in Alabama, merely call for a petition without specifying details.[184] All states require that petition signees be registered voters.

States vary somewhat drastically in the number of required signatures. Washington, with one of the lowest requirements, asks for only 188 petition signatures, whereas some states like South Dakota and North Carolina require a number equaling 10 percent of the past gubernatorial vote, or 5 percent of the presidential vote in California.[185] Some states—Nebraska, Michigan, Utah, and Iowa among others—levy a further regulation in that the required number of signatures must be distributed among the state's counties or congressional districts. Appendix A gives a listing of petition requirements in terms of the number of signatures for each state. The requirements vary by state, as does the percentage required of either registered voters on a petition or of electoral turnout in a previous state or presidential election.

Once a petition is completed, it is handed to the election board or secretary of state who checks the submitted signatures for eligibility. Therefore, some states have set a maximum for the number of signatures.[186] This places a further hindrance on minor parties. Since, in an effort to ensure the minimum percentage, even after the determination of eligibility, minor parties will gather an excess of signatures.

Verification of the eligibility of petition signers varies among the states. The most common restriction is the exclusion of signers of other petitions and primary voters, regardless of party.[187] Verification of petitions are by the secretary of state and or an election board. These officials are almost always elected on a major party ticket or are selected by the executive who was elected on the ticket. Thus, "the burden of verifying petition signatures seems to fall upon groups who want minor parties kept off the ballot."[188] One final obstacle can be found in Ohio. An oath must be filed stating that the candidate is not a communist and does not support communism.[189] Obviously, the Communist Party cannot get on the Ohio ballot.

The filing deadline for the collection of signatures is the next stage of the ballot access process. Some states require that a minor party wishing to be on the ballot begin their petition drives up to a year before the general election.[190] By January and February of the election year, most states have already begun to collect final petitions for the November election. The major parties have no such requirements. For example, Michigan requires minor parties to have their petitions filed with the secretary of state in November of the previous year, whereas the major parties do not have to file until early March. This type of requirement places an urgency on a minor party. Maryland and Ohio required 18,500 and 5,000 signatures respectively, to be turned in by March 1980 for the November presidential election.[191]

Besides petition requirements, filing deadlines, and past voting percentages, one final requirement is placed upon minor parties in order to permit them ballot status. Party nomination conventions are required in many states, either before or after the petition deadline.[192] At these conventions, whether state or national, both candidates and electors are to be selected, with the results reported to the appropriate state officials.

In conclusion, it can be observed that a minor party must face a vast array of requirements just to appear on the election ballot. Various state access methods result in an increased cost for any minor party effort. Calls for legislation that would standardize the system through a national plan have been numerous, but up until now, unsuccessful.

In response to what they deem to be unfair restrictions, many parties have used the courts to gain access. "While legislatures are reluctant to legislate additional restrictions on ballot access, judicial decisions are encouraging state action toward greater leniency."[193] However, there is still no guaranteed right to candidacy, or an assurance of a place on the ballot. The Supreme Court has ruled that the state has a compelling interest in composing the ballot in order to present a ballot that allows the voter a clear, easy, and meaningful choice.[194] Therefore, a state can limit access to the ballot.

This issue arose in a 1968 challenge to Ohio's ballot access requirements. The suit was brought on appeal to the U.S. Supreme Court by the American Independent Party (AIP) and the Socialist Labor Party (SLP). The two parties argued that Ohio's ballot access requirements, passed in 1948 to keep Henry Wallace off the ballot, were so stringent that they made it almost impossible for any minor party to achieve a place on the ballot. Ohio required a new party to obtain petitions signed by 15 percent of the total number of votes cast in the last gubernatorial election. The two major parties merely had to obtain 10 percent of the votes in the election and did not need to file any petitions. Besides the petitions, new parties had to file by February, nine months before the presidential election. The AIP demonstrated its numerical strength by getting 450,000 signatures, more than the needed 433,100.[195] The SLP conceded that it could not meet the 15 percent requirement, but filed as a coplaintiff anyway. Still, the Ohio secretary of state denied the AIP a place on the ballot, even though the state acknowledged that the AIP had the required number of signatures.

Ohio claimed that it had a compelling interest and absolute power over ballot access with the intentions to "promote a two-party system in order to encourage compromise and political stability."[196] In order to do this, the state of Ohio imposed heavy burdens on new parties, thus giving a permanent monopoly to the Democrats and Republicans. Justice Black, delivering the majority opinion, stated that "Ohio's burdensome procedures, requiring extensive organization and other election activities by a very early date, operate to prevent such a group from ever getting on the ballot and the Ohio system thus denies the 'disaffected' not only a choice of leadership but on the issues as well."[197] Therefore, the ballot restrictions are a violation of the U.S. Constitution's Fourteenth Amendment's "equal protection clause" and the First Amendment right of association. A 6–3 majority concluded that "these barriers of party, timing, and structures are great obstacles. Taken together they render it difficult, if not impossible, for a man who disagrees with the two major parties to run for President in Ohio, to organize an opposition, and to vote a third ticket."[198] The favorable ruling for the AIP did not extend to the SLP. The Court, therefore, gave little weight to the argument of limiting minor parties in order to promote a strong and stable two-party system. A balance must be reached between a party's rights of association and speech and the state's right to limit electoral confusion.[199] Still, some states have tipped the scale in favor of the major parties.

The decision in *Williams v. Rhodes* is only one example of recent minor party challenges to state ballot laws. The American Party challenged the ballot laws of Texas in 1971.[200] The American Party, an offshoot of the AIP, claimed that the Texas requirements were too stringent. The Texas law required a new minor party to have a petition equal to 1 percent of the votes cast in the last gubernatorial election. In addition, each person who signed the petition was required to take an oath before a notary public at the time of signing, and all petitions had to be filed in February.[201] The American Party argued that this denied Texas voters equal protection and their right to vote for whomever they pleased. The Court agreed with the American Party, and permitted the party access to the ballot.

Not all ballot access challenges end in success. The Socialist Workers Party, among others, challenged the ballot laws of Georgia. Georgia law stated that any party that had not received 20 percent or more in the preceding gubernatorial or presidential election may have its candidates on the ballot only by a petition of at least 5 percent of the eligible voters. The time span for circulating and filing the petition was 180 days.[202] The challenge of the appellants was rejected and the Court ruled that the Georgia law was not a violation of the Fourteenth Amendment's Equal Protection clause. The Georgia requirements were neither unreasonable nor a scheme to prevent minor parties from the ballot, as was the case in the 1968 *Williams* case. Since Georgia permitted write-in ballots, its laws could be distinguished from the Ohio laws which had no such provision. In addition, the filing date was not as early, and Georgia permitted a person to sign more than one party petition.[203] The Supreme Court found that, "in a word, Georgia in no way freezes the status quo, but implicitly recognizes the potential fluidity of American political life."[204]

Even though the Supreme Court seems willing to permit variations in state ballot laws, providing that these laws do not exceed reasonable limits, it has never clearly defined what is reasonable. "What the courts have been doing since *Williams v. Rhodes* (1968) is to give clues as to maximum stringency for requirements, although the limits are by no means clear."[205] Justice Marshall, dissenting in a 1986 case where the Socialist Workers Party was unsuccessful in its challenge of Washington's ballot access laws, stated that "limitations on ballot access burden two fundamental rights: the right of individuals to associate for the advancement of political beliefs, and the right of qualified voters, regardless of their political persuasion, to cast their votes effectively."[206] Despite this, the Court has justified the state in its imposition of some limits in order to prevent frivolous and fraudulent candidacies.[207] However, Justice Marshall insists that the Court has failed to adequately indicate just how much impingement would be acceptable for a state to have an interest in limiting ballot access to those parties with some level of popular support.[208]

Therefore, as long as there are fifty-one different ballot access systems, any minor party will face a costly and time-consuming campaign just to get on the ballot. As Bell notes, "Any minor party with authentic national aspirations faces over fifty different sets of bureaucratic and statutory difficulties such that merely being on the ballot can represent, to a small party, an electoral victory in itself."[209] In conclusion, in *Munro v. Socialist Workers Party* (1986), Justice Marshall addresses this point and states,

> Since *Williams v. Rhodes*, this Court has recognized that state legislation may not ensure the continuing supremacy of the two major parties by precluding minor party access to the ballot as a practical matter. Yet here the Court sustains a statute that does just that. The Court thus holds that minor parties may be excised from the electoral process before they have fulfilled their central role in our democratic tradition: to channel dissent into that process in a constructive fashion.[210]

If a party is to convince the electorate of its political force and seriousness, it must have candidates for a wide range of offices on a substantial number of ballots. Mounting numerous petition drives and court litigations can drain a party's treasury very quickly, leaving few resources for campaign efforts. As if in a chain of dominoes, if there is no ballot status there is little sense in staging a campaign, and if no campaign, there is no support either in votes or resources. The eventual result is the demise of the party within that state and, possibly, nationally.

Even if a minor party is capable of gaining ballot status, the American single-member district/plurality system virtually assures electoral defeat. As Key has noted, "In a single-member district only two parties can contend for electoral victory with any hope of success; a minor party is doomed to perpetual defeat unless it can manage to absorb the following of one of the major parties and thereby become one of the two parties itself."[211]

In a single-member system, the single candidate with the plurality vote wins; thus, even if a minor party were to receive 20 percent of the popular vote in every state, they still may not elect a single candidate.[212] What is more, since voters tend to believe that a minor party has, at best, only a slim chance of winning, they do not want to waste their vote on it.[213]

Clearly, a system of proportional representation would at least enhance the potential for success of minor parties. An example may serve to demonstrate the different effects of the single-member and proportional-representative systems on minor parties. Rossiter cites how in 1936, having reduced the number of members on the city council, the voters in New York City decided to initiate the system of proportional representation. The 1945 election resulted in 14 Democrat, 3 Republican, 2 American Labor, 2 Liberal, and 2 Communist party representatives on the city council.[214] The voters reacted negatively to the Communist council members and in 1947 reverted to the single-member district system. The 1949 election resulted in the election of 24 Democrats and 1 Republican, with no minor party victories.[215]

As Rosenstone, Behr, and Lazarus have commented, "The single-member-district plurality system not only explains two-party dominance, it also ensures short lives for third parties that do appear; it is the single largest barrier to third party vitality."[216] If a minor party cannot offer victories to its members, disillusionment will follow and most likely a decline in the number of supporters until the party eventually fails.

The electoral college system is a unique variation of the single-member/plurality system. Although minor parties have risen from time to time and exerted some influence on governmental policy, the two major parties have been the only serious contenders for the presidency. One reason for this status quo is the electoral college system. The winner-take-all structure of the electoral college limits a minor party's hopes of influence to that of forcing the selection of the president into the Congress.

The electoral college does not favor regionally supported parties that can only garnish enough votes in a few states. As Schattschneider notes, minor parties do not necessarily fail due to the single-member system but due to the fact that the presidential elections are not regionally, or sectionally based as is most minor party support.[217] The major parties have a wider support base and thus a much better chance of winning the presidency. Consequently, a minor party's hopes rests with the idea of deadlocking the electoral college, preventing an absolute majority for either major party, and having Congress decide the next leader of the United States.[218]

Besides ballot access, single-member districts, and the electoral college, probably the greatest institutional barrier that minor parties must face are federal campaign finance laws. The 1974 Federal Election Campaign Act (FECA), although originally designed to limit the influence of wealth in the electoral process, has in reality become "a major party protection act."[219]

To understand the barrier that this act erects against minor party electoral success, a brief review of the FECA and some of its key components is needed. When the FECA was initiated in 1974, the two major parties qualified immediately for public funding of their 1976 presidential campaigns. The act established definitional criteria for a major party, one that receives over 25 percent of the popular vote, and a minor party, 5 to 25 percent of the popular vote in the preceding presidential election. Funds are distributed according to this status, except that minor parties receive their election funds, if any, after the November election. The amount of a minor party "grant is to equal an amount that bears the same ratio to the amount granted to the major party candidates at the beginning of their election campaigns as the number of votes cast for the minor or new-party candidate bears to the average number of popular votes cast for the major party candidate."[220] For example, if the two major party candidates each receive 40 percent of the popular vote, and a minor or new party candidate receives the remaining 20 percent, the minor or new party candidate qualifies for 50 percent of the federal funds that the major-party candidates received.[221] Furthermore, a minor or new party must be on the ballot in at least ten states and receive 5 percent of the total popular vote to be eligible for FECA public funding. Any minor party that qualifies will receive the funds during the *next* presidential election. Therefore, minor parties can only qualify retroactively.[222]

Besides receiving a substantially lower amount of money, if any, in public funds, the delay in payments puts a minor party at a disadvantage. Polsby and Wildavsky argue that "to the extent that past presidential elections are used as a basis for calculating support, there is also a danger that a lapse of four years will distort a party's popularity, and the outpouring of third-party sentiment in one year will subsidize the perpetuation of the party four years later, when popular sentiments have shifted."[223] Even if the party had qualified for funding, a shift in voter preferences could cause the party to lose ballot status and any chance of continued success.

It is less difficult for minor parties to receive federal funds during the primary season. A candidate must gather $5,000 in individual contributions in increments of $250 or less in twenty or more states. In addition, the candidate must "prove" to the FEC that they are seriously seeking election.

The Citizens Party, the first minor party to get federal funds, qualified for $193,735 in funding after the 1980 election. Sonia Johnson received only 228,796 votes in 1984, a 71.7 percent drop from the 922,001 that Barry Commoner received in 1980.[224] This is an indication that the premise is true that a wait of four years for funding may be too late to keep voters interested in continuing their support for a party. Lenora Fulani of the New Alliance Party received approximately $900,000 in matching funds from a reluctant FEC for the 1988 primary election cycle.

The FEC vote to give matching funds to the Fulani campaign was not without debate. Joan Aikens abstained from the final decision, stating that she was concerned about a minor party candidate receiving funds before the general election. According to her, it is everyone's right to run for president, but not to get matching funds even if they meet the qualifications.[225] This attitude reinforces the argument that the FEC utilizes its power and purse to maintain the two-party status quo regardless of whether this is their legitimate role or not, and regardless of the impact upon democracy.

Only one independent candidate has qualified for FEC funds. In the 1980 election independent candidate John Anderson's National Unity Campaign received a popular vote of 6.61 percent. He became the first independent candidate to qualify for public funding, a total of $4,242,304 which his campaign received after the fact.[226] Although the amount seems adequate, Anderson's campaign spent well over $14.4 million for fund-raising efforts, ballot and petition drives, and for legal fees.[227]

Despite only one minor party receiving federal funds, the total amount of money that minor parties have spent increased. Minor parties spent only $2 million in 1976, but close to $20 million in 1980.[228] Since no minor party received public funds for the 1976 election, the increase in spending must be attributed to other factors. One factor was a 1976 Supreme Court case in which portions of the FECA were challenged as unconstitutional. Even though minor parties almost never receive any public funds under the FECA, they are still bound to the act's disclosure rules and contribution limits. One such contribution limit was on the amount of money candidates could contribute to their own campaign.

Buckley v. Valeo (1976) challenged the constitutionality of the federal election finance laws.[229] The Supreme Court had to balance the First Amendment liberties of free speech and association against the asserted right of Congress to enact limits and laws designed to protect the integrity of the election process. The plaintiffs represented a wide range of political ideologies, from conservative to liberal. They asked the Court to rule on the fundamental issue of the relationship between money and electoral success. Herbert Alexander suggests that the Supreme Court had to solve the riddle: "Is money speech and speech money?"[230] The Court decided that limits on independent spending by individuals and groups could be considered a limit on the right of free speech. The spending could only be independent, unconnected to any campaign organization or group. Therefore, personal spending limits are unconstitutional, but the court upheld the constitutionality of outside contribution limits and disclosure as only marginal and reasonable restrictions.[231]

This ruling has led minor parties, most notably the Libertarian Party, to nominate candidates who are wealthy. The Libertarian Party nominated Edward Clark for president, and millionaire David Koch who donated $2.1

million of his own money toward the 1980 campaign.[232] "The vice-president for the Libertarian party is usually selected for his strength as a private philanthropist who can add some financial strength to the ticket."[233]

Other aspects of federal and state campaign laws have a detrimental effect on a minor party. During the 1972 presidential campaign, the Socialist Workers Party refused to comply with state disclosure laws and would not provide a list of contributors' names and addresses. The SWP feared that contributors would be harassed by government agencies, and it brought civil suits in many states to protect the contributors' right to privacy. Although such harassment was dismissed as improbable by state election officials in 1975, it was disclosed that the FBI had indeed been systematically harassing party members and supporters.[234] The SWP was exempted from these requirements for the 1976 presidential election.

Finally, media exposure constitutes the last institutional barrier that minor parties must face. The lack of campaign exposure means diminished public esteem and legitimacy for a party which translates into few, if any, votes.[235]

The media utilizes two main arguments against lending coverage to minor political parties according to Ernest Evans. First, many believe that all minor parties are kooks and extremists, and as such, are unworthy of coverage. Secondly, since minor parties have no real chance of winning the election, they do not deserve any attention.[236] However, both positions are inherently one-sided, if not outright wrong. As pointed out, minor parties provide many issue ideas that later appear in one of the major parties' platforms. This is hardly the result of lunacy or extremism.

In addition, by not covering the other parties because they cannot win, it is automatically assumed that coverage should only center on preselected top contenders. In other words, the media is prejudging every election for the American electorate. This totally ignores the fact that the election process ought to be a forum where ideas are discussed and debated. Besides, what right does the media have to predetermine who may win and thus be deserving of coverage?[237] This makes the media appear elitist and wholly undemocratic through its insistence on choosing the "right" candidates and the "proper" issues to which the public ought to be exposed. This completes a vicious cycle for minor parties. Without proper media coverage, they have little chance of getting their ideas out and, as a result, receive few votes on election day.

With regard to the print media, there are no guarantees of coverage for any party, but this differs for television. Section 315(a) of the Federal Communication Act of 1934 established the equal time doctrine. It stated that a broadcast licensee who provided time to any legally qualified candidate must allow all other candidates for the same office an equal opportunity to broadcast time. As Smallwood notes, "This equal-time requirement which was originally used to protect third-party and independent candidates, explicitly guaranteed candidates equal access to the broadcast media, although it did not guarantee equal exposure of all candidates."[238] The purchase of air time became a guarantee of the FECA. If the equal-time provisions are ever revoked by an act of Congress, the networks would "be able to give or withhold legitimacy to minor-party candidates more or less at will, and this greatly affects the capacity of such candidates to mount a credible challenge to the two major parties."[239]

In 1976 the issue of equal time became centered around the series of televised debates sponsored by the League of Women Voters. The Federal Communications Commission was forced to decide whether the debates had to include minor party and independent candidates. The FCC ruled that the debates were a news event and thereby exempt from the equal time requirements, thus excluding any candidate except those invited by the League of Women Voters.[240]

The League of Women Voters later developed guidelines for determining if any minor party or independent candidate should be extended an invitation to the debates. A candidate had to meet a 15 percent standing of support, as measured by national public opinion polls, and be on enough state ballots to have the possibility of winning sufficient electoral votes to become president.[241] Only independent John Anderson met these criteria, but Carter refused to lend legitimacy to Anderson's campaign by participating in a debate with him.[242] As Alexander notes, although Anderson was excluded from a debate with both major party candidates, it is impossible to clearly determine what effect Anderson's exclusion had on his National Unity Campaign.[243]

Both the Libertarian and Citizens' parties have publicly criticized the debates held by the league. The Citizens' Party filed suit with the FEC to be included in the debates, which was rejected, and "the [then] new party's lack of funds prevented it from seeking judicial review of the commission's decision."[244] Libertarian Ed Clark condemned the debates as exclusionary, partisan, and a disservice to all Americans.[245] The Citizens' and Libertarian Party candidates did debate each other, but received little media coverage.

A new twist to the debate issue was added in 1988. A bipartisan Commission on Presidential Debates was created, essentially taking control from the League of Women Voters. This upset the league, which claimed that it should be in charge of the debates because of, among other reasons, its "ability to deal with third party candidates."[246] Its ability to simply deny a place to third parties can hardly be deemed a worthy reason for its maintaining control of the debates, especially since it never has had any intentions to include these candidates in any debates (nor would the commission). Once again, a hurdle has been established by an organization subjectively deciding what candidates would be included in the debates under the guise of a democratic arena.

The question, still largely unanswered, is whether an informal, voluntary organization such as the League of Women Voters should be permitted to determine who appears in a televised debate. As long as the invitation criteria remains subjective, minor party and independent candidates most likely will remain excluded in order to perpetuate a two-party debate monopoly. This not only deprives the American voter of an opportunity to choose a candidate from a larger field, but is an arbitrary decision to deny democracy in its basic form (the free and open exchange of ideas) in order to guarantee the status quo. Lacking the opportunity for public exposure that the debates provide, minor parties will continue to experience extreme difficulty in their efforts to build public awareness of their ideas and thus survival.

In addition to the many institutional obstacles, minor parties must overcome an array of social and cultural barriers that exist in their path of electoral success. These barriers consist of the "wasted-vote" idea; the political socialization process in the United States; and the general social consensus and dualism of American politics. Of these, the idea that voters are wasting their vote by supporting a party other than the Democrats or Republicans is probably the most difficult to overcome.

The concept of the wasted vote is linked to the performance of minor parties in the American electoral system as a whole. As the major parties consistently point out, voting for a minor party that has little or no chance of winning is a wasted effort.[247] It seems clear that while there is objective truth in the idea of the wasted vote, the concept is also used by the major parties to ensure loyalty to themselves and not to some other party.[248]

This tactic has the secondary purpose of delegitimizing minor parties as resting on the political fringe and led by those with unacceptable credentials as leaders.[249] In 1948 President Truman argued before an audience that the challenging Progressive Party could not achieve peace because it was powerless and a vote for it was simply wasted.[250] Both major parties have utilized this "wasted vote" fear to their advantage in several elections. The major parties point to the political inexperience of minor party candidates, and by preaching on the sacredness of the two-party system, they attempt to delegitimize minor parties, subvert their challenges, and thus discourage voters from supporting them.[251]

As long as a minor party cannot raise the possibility of winning at least 270 electoral college votes, the charge that "a vote for X is a wasted vote because he cannot win" will be leveled by the major parties.[252] Although it is difficult to provide direct evidence that this charge causes a decline in minor party voting, it seems obvious that it contributes to and reinforces the belief that minor parties cannot win at the polls. The resulting weak electoral performance by the minor party thus becomes a self-fulfilling prophecy, and reinforces the losing image for future efforts. In other words, "people expect third parties to do poorly because they have always done poorly, so only weak candidates run—and the cycle continues."[253]

This fear of the wasted vote is interrelated with the political socialization process in the United States. The socialization of children into accepting the legitimacy of the dominance of the two major parties is taught in schools and through the media. Children learn their political allegiances from these sources, but more importantly from their parents. In addition, parents transmit their allegiance, usually to one of the two predominant parties, to their children. As Smallwood has commented, "This self-fulfilling, self perpetrating process [has] gained momentum over time and [has] enabled the two parties to maintain—and even expand—their respective positions."[254] Consequently, voters acquire the belief that the two-party dominance and structure is essential, and that party diversity is somehow un–American.

This social consensus represents another noninstitutional barrier that minor parties must overcome in their quest for elected offices. The American public's innate conservatism and confidence in the prevailing two-party pattern not only places a limit on conflict, but also encourages a preference to solve problems through the two existing and established parties.[255] As Schattschneider has somewhat understated, "Once a two-party system is firmly established the major parties automatically have a monopoly of elections; they monopolize the greatest single channel to power in the whole regime. Control of elections gives the parties a very great position in the political system."[256] Since the major parties tend to graduate toward the middle ground in their political goals, any conflict tends to be minimized. Therefore, "the two major parties have preempted this middle ground and thus blocked the emergence of more radical third parties."[257]

In sum, minor parties face a series of social barriers in addition to the many barriers already described. Given these barriers, Rosenstone, Behr, and Lazarus assert that "to support a third-party challenger, a voter must awaken from the political slumber in which he ordinarily lies, actively seek out information in a contest whose outcome he cannot affect, reject the socialization of his political system, ignore the ridicule and abuse of his friends and neighbors, and accept the fact that when the ballots are counted, his vote will never be in the winner's column."[258] As long as the American system stresses political moderation, consensus, and party dualism, minor parties will lack influence in the election system. As Lawson explains, "The average American political ideology, that mild blend of consensus and apathy, acts unfailingly as a centripetal force to limit decisive inter-play conflict to the unradical center, and to keep the doctrinaire third parties confined to the sidelines of meaningful political action."[259]

Minor parties decline due to external factors found in the election system and society. They also decline due to a variety of internal factors and problems, including such elements as low financial resources, difficult membership requirements, a narrow clientele, the lack of volunteers and workers, and the ideological extremism of their platform stances. These internal or organizational factors are interrelated. For example, the extreme ideological positions that minor parties sometimes present may appeal to only a small segment of the electorate, which explains the narrow clientele and the lack of resources the party may have at its disposal.

Minor party problems with the lack of resources due to the FECA have already been referred to above. The low treasuries of minor parties prevent purchasing media time and advertising, financing adequate polls and campaigns, and initiating ballot drives in several states. Minor parties have always been outspent by the two major parties.

As mentioned earlier, the major parties already enjoy ballot status in all states, but minor parties usually have to file petitions and sometimes endure costly litigation just to get on the ballot. After Eugene McCarthy finished his ballot drives and court battles to be on thirty state ballots, his treasury was down to only $100,000 for campaign travel and advertising.[260] This financial problem is not new. Despite massive efforts at fund-raising, the 1936 Union Party could only raise $20,000 for its campaign.[261] If a party must use its war chest on ballot access drives, the amount of money remaining for media time, advertising, and polls is minimal.

Even though minor parties do not receive the millions of dollars in matching public funds that the major parties do, they still must subscribe to the limits imposed on contributions by federal law. Minor parties rely upon membership dues and small contributions to survive, and empty or near empty treasuries mean a thin campaign.[262] Since most minor parties only appeal to a small segment of voters for a variety of reasons, the number and amounts of contributions are low at best.

Some minor parties go to the extreme in fund-raising attempts, even to the point of illegality. Lyndon LaRouche has run for president since 1976. "In 1980, he collected 185,000 votes in fifteen Democratic Party primaries and received $526,000 in funds from the FEC. His campaign committee was forced to repay $55,751 and a fine of $15,000 after some irregularities were discovered in campaign records."[263] LaRouche's National Democratic Party, as the group became named in 1976, solicited contributions from people in numerous ways, some of them fraudulent. Phone solicitations were made for funds during the 1984 presidential election. Representatives of the National Democratic Policy Committee (NDPC) would ask for money, donations, or loans from the voter on one of their major credit cards. Several contributors who used their credit card later discovered that instead of the pledged $15 or $20 donation, they were billed for $500, $1,000, or even more.[264] The FBI and a Boston Grand Jury probe investigated and affirmed that the NDPC had indeed used "unauthorized credit-card numbers resulting in unauthorized charges apparently totalling hundreds of thousands of dollars."[265] Many loans the NDPC received were in the amount of $100,000, and many of these have already been defaulted on.[266] As a result, LaRouche and several of his top aides are presently serving time in federal prison for conspiracy and fraud.

The fraudulent activity of LaRouche's NDPC may have implications for other minor parties by making their electoral efforts seem likewise illegitimate. Voters may believe that if the NDPC is unscrupulous in its activities, all minor parties must be the same. Voters may be more reluctant to contribute time, money, and support to a minor party now more than ever. The level of respectability for minor party efforts may have been damaged.

The organization and structure of minor parties tends to be a drawback in their seeking electoral success. Minor parties not only have trouble in securing adequate funds to mount a reasonable campaign, but have difficulties in attracting and mobilizing committed workers over a long period of time, especially between presidential elections.[267] Most national minor parties have had a national headquarters, but few have maintained state and even fewer have had local headquarters. "Unlike the major parties they have not developed strong state and local organizations to serve as bases for their election-contesting activities, and this comparative advantage on the part of the major parties has consistently reflected itself in the election returns."[268] It is obvious that if a minor party cannot achieve ballot status in a state, its organization there will be weak or nonexistent.

Whereas the two major parties make requirements for membership as simple and undemanding as possible, some minor parties almost seem to want to exclude people from joining. Minor parties, like the Socialist Workers, Communist, and the African People's Socialist Party require a formal application in order to join. Each new applicant has to promise to adhere to the party's ideology, organizational principles, and disciplinary structure. The Communist Party even goes as far as to require new members to be union members, if possible be registered voters, and pay an initiation fee and yearly dues to maintain their membership.[269]

The Communist Party is a prime example of a party that has difficulty in recruiting and keeping members. It has had a very unstable membership and suffers from high turnover rate.[270] The CPUSA has been plagued with an inability to lead, retain, control, and direct its membership.

Regardless of what motivates a person to join the CPUSA, whether it be the need of social companionship, ideological attraction, or an agreement with its political and social objectives, members left for many reasons. The main reasons for defections have been internal ideological or political differences, the poor organizational structure of the party, and U.S. government policy toward communism and the CPUSA.[271] The key handicap of the CPUSA has been its inability to recruit and retain sufficient members.[272] It has attracted more people than it has kept, due to the fact that the party has had organizational difficulties, poor lower-level leadership, and has placed a high level of financial demands upon the members.[273] This had led to an unproductive structure and a party hampered by a pattern of weak commitment by its members.

Defections and expulsions from the party over political or ideological differences have also depleted its ranks. The two highest periods of exodus, 1929–20 and 1957–59, resulted from intraparty ideological disputes and almost ruined the party.[274] In fact, by 1959 the rolls of the party dropped from 22,000 to 3,000 members due to differences in maintaining a pro–Stalinist focus in the party.[275]

Finally, governmental policy toward communism and the CPUSA can be noted as a factor of members abandoning the party. Since "the CPUSA has been stigmatized as disloyal and un–American," the party has been politically isolated, especially during the 1950s.[276] The 1954 Communist Control Act declared the party a clear and present danger to national security and totally deprived it of any political organization rights. Federal and state government attacks on the party including mass arrests, deportations, and harassment of members, have caused people to leave the party and has frightened away prospective members.[277] Therefore, the CPUSA has suffered from so many problems in attracting and keeping members that it remains largely impotent as an electoral force.

It can be observed that membership in some minor parties is demanding and difficult. While the membership criteria may be high, the value of membership is low. If a person can overcome the social stigma usually placed on being a supporter of a minor party, the psychological returns can be few. Members and party workers must overcome the idea of not being able to capture a majority of the offices for which they have campaigned. Disillusionment can easily make members defect from the party and cause the party to eventually fail.

Minor parties cannot offer the type of incentives to their members and supporters that the major parties can. These can be typed as material incentives—tangible rewards for party work such as wages and jobs; solidary incentives—intangible rewards with no monetary value such as status needs, a sense of membership, and a desire for political power and party identification; and purposive incentives that encompass the goals and purposes of the party that caused a person to join.[278] Minor parties, as mentioned, do not have much to offer in terms of material incentives to its members. Treasuries are usually low, a great amount of the work is done by volunteers, and the short life of many minor parties does not offer stable employment for members. The two major parties are just the opposite in that they can afford to pay workers, their continued existence is assured, and at least some patronage is available to reward party activists.

Solidary incentives are important in party recruitment. The desire for power, social status, and prestige are incentives that the major parties can offer. For minor parties, though, these incentives are less important for a number of reasons. First, the chances of electoral success are slim for explanations already cited. Constant failures at the ballot box are hardly conducive to one's status and prestige, and with no wins, one's power cannot be increased.[279]

Finally, the purposive incentives for joining a minor party are the most salient. Minor "parties are quite different from the larger parties in that they arise to express concerns over critical issues that the major parties are either ignoring or answering with unsatisfactory solutions."[280] This means that the initial focus of the minor party is on future political goals and purposes. They accentuate policy and issue concerns, usually on a much different ideological plane from the major parties. The major parties often "blur or mute ideological concerns."[281] Therefore, due to the fact that many minor parties are short-lived and lack an established organization, the material and solidary incentives that a minor party can offer are few, implying that the party probably exists solely on the basis of its purposive incentives of policy goals.[282] Members are motivated by an ideological commitment to join and work for a minor party.

Electoral support for minor parties is another explanation for their weakness and decline over time. Support for a minor party tends to be regional or sectional.[283] As Sorauf notes, "Minor parties in the United States throughout American History have been the parties of localism and regionalism, and these local pockets of strength which have supported them are being slowly obliterated in the nationalization of life in the United States."[284]

Several minor parties arose to protest a particular policy or issue. This is particularly true of the midwestern parties such as the Minnesota Farmer-Labor, the Granger, and other agrarian-based interest parties. In fact, minor parties seem to have more success if they limit their electoral efforts to the needs and desires of a given area.[285] As the sectionally based issues that brought a minor party into existence decline in importance, the minor party atrophies. American society has become less regional both in its economic and social makeup. It has become diversified. Minor parties have tried to follow suit, but their organizational structures are not set up for a national campaign endeavor. A larger, multistate campaign costs more money than most minor parties can afford, yet without a national campaign a minor party has little chance of electoral success at this level. Without electoral successes, voters and members become disillusioned with the party and it will wither in size and impact, possibly disappearing altogether. Thus the party has failed.

Finally, the ideological base, or doctrinal position of minor parties is another organizational factor that causes these parties to decline and eventually collapse within American politics. The extremism of many parties repels voters from supporting them. The ideologically extreme parties realize they have little or no chance of inclusion in the government and reflect this in their action and ideas.[286] If a party does not have natural support in the electorate, it must engineer support through the promotion of its policies and goals.[287] Politically and ideologically extreme goals, whether left or right, will only appeal to a small segment of the electorate. This amount of support is hardly enough to sustain the party over long periods of time.

There are many examples of minor parties that have formed around extreme political positions. These parties express positions that are contrary to the norm of American self-conception of equality, individualism, private property, and democracy. Any attempt to revamp the legitimacy founded in the American social or political institutions will be considered as extreme and will attract only a few voters to the cause.[288]

Seymour Lipset and Earl Raab state that, "historically, extremist movements are movements of disaffection."[289] These groups believe they have been deprived of something and believe themselves to be politically isolated from the mainstream. Sometimes these extremist groups appear during periods of party realignment.[290] Most times, extremist parties are "preservist" in nature, hoping to halt changes in society and politics.[291] Extremism can be defined as any political program that in a radical or reactionary fashion challenges the norms, legitimacy, and consensus of the American political system.

There are several extremist minor parties from the right of the political spectrum. The American Nazi Party, formed in 1958 by George Lincoln Rockwell, claimed it would have a president by 1972.[292] Although the correlation between the ANP's platform and ideology and its failure at fulfilling its goal may be difficult to empirically substantiate, it is logical that this was the case. The ANP's ideology was anti–Semite, anti–Communist and anti–Negro. The party blamed Jews for controlling the country's financial institutions and government, and for instigating black Americans to riot and march for civil rights.[293] The party never achieved national election ballot status and has only appealed to a few extremists as supporters.

The Christian Nationalist Party ran the Rev. Gerald Lyman Kenneth Smith for president in 1944. Smith received only 1,780 votes on his anti–Semite, anti–Negro platform.[294] Again, whether or not the CNP's extremist platform repelled voters or not, one can only speculate.

Some extremist minor parties claim to be saving the United States from itself. One such party was the National States Rights Party (not to be confused with the Dixiecrats), which formed in 1958 from a paramilitary group. The party proposed to save the United States from internal threats of destruction by ridding the country of Jews, Negroes, Catholics, and other groups that it deemed undesirable.[295] The party lasted only a few years.

A prime example of an extremist party was a fascist movement in the U.S. led by Father Charles E. Coughlin. During the 1930s, Coughlin had a weekly radio broadcast in which he began to talk about political matters. He was anti–Communist while at the same time denouncing American capitalism for its exploitation of workers.[296] He called for government intervention to help the unemployed and reform the business and banking systems.

By 1934 Father Coughlin had developed a system that he labeled "social justice" that "advocated government ownership and control of the banks in order to guarantee full employment at reasonable wages, and though it approved of trade-unions, it opposed strikes and lock-out as unnecessary."[297] The new system of social justice was to replace capitalism and democracy which, in Coughlin's view, had no hope in the United States. Coughlin's policy was extremely nationalistic, isolationist, and anti–Communist and his new Union Party entered politics in 1936.

The Union Party claimed to have over 5 million members, but only received 900,000 votes.[298] After this disappointing show of support, Father Coughlin announced that his mistake was to believe democracy could work and his policy ideas became increasingly fascist in nature. Coughlin advocated the abolition of political parties, a corporate state, and stronger support for Mussolini and Hitler and their policies, including Hitler's persecution of Jews.[299] Coughlin and the Union Party ended in 1942, after the Church and several government officials ordered him to cease his political activities.[300]

Support for Coughlin and the Union Party was mainly due to economic dissatisfaction. The constant condemnation of the banking and business system by Coughlin appealed to those people who were discontented with their economic situation, especially the working class and unemployed. Coughlin's appeal and following decreased drastically as the United States entered into a war against leaders that held ideological positions similar to Coughlin's.

A more recent case of ideological extremism in a minor party can be found in Lyndon LaRouche's National Democratic Policy Committee. The NDPC's most notable achievement was having two of its members win the Illinois Democratic primary for the offices of lieutenant governor and secretary of state, forcing Adlai Stevenson to run on a minor party ticket to avoid being associated with these NDPC extremists.[301] LaRouche, who began his political career as a Marxist-Leninist and member of the Socialist

Workers Party, espoused far-right ideals.[302] His politics bordered on the far edge of the spectrum, claiming that Jewish bankers, the Chinese, the Soviets, and the queen of England, among others, were involved in a worldwide conspiracy to deindustrialize the world and make it dependent on drugs.[303] LaRouche and the NDPC were staunchly anti–Semite and racist in policy positions. Several authors describe LaRouche and his followers as a fanatical cult, rather than a true political party.[304] Whatever term best describes LaRouche and the NDPC, they made an impact in the 1986 primaries in many states.

LaRouche supporters ran in numerous primaries of both major parties in many states. One count put the number of candidates at close to 800 in as many as 29 states.[305] NDPC candidates took the opportunities of running in unopposed Democratic or Republican primary elections. Voters seemed confused about the party's name, or did not realize that the candidate listed under a major party ticket was in actuality a LaRouche supporter. The NDPC will not be a force to deal with in the future because of the imprisonment of LaRouche in 1988.

Robert A. Dahl best describes the extremist groups in the United States by stating that these "oppositional groups shade off into an indeterminate collection of alienated Americans whose opposition is even more out of line with the pattern of normal opposition. There are, and probably always have been, Americans who reject some or most of the key elements in the dominant ideology and some or most of the major institutions."[306] Usually, these groups have a difficult time expressing their extreme views through the American political process, so they resort either to other methods, or quit the political system altogether.[307]

No political party that has opposed democracy and the prevailing political and social ideals of America has ever had its candidates elected. If the party does not accommodate itself to the prevailing ideology, the voters will perceive it as being too radical and unrealistic in its goals.[308] As Dahl explains, parties that fall outside the prevailing consensus usually have a small following "made up of a disproportionate number of people low in political skills, realism and effectiveness."[309] For these political dissenters, continued political impotence and rejection breeds frustration which causes them to withdraw from the party or politics completely. The end result is that the party fails from a lack of support, and the members become alienated, hostile, and even resentful of parties and the political system.[310] Extremism will repel voters and cause a party to collapse.

As can be observed, there are many explanations for the failure of minor parties that can be found in the internal workings of the party. Poor organization, a lack of resources, sectional rather than national support, few volunteers and workers, and the ideological extremism are all internal factors that can cause a minor party to decline over time. There are two final explanations concerning the demise of minor parties, that of fusion and or cooptation of a minor party by one of the major parties; and that of fission or splintering within a minor party.

Fission is caused by a lack of unity within the party. Minor party schisms are detrimental to the party, causing it to disappear completely or forming new, but smaller, minor parties.[311] This was the case in the split between the Socialist and Socialist Labor parties. Since both parties have very similar platforms, any voter considering supporting their ideals would be torn between the two parties. Supporters may simply become disillusioned with the party's factionalism, and thus return to supporting a more stable party, minor or major.

Finally, "to the leaders of minor parties fusion [with a major party] often seems the open door to real political power; but fusion has probably been more often fatal to such parties than any other cause."[312] Fusion is the process in which a minor party joins with a major party and agrees to support its candidates. It is a surrender of the party's platform, issues, and goals to a major party through cooptation.[313]

Minor parties often base their campaign on policies and issues that the major parties ignore. If there does seem to be a national response to the minor party platform, the major parties will move to accommodate these issues in order to capture this support. In other words, the major parties wait for the minor parties to experiment with various issues in order to know whether or not it is feasible to absorb these issues into their platforms.[314] "Minor parties bring about their demise by the very support they attract. They usually lose the battle but, through cooptation, often win the war by having their issues adapted into policy via a major party."[315]

Extremist minor parties are usually immune from this threat of fusion. In fact, Rosenstone, Behr, and Lazarus conclude that "the longevity of the five ideological parties — Prohibition, Socialist, Socialist Labor, Socialist Workers and Communist — can be attributed in part to their extreme stands and narrow basis of support."[316]

Mazmanian notes that "usually after a strong showing by a minor party, at least one of the major parties shifts its position, adopting the third party's rhetoric if not the core of its program. Consequently, by the following election the third-party constituency has a choice between the 'extremist' third party with little hope of victory, and a major party more sympathetic to its needs."[317] Therefore, electoral success can breed failure for a minor party through major party cooptation. Once it is demonstrated that a principle gets votes, one of the major parties adopts it and, if the demand has merit, it will probably be translated into policy by the major party.[318]

Fusion, as referred to earlier, can also mean that two or more parties support a single set of candidates. This usually involves a temporary alliance between a minor party and the weaker of the two major parties.[319] The

Greenback Party during the 1884 election attempted fusion with the weakest major party in many states.[320] Even though the party's leadership had forbidden its members from forming alliances with any other parties, this directive went unheeded. Fusion had weakened voter attachment to the original Greenback Party and ultimately resulted in the party being absorbed into the Democratic Party.[321]

Although fusion helped many minor parties win, it also helped maintain a significant minor party tradition by providing a guarantee that a dissenter's vote would be more than a symbolic gesture of protest by voting through a major party.[322]

Because minor parties held the balance of power in many state elections between 1878 and 1892, fusion became an objective for leaders of both minor and major parties in order to secure electoral victories.[323] By doing this, some states — particularly Michigan — in order to purify elections and prevent fraud, passed antifusion laws that prevented two or more parties from backing the same set of candidates.[324] However, this fusion negatively affected the support of some minor parties, such as with the Populists. It has caused a lack of identity for minor parties, its members, and for the voters. Voters find the issues proposed by the minor party appearing in the major parties simultaneously. This may cause an exodus of supporters from the minor party camp to the major party because it is believed that the major party has a better chance of election. To this point, the Populist fusion with the Democrats in the late 1800s provides a prime example.

In the 1896 presidential election the Democratic and Populist parties ran a fusion campaign in support of William Jennings Bryan. Depending upon the state, Bryan appeared on either the Populist or Democratic ballot. Antifusion laws prevented Bryan from being listed on either ticket in some states. Populist party members, and some Democrats, feared that the fusion would in actuality be absorption of the Populists by the Democrats; and even more staunch Populists refused to vote for Bryan on the grounds that this would dilute the principles of their party.[325] Nevertheless, in some states Populist candidates were forced to declare themselves as Democrats in order to gain a place on the ballot.

The consequences of this fusionist campaign were numerous. The Populist Party lost many supporters who refused to vote for the Democratic-Populist ticket. Secondly, the Populist party lost enough votes in the 1896 election to require requalification for ballot status through the petition process in subsequent election years.[326] The campaign also caused a temporary split within the Democratic Party. There seems little doubt that fusion was a contributing factor to the Populist decline, as it has been in the case of most minor parties.

In concluding this development of the explanatory framework, one can observe how the three phases of a minor party's span can be analyzed through historical examples. A minor party's formation, function, and failure do have precedents within political history and do permit a synthesis into an analytical tool.

In the following chapter the explanatory framework just developed will be described in relation to a contemporary minor political party. The Libertarian Party will be utilized as a case study to systematically analyze the numerous explanations found in each of the three categories of the explanatory framework. This effort will permit evaluation of the individual explanations, and thus determine which are feasible in explaining the development, performance, and future of the Libertarian Party.

3

The Libertarian Party

*I am ashamed to think how easily we capitulate to badges
and names, to large societies and dead institutions. Whoso
would be a man must be a nonconformist. . .[and] for nonconformity the world whips you with its displeasure.*
— Ralph Waldo Emerson, 1841
Essay on "Self Reliance"

As if to respond to Emerson's cry for a true nonconformist in society —
someone willing to face the odds even though defeat is almost always
certain — minor political parties have appeared in American politics in just
about every election. It is true that minor parties have suffered the
displeasure of being the nonconformists since they seldom capture the
offices for which they have campaigned. One party in particular, though,
has gladly embraced this role of nonconformity, and yet has had some success in its many electoral endeavors. The Libertarian Party espouses some
untraditional political ideas, but it has made an impact on the American
political system. This nonconformist political party, the Libertarian Party,
will be examined in detail in this chapter.

In Chapter 2 the many explanations that involve minor parties were
systematically organized into three categories and then were reviewed in
detail. In this chapter the many explanations will be examined in relation
to a single contemporary minor party. The history and future of the Libertarian Party will be elucidated by the explanatory framework. It is important to remember that the purpose of this study is not to define American
libertarian philosophy, but to examine a political party that has labeled itself
as libertarian. However, a brief definition of libertarianism and some of the
more influential libertarian thinkers will enhance a better understanding of
the party's political, social, and economic ideas and goals. Thus, the first
section will concern itself with the philosophy and philosophers of libertarianism. Subsequently, the various aspects of the party, such as its formation, are examined in relation to the explanations that were reviewed and
categorized in the previous chapter. Only those explanations relevant in
describing the phases of the Libertarian Party are analyzed.

The Libertarian Party appears to be the most serious of the minor parties in its attempts at electoral success in that it is on more ballots and has won several more campaigns than any other contemporary minor political party. The party's mixture of liberal and conservative ideas appears to appeal to many voters in different regions, and thus enhances the party's attractiveness for research. Finally, the Libertarian Party is a relatively new and still existent party, thereby being a more appropriate case study for the understanding of several aspects of the explanatory framework.

The following section will briefly review and develop a clear definition of what constitutes libertarianism. As a means to better understanding the party's platforms, some of the libertarian thinkers that have had an impact on the party are reviewed. It is necessary to examine the libertarian ideology as it pertains to the party because, as Mark Paul has stated:

> Libertarians, unlike the major parties, are more than a sum of their programs, which to most voters look like an unlikely amalgam of left and right. A vote for the Libertarians is a vote for an ideology that is both unusually consistent and rigidly unwavering. Their ideology dictates that they support civil liberties and an end to militarism; it also leads them to the defense of a laissez-faire capitalism purer than anything that has ever existed in American history.[1]

Libertarianism: A Brief Definition

Libertarianism, as it appears in American philosophical thought, can trace its roots to John Locke, Thomas Jefferson, the Anti-Federalists, Rousseau, and John Stuart Mill among others. Because libertarianism is a mixture of various schools of thought, a clear and precise definition is difficult to discern. Karl Hess seems to best typify what is meant by libertarianism. Hess has stated that

> Libertarianism is the view that each man is the absolute owner of his life, to use and dispose of as he sees fit; that all man's social actions should be voluntary; and that respect for every other man's similar and equal ownership of life and, by extension, the property and fruits of that life, is the ethical basis of a humane and open society. In this view, the only function of law or government is to provide the sort of self defense against violence that an individual, if he were powerful enough, would provide for himself. The socioeconomic form of this radical revolutionary position is laissez-faire capitalism.[2]

Libertarian philosophy centers itself on the individual as being the key unit in any society. Since the main concern is the individual, almost anything that restricts or coerces him is an object of disdain and mistrust. Man must have liberty, which is an absence of coercion by other men and organizations.[3] This freedom from coercion is essential to man's personal and economic well-being. Man has a natural right to life, liberty, and property, just as Locke had stressed, and the libertarians utilize this as a basis for their philosophy.[4] Anything that infringes upon these rights through coercion and or threat, whether it be a man or a government, must be opposed on moral and political grounds.

The individual is considered to be a rational creature. In other words, each person through reason can decide their own morals, their path in life, and how to optimize their liberty through rational and voluntary decisions.[5] Libertarians are therefore laissez-faire in individual, religious, and economic matters.[6]

Libertarians level their most vehement opposition against the state and government. Coercion or the forceful limiting or deprivation of another's freedom is not only immoral, but also illegal. Government is the key source of coercion and force in society. It enters to enforce conformity through the use and threat of force and has a monopoly on legalized force.[7] This power places government in the role of an aggressor against individuals and this is a violation of man's personal and natural liberties.

The primary function of government is to protect the liberties and property of individuals. Unfortunately, governments have gone beyond this limited function of protection and have violated their citizens' freedom.[8] Governments are not abstract, omnipresent entities that exist independently from people, but are agents of the people, and therefore should be limited in their role to defending people's rights.

Since man has a natural right to do whatever he wishes to do with his person and property, any exchanges or transference of power and or rights must be on a purely voluntary basis.[9] As long as there is voluntary consent, no force is present. Force is a violation of liberty since it prevents an individual's opportunity of consent.[10] Governments use many types of force in the form of fraud, censorship, and tax powers. Since governments have been the primary source of coercion and force in society, they have been the principle violators of man's rights, especially the essential right to property.

Libertarianism is extremely interested and concerned with property rights. In fact, many libertarian thinkers place almost all human relationships in a property context. Since "every man has the right to be free and must not infringe on the rights of others," it is only through the exercise of this right that everybody will be allowed to voluntarily sell, buy, or trade any item.[11] There must not be any infringement on this economic freedom. Governments, by their very nature, limit and infringe upon this freedom. It seizes property through taxation, its powers of eminent domain, and numerous regulatory statutes. Through its use of coercion, government can be equated with a criminal, one who violates another's basic rights to property.

Since the individual is viewed as the most important unit in society, only in capitalism can an individual exert himself, or in other words, enjoy his natural freedom. Libertarianism stresses the need for individual economic freedom, and for a system that will permit this freedom to be exercised. Societal rights in the economy are nonexistent. It is the individual who produces, and consumes and therefore, the system must center on the individual. Thus, the necessity of the freedoms found in a capitalistic system are emphasized.

Capitalism implies that all exchanges within the system are voluntary in nature. Obviously, libertarians hope for a total laissez-faire system rather than some variation of a corporation-governmental economic system. Government intervention in the economy is considered a blight on the system.[12] A free-market system is envisioned as a system of peaceful and free competition on a strictly voluntary basis.[13] Governmental coercion is nonexistent in this "economic democracy."[14] The consumer can buy however and whatever as much as he wishes. The individual has the key power in that by buying a product he has in actuality voted for that capitalist to keep on manufacturing. If the quality of the product is poor, the capitalist will either have to improve it, or lose votes and risk going out of business.[15] Capitalism permits each individual the freedom to pursue, on a noncoercive basis, what he believes to be in his or her best economic interest. In an idealistic manner, libertarianism foresees greater prosperity for individuals in an economic system that is competitive, noncoercive in that each has a choice of what product to purchase, and is totally free from government intervention and interference.

The present economic system is characterized by coercion. As previously alluded to, libertarians argue that the prime source of this coercion is government itself. Government disallows and severely limits competition in some areas by monopolizing that area for itself.[16] It also awards monopolies to corporations and does not permit the market system to freely operate. Prices are artificially inflated through government subsidy programs. Furthermore, present tax laws penalize the producer for making profits and thus, in the long run, penalize efficiency.[17] Without this profit incentive, producers will not make products in an efficient manner.

Crime is defined as an invasion of rights. The government, since it has a monopoly of control over the tools of force — the police and the military — attempts to gain and maintain control over man's basic economic rights and liberties. "The state maintains its revenues by coercion, and by threatening dire penalties should the income not be forthcoming."[18] This coercion can be seen in the involuntary taxing system that makes taxation the equivalent of theft. As Murray Rothbard notes, the "state by its very nature, must violate the generally accepted moral laws to which most people ascribe."[19] Rothbard continues and states that "the state is a criminal organization that subsists by a regularized large-scale system of tax-theft and gets away with this by engineering majority support."[20] Majority support does not make it any less of a crime. The only possible solution is to erase or drastically reduce the power of government.

What form of government, if any, would libertarians be satisfied with? Obviously, some libertarians border on the realm of anarchism. Others would argue for a limited government, a minimal state, a belief called minarchism. The only form of government that would be tolerated by most libertarians is one that exercises only retaliatory force against someone who initiated force on another individual.[21] In other words, government may only exert its protective powers. It is to provide police powers, contract arbitration services, and contract enforcement only when necessary. If government oversteps this authority, it becomes an aggressor and a criminal since it is violating man's rights and liberties.

A reliance upon voluntary associations is integral to libertarian thought. Only those agreements, relationships, and associations that have formed out of volunteerism are in fact acceptable and legal. Nothing is to interfere with this right since that would have to be construed as an infringement upon personal rights and freedom. Libertarians do not rule out government per se, but only that form of government which may hinder or limit man's liberty and voluntary decisions. Voluntary cooperation is never a threat to a person's rights to be in control of his life, body, and property.[22] This system of voluntary cooperation is the only feasible alternative to that of government. Government must, therefore, be restricted or eliminated, and the free-market system allowed to operate.

The individual is the most important unit, but is not necessarily isolated from society and the community as a whole. Man is the only being capable of thought and action, but all individuals interact with society and are interdependent with it.[23] However, libertarians do dismiss and despise any values, relationships, or associations that are enforced collectively and coercively. Instead, a system of voluntary cooperation among individuals is stressed as necessary for the preservation of man's natural rights to life, liberty, and property.

As Rothbard has noted, libertarianism is a political theory and not a moral or aesthetic philosophy.[24] Its focus is primarily on the proper roles and duties of government — to protect and defend the rights of life, liberty, and property. Morals and values are an individual matter of choice. Man has the personal liberty to decide for himself what values and principles to adopt and how to act.[25] The only limit is when he infringes upon the liberty of another person. Put another way, libertarianism avoids prescribing an ethical system because of its belief in the individual, and the abilities and rationality that man possesses. This includes the acceptance of any consequences that result from one's decisions.

Libertarianism focuses on economics and property and holds that man is a rational individual. Man has a natural right to property and may do what he pleases with this property. Limiting what a person may buy or sell infringes upon his rights and liberties. No government, or group for that matter, can decide for an individual what to buy or sell. No one has the right to take away on a coercive basis the fruits of one's labor. Therefore, libertarians are capitalistic in that this is the only system of economics that will protect a person's liberty. Governments are coercive in nature because they take the fruits of labor through its tax system and other powers.[26] All men must have the right to pursue their own economic interests, whatever they may be, and a market system free of government intervention will permit this to take place.

Libertarianism opposes any form of collectivism. Collectivist philosophies, such as communism and socialism, destroy the individual and his rights.[27] Socialism and communism attempt to remold man's nature into a collective mind-set, thus limiting necessary individual liberties.[28] A regime of liberty, on the other hand, will enhance the emergence of the good side of man. Rothbard argues that "liberty and the free market discourage aggression and compulsion and encourages the harmony and mutual benefit of voluntary interpersonal exchanges, economic, social and cultural."[29] This is not necessarily idealistic, but, as Rothbard argues, is simply based on common sense.[30] If man is totally free in the social and economic spheres of life, then he will realize the benefits of being good and will act accordingly.

In conclusion, libertarianism in American thought can trace its roots to John Locke who proposed "one of the first systematic elaborations of libertarian, individualistic natural rights theory."[31] In fact, many libertarians depict the American Revolution as a libertarian revolution in that the two major propositions were the natural rights of man and the government's protection of these rights.[32] It is obvious that Jefferson reflected these thoughts in the Declaration of Independence. Libertarians today seek to return to these basic principles. Rothbard notes that "Libertarianism [then], is a philosophy seeking a policy."[33]

Libertarianism, as a political philosophy, is not without its critics. Liberal and conservative thinkers criticize libertarian thought as being overly optimistic and philosophically misguided. Libertarian reliance on the philosophies of Locke, Rousseau, Jefferson, Mill, and the abolitionist Spencer, among others, along with the social contract metaphor, tends to alienate most conservatives and liberals.[34] In fact, some writers charge that the libertarians carry the doctrines of these philosophers to a new level of absurdity.[35] They dismiss the libertarian quest for almost absolute freedom from authority by stating that "the perennial libertarian, like Satan, can have no authority, temporal or spiritual. He desires to be different, in morals as

in politics. A typical libertarian delights in eccentricity and genuine libertarians are lunatics and lunacy repels and political lunacy especially
repels."[36] Most criticisms of libertarianism can be summed up in the claim
that "libertarianism is a social and political theory full of noble sentiment,
but lacking in depth and possibility."[37]

Despite the rejection of libertarian thought by the political and
philosophical mainstream in American thought, libertarianism retains a
continuing intellectual and political appeal to some sectors of the American
electorate. The following section briefly reviews several libertarian writers
who have had some impact on the platforms and political positions of the
Libertarian Party.

Libertarian Intellectuals: A Brief Survey

Libertarian thought is not a united front within the American political
system. It is a movement made up of many diverse, and sometimes unrelated, political and economic doctrines. American libertarianism as it has
appeared in recent decades can be separated into two main schools, each
with its representative philosophers. These two factions are the anarchists,
and the minarchists.

The minarchists, or minimal state libertarians, have had the most influence upon the early stages of the Libertarian Party. Writers such as Ayn
Rand, John Hospers, Robert Nozick, Friedrich Hayek, and Jerome Tuccille, among many others, are the best representatives of this version of
American libertarian thought.

Ayn Rand (1905–1982) has, through her writings, contributed a defense
of individualism and laissez-faire capitalism to the American libertarian
movement. The free-market system is interrelated to man's achieving virtue
and excellence since it is the only system that permits free and rational
choice.[38] Rand explained that man's "virtue and liberty are inherently
related and laissez-faire capitalism is the only economic and political system
that recognizes this connection."[39]

The importance of Rand's thought cannot be stressed enough. Her
philosophy provided a moral justification for capitalism that libertarians
constantly praise.[40] Rand's ethics of naturalistic humanism connected an individual's chance for moral perfection through freedom of choice in the
marketplace. The potential for excellence is present in all people, but in
order for this to be fully developed, the freedom of choice is required,
especially with regard to determining one's own self-interests.[41] Therefore,
liberty must be the most important and highest social and political value of
mankind.[42]

Rand transformed selfishness from a vice into a virtue. Man's reason leads him to act out of self-interest, and such action is one of the highest and noblest expressions of human dignity and creativity that exists.[43] Those people that are productive, or capitalistic, owe nothing to those that refuse to produce. Charity, especially coerced charity through a governmental structure (welfare), is morally wrong since it is destroying the dignity of the recipient.[44] If a man does wish to be charitable, it must be on a voluntary basis, not on a state compulsion basis. Thus, in conclusion, whereas the defense of capitalism had previously rested on its technology and efficiency, Ayn Rand provided a moral defense for the system by relating it to man's personal liberty and rationality.

Whereas Ayn Rand provided a moral foundation for libertarians, Friedrich Hayek provided an economic foundation. Fearing and condemning any form of state economic planning as being nothing more than a new form of serfdom, Hayek argued for the only justifiable alternative, that of economic individualism.[45] In Hayek's terms, "Economic planning by the state leads to the creed of unrestrained egalitarian collectivism."[46] In contrast, the free-market system leaves men free and therefore satisfied, and this will ensure that a nation will remain stable.[47] Only the free-market system is capable of raising the living standards of individuals.[48] Nothing should determine a man's share in the market except that the manner in which the individual utilizes this economic and political freedom. The strife for social justice through government has had the detrimental result of destroying individual freedom.[49]

Hayek laments about the increased size, power, and role of government in society and the economy. The legislative power of the government is no longer limited, either by law or principles. Under the influence of special interests and parties, legislatures are less concerned with general principles than with special interests and less concerned with being truly representative of the people. Legislation should be directed toward the preservation of personal and economic freedom in accordance with a set of prescribed laws and not with attempts to collectivize society in order to achieve social justice.[50]

Hayek advocates a minimal form of government based on the rule of law. The role of government is limited to providing a national defense, protecting man's rights, preserving law and order, and enforcing contracts.[51] Support for these services should come from a uniformly scaled taxing system, but it must be stressed that none of this revenue is to be used for any plans that entail the redistribution of wealth.[52] The private sector must be allowed to operate in as much freedom as possible within the bounds of the laws. Liberty, or the absence of coercion, must prevail.[53]

John Hospers follows Hayek's line of reasoning in his own writings. The individual is the key, and the only true unit of concern. There are only individual rights not social rights since society is not a separate entity.[54] The individual is the focus of concern and anything that hinders that person can be labeled as illegal and immoral.

Individual liberty in the social and economic spheres is essential for citizens to reach their full potential. Any form of compulsion or coercion that forces them to do something involuntarily is evil. Echoing John Stuart Mill, Hospers argues that "every man has the right to be free as long as he does not infringe upon the rights of others."[55] Governments have constantly increased the amount of control over citizens' lives and must therefore be restricted to the minimal role necessary to the full exertion of freedom by the citizenry.

A limited government can supply the indispensable need of men living in a society, that of a rule of law.[56] Its function is to keep the peace, protect one's rights from affronts, and arbitrate disputes between individuals according to a prescribed, carefully defined constitution.[57] Hospers points out that libertarianism's view of the role of government is not anarchism; rather, it is limited government along the lines and wishes of Jefferson and Madison.[58]

Obviously, Hospers praises the laissez-faire capitalistic system as being the most desirable. Again, this permits the maximum amount of individual freedom. Government must not exploit the earners through involuntary taxation so that another class may live off their proceeds.[59] Charity must be a voluntary act taken from one's own surplus and given to what the individual believes are worthy causes. Forced charity in the guise of taxes and welfare is the equivalent of theft.[60] This must be stopped, and the free-market allowed to flourish and provide the necessary services that the consumers desire and need. Governmental services are to be provided by private enterprises in this new society.

Robert Nozick is the third minarchist to be examined. Nozick, relying heavily on Lockean contract theory, attempts to justify and explain the minimal state. Rothbard describes Nozick's philosophy as follows: "Beginning with a free-market anarchist state of nature, [he] portrays the state as emerging, by an invisible hand process that violates no one's rights, first as a dominant protective agency, then to an ultra-minimal state, and then finally to a minimal state."[61] This minimal state has the duties of protecting man from force, theft, and fraud, as well as the duty to enforce contracts.[62] In other words, the state fulfills the role of a night watchman in Nozick's minarchist philosophy. Nozick notes that "the minimal state is the most extensive state that can be justified. Any more extensive state power violates the rights of the people."[63]

For Nozick, the minimal state developed out of a voluntary contract among persons to create a state charged with the limited role of protection of individual rights. The economic system would remain a laissez-faire system since individual liberty is integrally related to economic liberty.

Not all libertarian writers are minarchists. A second school of thought exists within the libertarian movement. This school, that of anarchism or, better yet, anarcho-capitalism stresses the free-market system to the point of excluding the very existence of any form of governmental structure and authority. The principles of capitalism and the marketplace would be relied upon to provide all of man's basic needs. The best representative of the anarcho-capitalist libertarians is Murray Rothbard. Even though the majority of libertarians are not anarcho-capitalists like Rothbard, this group has greatly influenced the opinions and ideas of the Libertarian Party.

As with the minarchists, Rothbard bases his ideas upon a Lockean foundation. He relies on Locke's natural rights and state of nature theories, especially regarding the rights of property, as a method of elaborating his version of the libertarian creed.

Man has a natural right to property, including the property of his own body, and from this property right stems all freedoms.[64]

Each individual is to be free to choose his own goals, the methods of achieving these, and applying his labor toward these goals as he deems fit.[65] All human rights and freedoms can be envisioned as property rights for, as Rothbard notes, "There are no human rights which are not also property rights."[66] As an example, the freedom of speech means the right to rent a hall and talk about anything to anybody who enters the hall to hear that person speak. The renting of the hall is a voluntary contractual transfer of property from the owner to the speaker. Since the hall is private property and the transfer of temporary control voluntary, the speaker may address any topic desired. Thus, the freedom of speech is in reality a right to property and its control.[67]

Rothbard carries this property logic to what some libertarians claim is an extreme. For example, abortion is justified in this context, in that the fetus is the property of the woman and she may dispose of her property as she sees fit.[68] Using this logic, he would even justify the selling and buying of children on a free-market basis.[69] Thus, the rights of property replace the rights of citizenship in the absence of a state.[70] Only in a property context can individualism be secure from collective or egalitarian affronts.

According to Rothbard, man has the basic right to self-defense. Again, this right must be examined in the framework of property. Any aggression against a man's property or the property of his self can be met by a reciprocal and proportional counteraction. Anyone or group that uses aggression against another person or another person's property is a criminal and the victim can defend his person or property.[71]

Rothbard addresses most of his criticism at the state. After explaining that the use of aggression and force is criminal and that only legitimate agreements can be based upon voluntary contracts, he labels the state as a criminal since it uses coercion and aggression against the citizenry. The state, through a "monopoly of the use of violence," is inevitably an aggressor, and thus a criminal of the highest degree.[72] "The state is a coercive criminal organization that subsists by a regularized large-scale system of taxation-theft and gets away with it by engineering support of the majority."[73] The state subsists by collecting revenue or property from the people on a compulsory basis. This system is based upon force and the threat of force to collect the revenues. It is involuntary in that no one may opt out of it. Therefore, taxation by the state is the crime of theft.[74]

The state, "by its very nature, must violate the generally accepted moral laws to which most people adhere."[75] People deem robbery as immoral, but the state does it and calls it taxation. Murder is immoral, but the state murders and labels it as capital punishment or war. Slavery is immoral and against the natural rights of man, but the state is able to enslave men through military conscription. Therefore, because the state is a criminal, it must be eradicated. This is the only acceptable solution. A constitution cannot guard against the numerous infractions of a government upon man's rights. Rothbard as an anarchist believes in the sanctity of the free-market capitalist system. Any enterprise, from roads to defense, must be performed on a free-market, private basis.

Rothbard goes on to deny any contradiction between the values of laissez-faire capitalism and an anarchist social environment. Not only are capitalism and anarchism compatible, but they are desirable, for to be a pure capitalist, one must also be an anarchist. Rothbard's philosophy of anarcho-capitalism rests upon the central axiom that no man, or group, may use aggression against the person or property of another.[76] Man has the right to be free and only in a stateless society with a laissez-faire market system can he truly achieve his full potential as a human being.

As unique as the various brands of libertarianism may appear, they have had an active role in shaping the platforms and goals of one particular party. It is obvious that much of the expression of ideas are outside the U.S. political mainstream, yet the core elements of the libertarian creed rest upon the consensual concepts of the American political creed, those of individual liberty, consent, equality, and due process.[77] The thoughts of Locke, Jefferson, the Anti-Federalists, de Tocqueville, Rousseau, Spooner, Garrison, and John Stuart Mill are echoed in the party's philosophy on a more contemporary scale. The Libertarian Party has attempted to educate and elucidate the meanings and implications of libertarianism in its platforms. This party also prides itself in being nonconformist. It believes its political goals are suitable and desirable for all individuals and that they reflect the basic values of the American political creed. In the following sections the Libertarian Party is examined in more detail. It will be described in accordance with the three categories of explanations found in the explanatory framework.

The Libertarian Party: Its Formation

As explained earlier, one of the chief objectives of this study is to review the literature concerning minor parties and to develop a framework for the systematic analysis of a contemporary minor political party, as presented in Chapter 2. The Libertarian Party was selected for case study analysis to serve as a model for the application of the three phases of the framework related to contemporary minor parties.

It is nearly impossible to pinpoint one single cause or combination of causes for the formation of the Libertarian Party. However, since the party was formed only twenty years ago, those formation explanations that are deemed feasible can be readily noted.

The Libertarian Party, the self-proclaimed "party of principle," was formed in 1971.[78] "The target of the libertarians is coercion of any sort that would impinge upon that liberty of the individual; but their real focus is the government and the cult of the omnipotent state."[79] Tuccille attributes the formation of the party to a split in the traditional conservative ranks stemming from an abandonment of the concepts of individual liberty for one of anticommunism in a paranoic, fanatical manner.[80] After the 1968 presidential election, there was a further rift in the conservative ranks. The Libertarian Party formed out of disgruntled Republicans, bitter Democrats, anarchists, socialists, and members from the SDS and Young Americans for Freedom (YAF).[81]

As will be recalled, the first set of explanations in the framework consisted of three crisis explanations for the formation of minor political parties. These crises were political, social, and economic oriented. It is difficult to qualify the origin of this party as being caused by any type of crisis.

The Libertarian Party can trace its roots to a philosophical movement in America rather than to any one particular crisis. As stated in previous sections, libertarianism can trace its origins back to Locke, Jefferson, and other philosophers. Its twin pillars of pure capitalism and antistatism attracted a wide spectrum of adherents. It desired the minimal state of the classical liberals and condemned the modern state as aspiring to omnipotence in the prescription of individual morality and personal conduct in social and economic affairs, and then dividing profits among undeserving people in the name of social justice.[82] It has retained the dominant theme of individual rights and liberty in all spheres—personal and economic.[83] Up until the 1950s and 1960s, the libertarians consisted mainly of free-market economists and intellectuals. However, as David Bergland notes, "The number of people who, in a knowledgeable way, came to call themselves 'libertarians' grew at a slow but steady pace. At the time, there was no organized political movement to implement libertarian ideas in the American political arena."[84]

By the late 1960s, the various groups of the libertarian movement began to press toward partisan politics, a movement that culminated in the formation of the Libertarian Party during the late 1960s and early 1970s.[85] The social, political, and economic setting of the time seemed appropriate to motivate the formation of a minor political party that would agitate for the libertarian ideals of personal liberty and a free-market system.

Whether or not there was a crisis of any sort at this time is hard to prove. By 1968 many issues were permanent enough in American politics to cause major gulfs between groups of voters. The 1968 election itself, with Wallace's AIP campaign, demonstrates this point. There was concern over the war in Vietnam, civil rights, disillusionment with the Great Society programs, and, after Watergate, a growing suspicion of the two major parties and politics as a whole.[86] In 1969 the YAF split over the issue of resisting the military draft. The new splinter group, calling itself the Libertarian Society for Individual Liberty, was united in its belief in noncoercion, especially as it pertained to governmental intervention in personal or economic freedom.[87] Other groups began to be enticed by the chance of injecting their political, social, and economic ideas in the political system. Members from the SDS, remnants of the New Left, and Randian Objectivists coalesced in the libertarian movement and entered partisan politics.[88] Efforts to form a clear-cut and united libertarian movement in 1969 failed in the sense that no viable political party could be formed out of the many disjointed and disorganized groups.[89]

Bergland states that in 1971, "Richard Nixon created some of the motivation for the new political party which would work for everyone's liberty on every issue."[90] This was the year in which wage and price controls were instituted by executive order. As Bergland notes, this was the primary act that ruined any hopes that Nixon and the Republican Party would reduce government intervention in the marketplace in accordance with libertarian goals.[91] This action, coupled with the growing opposition to U.S. involvement in Vietnam, as well as instances of government harassment of antiwar groups, led to a convention that eventually developed into the present Libertarian Party.

Under the leadership of David Nolan, the founding convention of the Libertarian Party was held in Colorado Springs, Colorado, in December 1971. The party became formally organized in June 1972, when it met in convention, and nominated candidates for the offices of president and vice president. At this time, the party also formulated a Statement of Principles that has served as a foundation for all of the subsequent platforms.[92]

The Libertarian Party was initially dominated by minarchists and followers of Rand's objectivism, but soon Rothbard and other anarcho-capitalists became top party strategists.[93] The debate between the two factions as to the proper role and course for the party would continue and eventually take its toll. This has led to the party being a coalition of various philosophical trains of thought rather than a single, unified front in partisan politics. However, despite its internal philosophical disputes, the party hoped to rise and fulfill a new role much like the Republicans did in their natal decade.[94]

As such, whereas crisis had been the catalyst for the formation of many minor parties in the past, this does not appear to be the case with the Libertarian Party. The American political, social, and economic settings in 1971–72 had not reached the necessary levels of conflict to produce such an effect.

For a political crisis to take place in which a minor party will develop, there must be a high level of intense conflict over an issue that will divide the electorate into an estranged minority alienated from the majority.[95] The minority position is not represented in either major party; therefore, they turn to a minor party, or create a new party as an outlet for their views and interests. This was the case in 1968. The political issue of involvement in Vietnam and the social issue of civil rights caused a division in the electorate. The minority—hawks and segregationists—turned to the American Independent Party to represent their interests in the political system.

By 1971 the political setting had calmed somewhat, and President Nixon was able to "fulfill his promise of aggressive action in foreign policy."[96] As promised in his February 1970 "State of the World" message, Nixon continued the peace negotiations with North Vietnam while at the same time reducing the U.S. role in the conflict through a policy of Vietnamization.[97] This appeased the antiwar factions in society. Those groups that remained hawkish in policy interests were still represented by the AIP. Both major parties had begun to represent the peace movement. Sundquist notes, "As the Democrats swung against the war, the Republican Party moved in that direction, too, though less quickly and decisively."[98]

Nixon was also able to make gains in the area of a nuclear arms treaty by getting the Soviets to agree to concentrate on limiting ABMs (antiballistic missiles) at the Helsinki SALT (strategic arms limitation talks) meetings. Probably Nixon's greatest achievement was opening a door to China, and reaffirming this new policy by visiting Peking in February 1972. Thus, it would be safe to assume that the conditions for a crisis over Vietnam or other foreign policy issues were not present in 1971–72.

Crisis in the social sphere is also inadequate for explaining why the Libertarian Party was formed. In 1968 the key social issues were civil rights and its corollary, law and order. Law and order as an issue was really a middle-class reaction to keeping black disorder and unrest out of their communities.[99] Ghetto and campus riots, peace marches, welfarism, drugs, and everything else deemed undesirable merged together as resulting from a breakdown of law and order. As stated earlier, the AIP had represented the segregationist and strong law and order interests in the 1968 election. By late 1968, though, both major parties had adopted a favorable stance toward civil rights and law and order. Thus, the AIP remained the party of white backlash against the civil rights stance of the two major parties.[100]

The black vote was being courted by both major parties in the early 1970s. According to Sundquist, "The fading of the race issue had made it possible for the Democrats to set out deliberately to construct such a black-white coalition by waging neo-populist campaigns, appealing to working-class voters and small farmers, and fashioning an attack, in one form or another, on powerful economic groups."[101] Race, as a catalyst of social crisis, was no longer a viable explanation of minor party formation by 1971–72. In fact, of the votes attracted to the AIP over the race issue in 1968, roughly 80 percent went to Nixon in the 1972 election.[102]

Therefore, by 1972 both major parties had yielded to the peace advocates and supporters of civil rights. Neither the war nor race provided the necessary campaign issues to win the 1972 presidential election. When McGovern attempted to win votes by stressing the differences between his and Nixon's stance toward the Vietnam conflict, he lost.[103]

Economic issues are more relevant in explaining the formation of the Libertarian Party, but again, these issues had not reached crisis proportions by 1971–1972. In the past, industrial and agricultural adversity had been the primary stimulus for the creation of many farmer-labor parties such as the Greenback, Populist, and Bull-Moose Progressive parties. Similar conditions were not present for the libertarians. Usually a period of adversity created an economically discontented segment of society for whom the minor party would direct its efforts. The Libertarian Party is not oriented towards representing this type of interest or clientele. True, it does desire and strive for a free-market system, but this philosophical endeavor does not draw upon any particular segment of economically discontented voters for support.

Instead, there were economic problems that, taken together, caused a political reaction from free-market thinkers in the form of creating a party based upon their principles. The foremost problem facing Nixon during this time was inflation and how to halt this, while at the same time avoiding a recession. In 1969 the unemployment rate was 3.3 percent, but it, along with the cost of living and interest rates, was increasing.[104] In order to halt the recession, in August 1971 Nixon instituted a ninety-day wage and price freeze. At the same time, tax cuts were proposed in order to create jobs; the Cost of Living Council was formed to administer the freeze plan; and in order to stimulate the sales and production rates, the automobile excise tax was ended and personal tax deductions increased.[105] In order to stabilize the dollar's value overseas, Nixon "suspended the convertibility of dollars into gold until foreign nations made proper adjustments" in their rates of exchange.[106]

The freeze plan upset labor leaders, especially the AFL-CIO, but reluctantly they eventually supported the plan.[107] The actions of Nixon with regard to the wage and price freeze did not create the high level of intense conflict in the electorate characteristic of a crisis. What did happen was that these actions did offend some conservative elements in society who were opposed to government intrusion in the marketplace. It was these elements, the libertarian conservatives, who would form a new party to protest what they deemed as a betrayal of their philosophical dedication to pure capitalism. The party did not depend upon a large, discontented segment of the electorate like the Greenback or Populist parties had in the late 1800s.

In concluding this discussion of the crisis explanations, there were prevalent issues in 1971-72, but none had the intensity to cause a crisis and thus divide the electorate. The Libertarian Party was formed out of opposition to the programs of Nixon that violated the group's philosophical dedication to the market system. The crisis explanations just cannot be substantiated. In fact, the party's poor start and low level of support in the 1972 election would serve to demonstrate the point that voters were not flocking to the party out of any crisis.[108]

The celebrity candidate and party splintering explanations can be quickly dismissed. No celebrity or popular personality appeared at the founding convention of the party in 1972. The party's first presidential candidate, John Hospers, was hardly a household name. The Libertarian Party was not, and has not been, a personality-oriented party. It has even strived to avoid becoming such a party. Nor did the party form as an offshoot or faction splintering from either a minor or major party. The party did attract many members of other groups and parties, but no one party split to form this new minor party.

The only appropriate explanation is that some degree of voter disillusionment or dissatisfaction with the major political parties was the catalyst for the formation of the Libertarian Party. The eighty-five delegates at the first nominating convention represented the leftovers and disillusioned members of the two major parties and several other political organizations. As stated, the convention had attracted SDS and New Left leftovers, disillusioned Buckleyites and right wingers, objectivists, remnants of the Liberty League and the YAF, and those who saw the need to have a political wing of the libertarian ideology.[109] What these people did have in common was a dislike of the growing centralization of power in government and the growth of infringements in personal and economic liberties. Kenneth Woodward characterized the party's ideological focus as a "blend of the hedonism of Epicurus, social Darwinism of Spencer, radicalism of Paine, objectivism of Rand, misanthropy of H. L. Mencken, laissez-faire economics of Hayek, and the antic anarchism of Abbie Hoffman."[110] Yet, Woodward

is also quick to point out that "anarchic as it sounds, libertarianism has sur-
faced in this election year [1974], as an ideology matched to the mood of
many disgruntled Americans."[111]

The Libertarian Party was believed by its members to be representative, a vanguard of a new American revolution. The party was launched
on the rising tide of antistatist sentiment and general dissatisfaction with
the modern state.[112] It hoped to capitalize on this disillusionment by ampli-
fying the Lockean themes for challenging statist practices and forcing
liberals and conservatives alike to justify their principles.[113] The role of the
state and its power needed reassessment and the Libertarian Party sought
to fulfill this challenge.

In 1978 Carl Polsgrove described the Libertarian Party's goals as a
comfortable, middle-class view of things.[114] He went on to note that the
Libertarian Party, "so audacious, so sweeping are their views, so puny their
power, that it is easy to dismiss them as armchair anarchists, utopian aca-
demics out of touch with reality. At the same time, their audacity attracts;
if they are crazy, theirs is an articulate, good-humored craziness."[115]

The goals of this party are seemingly idealistic and utopian. In this regard, Carey McWilliams states: "Nothing if not ambitious, the Libertarians
propose to change the course of history; they hope to fashion a society of unrestrained human freedom based on voluntary consent and a free-market
economy, without governmental sanctions or regulations."[116] His conclusion
is that this new party is important, and that its philosophy

> . . . does not mean that the Libertarians should be easily dismissed; they
> may well be able to tap a large national constituency made up of dis-
> affected, frustrated, none of the above, voters. Libertarian spokesmen are
> young, brash, intelligent, politically stylish and rhetorically resolute types.
> One gets the impression that they are ideological only in the sense that
> they emphatically reject consensus politics of the conservative-liberal-
> neoconservative variety. They are obviously not bigots or racists. They
> want to get government off their backs and ours; to them government is
> something separate from the people. They seem to be unaware of or in-
> different to the years of patient effort that went into the development of
> a system of rural free delivery and other important government services
> now taken for granted. At times they sound like anarchists without the
> social conscience that animated the anarchist movement of former years.
> Their attitude toward the down-and-outers seems to be: get up and start
> cooking.
>   Laugh not at the Libertarians. If the present vacuum in national politics
> is not filled with some semblance of responsible party leadership, we may
> well be in for a period of new parties, adventuristic politics and a kind
> of pragmatic anarchism. In a word, the existing political vacuum could
> grow larger until, in default of responsible political leadership, it would
> be filled by an authoritarian negativism of the None of Above variety.[117]

It would appear that the best explanation for the formation of the

Libertarian Party is that of voter disillusionment and dissatisfaction. Celebrity candidate and factionalism explanations are not applicable in this case. The crisis explanations are more difficult to dismiss, but all of the ingredients for a crisis development minor party were simply not present in 1971–72. As Mazmanian holds, crises have been responsible for the formation of significant minor parties. The Libertarian Party could hardly be labeled as significant after its 1972 start. Not until 1980 did the party have much of an electoral impact in terms of ballot access and the number of votes received.

Thus, of all the explanations, the disillusionment of the voters appears to be the most appropriate to explain the formation of the Libertarian Party. Certainly the delegates at the 1971 convention were not a cross section of the American electorate. They were dedicated intellectuals, radicals, and enthusiastic believers in a philosophy that remains somewhat outside the mainstream of American politics. Nevertheless, the voter disillusionment explanation being the most probable and most supportable of the categories, a corollary explanation for the formation of the Libertarian Party can be developed. This is necessary because even the disillusionment explanation seems inadequate in completely describing the formation of the Libertarian Party.

The libertarian philosophy is obviously a culmination of ideals — political, social, and economic — that can be found in many writers. It appears that the Libertarian Party was more representative of an ideological movement than that of a voter movement. The party members believed there was a gap in the usual liberal-conservative pendulum of the Democrats and Republicans. This ideological vacuum needed to be filled by a party that espoused the basic notions of the Declaration of Independence and the Bill of Rights.

This new party was formed out of representatives of dissenting groups that were motivated by a concurring idea of what should constitute a better political and economic system for the United States. Its interpretation of the meaning and intent of the basic American political creed can be said to represent a new political and ideological movement in America. Whereas the voter disillusionment explanation may be supportable in this instance, it must also be viewed within the notion that some doctrinal parties arise to fulfill what they perceive to be as an ideological gap in the political spectrum. This can help explain, in part, the somewhat similar formation of the Socialist Party in the late 1800s and early 1900s. The original members of the party envisioned the need of a more moderate, pragmatic socialist political party and were repelled by the Marxist orthodoxy of the Socialist Labor Party.[118] A split occurred, and the new party formed out of several groups that united for this ideological goal.

Therefore, the framework explanations that are most feasible and which also have some utility include both voter disillusionment or dissatisfaction and, a new idea, that of representing a philosophical movement or filling an ideological vacuum. Other explanations such as crisis, factionalism, and celebrity candidate, cannot adequately account for the party's beginnings in the early 1970s.

Before the function that the Libertarian Party performs in the American political system can be evaluated, an examination of the party's structure and organization is appropriate. The following section will consider this and how it has developed since its inception in 1972.

The Structure of the Libertarian Party

In this section the basic organization of the Libertarian Party will be examined. The first part deals with the membership of the party in terms of both numbers and the criteria for joining. From this, a look at the national and state level committee system and the duties of each committee will be described. An examination of the party's budgets and expenses will be done, especially as it pertains to the development and performance of the party. Finally, the convention and nominating process is described.

Membership

According to the bylaws of the party, to become a member of the Libertarian Party a person must pay annual dues and must certify in writing that they are opposed to the use of coercion to achieve political or social goals.[119] This certification is satisfied by merely signing a membership form that states: "I hereby certify that I do not believe in or advocate the initiation of force as a means of achieving political or social goals."[120] It is obvious that this is in keeping with the philosophical foundations of the party. Dues are nominal and have averaged between $10 and $20 per year. In return, members receive a subscription to the *Libertarian Party News*, the party's main publication. As with all American political parties, membership is really a formality since anyone may vote for the party on election day.

Criteria for membership are minimal in comparison with some other minor parties as described earlier. There is no probationary period or sponsorship by other members, and leaving the party simply means not paying the membership dues. The party obviously does not strive for doctrinal purity in its new members since there is no screening process; rather, it hopes to educate the member into accepting libertarian principles.

The number of voters that claim to be members of the party has varied from year to year. Claiming to be a member of the party and voting for it on election day are not the same thing. Therefore, the only manner to accurately determine the number of members in the party is to count the number of annual dues payers. It is difficult to ascertain the exact number of dues-paying members because of the party's loose organizational structure. Data on the number of dues-paying members are unavailable for the years before 1982, the first year in which the data was tallied and regularly reported. As of 1982 there were approximately 5,400 dues-paying members. By 1986 the number had dropped to 5,253. Dues-paying membership during the years 1983–85 was over 6,000 members. As of 1988, 6,402 members were registered with the party hitting its highest level in early 1991 with 9,745 members.[121] These figures demonstrate two points. First, the membership is fairly stable, only varying by a few hundred from 1983 to 1985, and has steadily grown since then, but not in a uniform manner since some states have gained members while others have lost them. Second, the number of national party, dues-paying members is small. Five to six thousand consistent members show that the Libertarian Party is truly a minor party in terms of size. The problem of declining membership and what this poses for the future of the party will be addressed in a later section of this chapter.

Party publications argue that joining can be profitable, at least in terms of providing its members a somewhat substantial information network concerning new ways in which to expand and protect their personal and economic freedom.[122] Besides this personal benefit, the party offers an access route to public forums on particular issues. Thus, this avenue of protest permits anyone who is a member of the party an outlet for the expression of libertarian ideas.[123] Finally, the party states that it offers new members a sense of community as everyone strives toward a free society.[124] Therefore the incentives for joining the Libertarian Party fall mainly into the purposive category.

Members are attracted to the party more for ideological reasons and fulfillment than for any tangible rewards. This is obviously a generalization. Since the party does have a small paid staff, a few people may be attracted to the party for material benefits. However, the amount of material or solidary benefits that the party can offer its members are limited. Therefore, an appeal is made to a person's individual beliefs and ideology in order to motivate and persuade them into joining the party.

State and Local Structure

In order for any political party to be viable on a national scale, the party needs a system of state and local organizations that allow the party to contest almost every election.[125] The Libertarian Party can be best described as a complex association of state and local affiliate parties directed by a national committee. As might be expected, it is a very decentralized organization. The state and local parties are independent in their own campaign and election efforts, as long as they remain within the national platform guidelines. The state and local committee members are not appointed by the national committee, but are free to choose whomever they wish to serve on these various committees.[126]

According to Article 6 of the Libertarian Party bylaws, it is up to the National Committee (NatCom) to grant affiliate party status to any group of ten or more people that petition for this status.[127] It is stated that there shall be only one affiliate party in any one state or territory. The independence of these state and local parties is guaranteed in the bylaws. In Section 6, it is stated that "the autonomy of the affiliate parties shall not be abridged by the National Committee or any other committee of the party except as provided in these bylaws."[128] The NatCom does reserve the right to revoke affiliate status from any party, but this can be appealed through a process provided for in the bylaws.[129]

Although there appears to be a separation between the many affiliate parties and the national party, this applies only in the areas of party management. The national organization does provide limited material and financial assistance to the state and local affiliate parties. In fact, a key concern of the National Committee has always been to help rebuild those state parties that are in a decline and it has instituted a data gathering program to discover what can be done to rejuvenate these parties.[130] Still the point remains, that many of the key functions such as membership drives and solicitations of funds are handled at the affiliate levels. If these units handle these important tasks in a poor manner, it has a detrimental effect upon the national party.

National Party Structure

With regard to the national level organization, the Libertarian Party consists of two major committees, the National Committee or NatCom, and the Judicial Committee. There are several subcommittees, but the main source of decisionmaking power within the party remains with these two committees.

The NatCom is composed of the officers of the party (chair, vice chair, secretary, and treasurer), the preceding chair, seven at-large members from the delegates at the national convention, plus "one member and an alternate from each region plus one additional member and alternate from each region containing between 10 percent and 20 percent of the total party memberships, plus another additional member and alternate from each region containing over 20 percent of the total party membership and alternatives to be selected by the regions herein provided."[131] There are a total of nineteen regions. The term of office for members of the NatCom is between

regular conventions, usually a four-year period. The regional representatives on the committee may be removed and or replaced by the action of
the affiliate parties.[132] This provides a link between the national structure
and the many affiliates throughout the country.

The duties and powers of the NatCom are ambiguous. According to the
bylaws, the NatCom "shall have control and management of all the affairs,
properties and funds of the party. . . [and] may delegate authority in any
manner it deems necessary."[133] The NatCom's main duty involves
educating the public about the party, its goals, and its philosophy, and
therefore hopefully increasing the membership of the party. This public
education function is supplemented by an internal education program to
explain libertarian solutions to economic, political, and social questions.
This internal duty falls to a NatCom subcommittee, appropriately called the
Internal Education Committee, or IEC.

The IEC was formed in 1981 by Alicia Clark, the national chair at that
time. Its primary focus was to educate party members on the goals of the
party and its policies concerning various issues. According to Friedman and
McDowell, "Such educational programs are particularly necessary to the
libertarian movement because of the simple fact that the strands of libertarian thought do not naturally make a tightly woven ideological fabric; it
takes effort to piece them together."[134] Since libertarianism encompasses
a wide variety of views, this educational program was essential to the ability
of the party to present a united front in elections. This internal education
program's purpose was not necessarily to recruit members, but to refine the
views of those who were already members of the party.[135] According to
Alicia Clark, the IEC and its state and local counterparts "must lead such
efforts to promote study groups to discuss and learn about the various parts
of the national platform as well as developing other educational programs."[136]

Clark defended and stressed the importance of this educational function as consistent with the party's claim to be based upon principles. If it
is a central goal of the party to educate the public, then this libertarian in-
struction should begin from within the party itself, thus enabling the party
to develop a solid and knowledgeable grass roots organization and ensuring
that the party's candidates will follow the principles of the party.[137]

A second subcommittee is the Outreach Committee. Formed in 1981,
its purpose is to develop campaign strategies, voter support polls, ballot access designs, and conduct issue education for the voting public. Publications and advertising are further duties of the Outreach Committee.

The Judicial Committee consists of five members who are elected at the
regular national conventions and serve until the next convention.[138] The
duties of this committee are primarily to rule on the question of suspension
of affiliate parties, officers, NatCom members-at-large, and if necessary,

presidential and vice presidential candidates. It also has the final decision
on challenges and disputes regarding NatCom decisions, platform planks,
and party resolutions that may arise.[139]

Party Budget

The operating budget of the Libertarian Party is set by the National
Committee. The goal of the party is to operate on a balanced budget system
and it has achieved this except in the 1980 and 1984 presidential election
years. Revenue for the party consists of membership dues, mail and phone
solicitations, fundraising programs, sales of publications and materials, property rentals, and subscriptions to the *Libertarian Party News*. The party has
attempted and has, for the most part, succeeded in avoiding operating on
a deficit basis.

In the first six months of 1986 the party had been on an even budget.[140]
A treasurer's June 1986 financial report states that the party is on schedule
in regards to fund-raising, but it is exceeding the expected costs of this
activity. The expected 1986 income for the party was $355,500 with a total
projected expense of $319,950.[141]

The Libertarian Party has survived the debts of the 1980 and 1984
presidential campaigns by relying heavily on individual contributions. In
fact, the Federal Election Commission's Report on Financial Activity shows
that from the period of 1981 to June 1984 the party received no money from
corporations, labor, or trade unions.[142] Contributions from individuals were
the only source and can be categorized into amounts. Almost 85 percent
of all contributions were under $500; 6 percent were between $500 and
$749; and roughly 9 percent were over the amount of $750.[143] Therefore,
the party relies exclusively on the individual for contributions, and most of
these are in small amounts. This resource base appears to be in line with
the principles of the party, for as one party official put it, "The other political
parties rely largely on stolen tax money to finance their operations. We
don't and never will. We provide a product — Libertarian political action —
in exchange for financial support."[144]

Party Conventions and the Nominating Process

The Libertarian Party holds a regular national convention every odd-
numbered year at a time and place chosen by the NatCom. It is at these
regular conventions that the party's business is conducted, and in the
regular conventions held in the year previous to a presidential election year
the party's presidential and vice presidential candidates are selected.[145]
Delegates to the convention are required to be members of the national or
an affiliate party. The allocation of delegates at the convention begins with

four delegates from each affiliate party; plus one for each 25 percent of the total national membership in that party's area and one for each 1 percent of the vote cast for the party's presidential candidate in each state in the previous election.[146] Each affiliate may also submit a list of alternates to the Credentials Committee at the convention. Each affiliate party is autonomous in its delegate selection process as long as the delegates are members of the party.

It is at the regular conventions that the platform is developed by committee and more importantly, the candidates for president and vice president are chosen. The candidates must be selected by a majority vote of the delegates at the convention. One option that the delegates do have is to cast their vote for "None of the Above."[147] If this is the delegation's choice for office, that position will remain vacant until the following convention. If this happened, the party would not offer a candidate for president, it would therefore lose ballot status in several states, and would effectively curtail and possibly even destroy itself as a national party. Thus, in effect, the delegates have the power to curtail the effectiveness of the party if they so wished.

A secondary function of the convention is the selection of the NatCom members and the officers of the party. Nominations for these positions are received from the floor and must pass by a majority vote of the delegates. Again, the "None of the Above" provision is allowed with the same stipulation that if this choice wins, the position remains vacant.

In the next section the party will be examined in the context of the second category of explanations that are concerned with the roles and functions of minor political parties in the American political system. In doing this, the presidential campaigns and platforms of the party will be described in detail.

The Functions of the Libertarian Party

In this section the party's performance, roles, and functions within the American political system are examined in the context of the explanations found in the second category of the explanatory framework. The first of these explanations concerns the notion that minor parties serve at times as issue educators, innovators, and providers of ideas to the two major parties.

It is difficult to empirically support the hypothesis that the Libertarian Party has provided platform ideas to the Democrat and Republican parties. Just because the Libertarian Party professed a particular idea or issue stance first, this does not prove that they caused the major parties to adopt the idea. With this in mind, an examination of the party's platforms and issue statements is made to determine what, if any, feasible and acceptable ideas the party may have provided. The following is a look at the role of issue educator and innovator.

Issue Educator, Innovator and Idea Provider

The goal of issue education is a central focus of the Libertarian Party, almost to the point of neglecting their electoral functions. This education is essential to ensure that the party remains philosophically sound while attempting to become electorally successful. As Alicia Clark stated in 1982, "As a party we have one central and overriding goal: spreading the ideas, principles and programs of libertarianism until they are triumphant here and around the globe."[148] This "spreading of ideas" involves an internal education program, to teach new members about libertarianism—as already described—and an extensive program to educate and convert voters to the ideals of the party. These party programs are coupled with the various publications and foundations that ascribe to the libertarian philosophy. A constant concern is to avoid compromising the libertarian philosophy through partisan politics.

A concern of the party has been to maintain doctrinal purity while advocating practical stances on various issues. Campaigns are to be run with candidates who are experienced and knowledgeable about libertarian positions. The key goal is educating the public and party members while remaining an active political party.

In order to ascertain which issues and platform ideas may have influenced the major parties and the voters as a whole, an examination of the party's platforms is in order. For the most part, the platforms of the party from 1972 to 1988 have remained consistent. The platforms can be divided into four sections: (1) Individual Rights and Civil Order; (2) Trade and the Economy; (3) Domestic Ills; and (4) Foreign Policy. Each platform, except for 1976, begins with a statement of principles.

The first platform section, Individual Rights and Civil Order, begins with a statement that reads: "No conflict exists between civil order and individual rights. Both concepts are based on the same fundamental principle: that no individual, group, or government may initiate force against any other individual, group, or government."[149]

In this section the planks concerning crime, the freedoms of speech, press, and religion; the rights to privacy, property, and to bear arms; criticisms of existing governmental policies in regards to secrecy, discrimination, and the draft; and children's and women's rights are explained in the context of libertarian philosophy. In order to better grasp the party's stance on some of these issues, the more relevant planks will be summarized. It must be noted that some of the planks do vary from year to year, but this variance is minor since they remain based on the same general principles.

Some of the first concerns of the party are those of crime, victimless crimes, and the guarantees of due process of law. The party's response to the increasing crime rate is to call for a more impartial and consistent law enforcement that protects individual rights as the manner best suited to suppress crime. Since only those actions that infringe upon the rights of others are really crimes, the party supports repeal of all laws against victimless crimes. The party advocates an end to laws regarding the production, sale, possession, or use of drugs; those laws regulating consensual sexual relations such as prostitution; and laws prohibiting gambling, euthanasia, and suicide.[150] Due process of law for those accused of a crime must be guaranteed and safeguarded. The party stresses the need to have law enforcement officials to have search warrants because they are essential to protecting individual rights. Restitution for any losses suffered by a victim of any crime became an issue supported by the party for the first time in 1976.[151]

The party opposes any form of restriction or censorship on the freedom of speech and press. Regulations of the broadcast industry are strongly opposed. Included in this plank is a call for an end to all antipornography and obscenity laws since these infringe upon an individual's rights to enjoy and purchase such materials. This plank has remained consistent from 1972 to 1988.

As each platform since 1976 states in regards to property rights, "There is no conflict between property rights and human rights. Indeed, property rights are the rights of humans with respect to property and, as such, are entitled to the same respect and protection as all other individual rights."[152] Obviously, this is in line with the basic outlook of libertarianism as was described earlier.

Not all of the planks of the party can be readily accepted by the political mainstream of voters. For example, it is unclear what the party intended by its 1980 support of the right to political succession of any state or group, as long as it does not violate the rights of others. In 1980, and in much more detail in 1984 and 1988, the party embraced the ideal of children's rights. Basically, this plank stated that children have all the rights of human beings and, as such, any law that may infringe upon their rights must be forbidden. In other words, children were to be granted full protection and rights under the law as adults. Laws that involve limits on labor, "status offenses" such as underage drinking and smoking, and compulsory education laws must be repealed since they infringe upon the rights of children.[153] In addition to this, this idea continues along its Rothbardian line of thought to consider the guardianship of children. Since children are to be accorded full rights as adults, they have the right, at any time, to seek their own guardians or assume full responsibility for "the administration and protection of their own rights, ending dependency upon their guardians and or parents."[154] Parents can likewise seek new guardians for their children, or in other words, market their children at any time they wish. Any law that impedes this process is opposed as an infringement upon the rights and freedoms of the child or the parent.

The party considered the issue of abortion in its 1984 platform. The issue was widely debated at both the 1983 and 1987 conventions, and was finally adopted as a plank in the context of a statement of women's rights.[155] The debate ranged over the right of the woman versus the right of the un-born child. Was abortion an infringement of the liberty and life of the fetus? In the end, the purists won the debate and placed abortion in a property context. Since a woman's body is solely her property, she may do with her property as she pleases, and this includes the termination of a pregnancy at any time. Any law that hinders this freedom must be erased, but at the same time, the state must not support through taxes the practice of abor-tion.[156] Therefore, the party assumed a pro-choice stance while at the same time keeping within its limited government ideal.

The party's views on trade and the economy are strongly stated within the platforms. This section begins with a statement that reads as follows:

> Because each person has the right to offer goods and services to others on the free market, and because government interference can only harm free activity, we oppose all intervention by government into the area of economics. The only proper role of existing governments in the economic realm is to protect property rights, adjudicate disputes, and provide a legal framework in which voluntary trade is protected.
>
> Efforts to forcibly redistribute wealth or forcibly manage trade are in-tolerable. Government manipulation of the economy creates an en-trenched privileged class—those with access to tax money—and an ex-ploited class—those who are net tax-payers.[157]

It is this laissez-faire concentration that leads the party to call for the reduction and eventual end of all taxes. Associated with this, various planks call for the repeal of all governmental controls on wages, prices, rents, and interest rates; the repeal of the Sixteenth Amendment as stealing the fruits of one's labor; ending all subsidy plans and antitrust laws; a clear separation of the state and banking industry to institute a free-market banking system; and the cessation of protective tariffs and trade quotas.[158] The 1980 and 1984 platforms call for the end of government-supported services and fran-chises such as garbage collection and utilities. These services should be offered on a free-market basis to the consumer. Finally, the 1984 platform supports an amendment to the U.S. Constitution requiring a balanced budget.

Domestic issues are also firmly stated. A statement precedes the planks and sets the tone of the issue stances and solutions offered by the party. The introductory declaration to this section states:

Current problems in such areas as energy, pollution, health care delivery, decaying cities, and poverty are not solved, but are primarily caused by government. The welfare state, supposedly designed to aid the poor, is in reality a growing and parasitic burden on all productive people, and injures rather than benefits, the poor themselves.[159]

Within this setting, the party covers such topics as pollution, energy, poverty and unemployment, education, health care, social security, the civil service, the postal service, consumer protection, campaign finance laws, and a None of the Above provision for ballots. The government is blamed for problems and the only reasonable solution is touted as being an exertion of property rights via a free-market system. For example, the problem of pollution can be traced to a poorly defined legal system of individual property rights to clean air and water. Pollution is a violation of these rights and must not be permitted. Individuals can sue offenders of these property rights and have them halt their pollution, or else pay suitable damages to the plaintiff. The party has, therefore, since 1976 called for the abolition of the Environmental Protection Agency since it goes beyond these rights and forces governmental policies on property owners. The EPA and other government regulators and regulations are to be replaced with strict and defined liability guidelines.[160]

Since 1972 the party has called for a complete separation of education and the state. Government schools are equated with indoctrination and hinder the freedoms of choice and thought. All governmental ownership, operation, regulation, and subsidization of schools and universities must end. This halting of government involvement in education includes laws that require busing and compulsory education. In place of the present system, the party called for a tax-credit system of private schools and a removal of school taxes for those people not responsible for the education of children.[161] Only those people with children should pay for education. Individual expenditures for tuition and other educational matters would be tax free, in order to permit the parents to send their children to school and for whatever length of time they wish.

In the plank regarding poverty and unemployment, the party exerts its free-market principles. Complete separation of the government from business and the economy is the only acceptable goal. Nothing short of complete cessation of governmental monetary and fiscal policies intended to affect the level of employment is acceptable. It supports the repeal of the National Labor Relations Act; all minimum wage laws; mandatory retirement laws; occupational licensure; and any regulation that limits the entry into or practice of any trade or profession by any person. The party states its opposition to the welfare system and states that it must be eventually eliminated. In its place, private and voluntary charitable institutions would assume responsibility, on a purely voluntary basis, for helping the poor.

Since 1976 the social security system has also been condemned by the party. It is claimed that the social security system is a massive fraud, is bankrupt, and is oppressive to all individuals since it is an involuntary system that forces one to pay into it whether or not they have a private retirement and medical plan. The system must be made a voluntary system, or in other words, all citizens must have the right of nonparticipation.

Campaign finance laws are opposed for several reasons. The FEC is described as a despot that suppresses voluntary support for a candidate or party and limits contributions to the party or candidate of choice. The federal subsidization of elections forces individuals to monetarily support and entrench the two major parties into the system, even if the parties do not adequately represent the views of the electorate. These laws have removed the government from public accountability by enabling it "to control the elections of its own administrators and beneficiaries."[162]

The party calls for the abolition of the U.S. Postal Service because it is a government monopoly and restrictive of free competition; the U.S. Civil Service because it creates an entrenched bureaucracy and a concealed system of patronage; and the Occupational Safety and Health Act since it invades upon the rights of liberty and property of both the employer and employee. Consistent with the party's philosophy, the platform proposes privatization of all government-owned lands and resources and turning all federal parks over to private ownership and control.

Probably one of the most unusual planks in this section first appeared in 1980. This plank calls for the establishment of the None of the Above provision to be placed on all ballots, regardless of the level of the government. If this choice wins in the election, the office is to remain vacant and unfunded until the following election.

In their final sections, the platforms cover foreign policy issues. The party states that all international relations should be guided by the principles of noninitiation of force and nonintervention. In conjunction with this view, the individual rights of unrestricted travel, trade, immigration, and negotiation must be upheld. This implies that while the party professes to be noninterventionist, they are not necessarily isolationist in that individuals still may involve themselves in international affairs.

As might be expected, the party calls for a complete cessation of all tax-supported foreign aid programs, and it favors U.S. withdrawal from the United Nations, the World Bank, and the International Monetary Fund.

As for the defense and military policies of the United States, the party calls for the withdrawal of commitments for military intervention, such as NATO, from around the world. No military bases are to be operated abroad. The party does recognize and support the need of maintaining a sufficient military force to defend the United States from attack, but this is the only permissible bounds of defense policy. In regards to the Presidential War

Powers Act, it is to be severely restricted. The president must not be able to initiate any military interventions for any reason. In its 1980 and 1984 platforms the Libertarian Party favored an amendment to the U.S. Constitution limiting presidential powers and roles as commander in chief to its original constitutional meaning as head of the armed forces only in times of actual and declared war.

The platforms conclude with policy statements pertaining to various regions of the world, such as the Middle East, China, and South Africa. The noninterventionist principle comes to the forefront in these planks. All governmental aid, whether military or economic, must be halted. All alliances or incorporations of these regions into the American defense perimeter are condemned by the party. As this interventionist principle relates to South Africa, the government is to not only halt all involvement in that nation, including military, economic, and political aid, but also to take no action that prevents or restricts American trade or investment in South Africa. Private support of any group in that nation is to be permitted.

Each platform of the Libertarian Party since 1976 ends with a statement about omissions. It reads: "Our silence about any other particular government law, regulation, ordinance, directive, edict, control, regulatory agency, activity, or machination should not be construed to imply approval."[163] With this, the party has covered all its bases.

As mentioned in Chapter 2, it is difficult to support the contention that simply because a minor party included an idea in its platform before a major party did, that this will explain why this same issue is now on the political agenda of a major party and the public. Some of the platform planks just reviewed have found their way into the present arena of political ideas, while others have been ignored. Briefly, this study will focus on two such issues that the Libertarian Party expressed many years ago as policy goals, that have now found their way into public debate via the Republican Party.

The fiscal crisis of the late 1970s and early 1980s has lent some plausibility to libertarian analyses and solutions.[164] Two solutions stand out from among the rest: the privatization of governmental services in order to cut the cost and size of government; and an educational voucher or tax-credit system to permit a higher level of the freedom of choice for parents and children while at the same time reducing the costs to the government. The Libertarian Party has been a leader in the movement toward privatization. Privatization has been the centerpiece of the party's 1976, 1980, and 1984 presidential campaigns. Besides this, the libertarian think tank, the Cato Institute, has issued a steady stream of policy studies dedicated to the cause of privatization since the organization's founding in 1977.

Roger MacBride, the presidential candidate in 1976, summarized the idea of privatization in his book outlining the party's purpose and platform.

Economic woes are the result of government interference and are not the result of a lack of government involvement. The only moral and practical solution, essential to the survival of the United States, is a totally free-market capitalistic system.[165] The poor manner in which government monopolies are managed and operated, and the costs incurred through these to the taxpayers, supports the contention that private enterprise can handle these services more efficiently and with less expense to the consumer.[166] Government interference obviously limits competition, which in turn means that the consumer is forced to pay whatever price the government decides to arbitrarily set. The consumer has no recourse, whereas in a free-market system he would by simply turning to a competitor with a lower price. In the 1980 campaign Edward Clark repeated this call for privatization. According to Clark, private enterprises are much more efficient and less expensive, and therefore are much more desirable to those services operated by the government.[167]

The libertarian version of privatization would not cease with a few, select services, but would eventually include all governmental functions except for national defense and the court system. At one time or another, libertarian writers have called for the privatization of welfare, social security, the postal service, police and fire protection, and numerous other governmental programs, all in the name of saving the consumer money and reducing the size of government. These goals are in keeping with the libertarian aversion to government intrusions into both the economy, and into the everyday lives of the citizenry.

The Reagan administration had considered the privatization of several federally operated programs and services ranging from TVA to the U.S. Coast Guard. Other targets included the U.S. Postal Service, Conrail, and the FHA. "There [were] two motives at work—the Reagan administration's philosophical aversion to Big Government and the necessity for reducing federal spending under the Gramm-Rudman deficit-reduction plan, which is now law."[168] Some authors state that the "genesis for the privatization parade has been largely philosophical: the perfect symbol of the libertarian belief that 'small is beautiful' when applied to domestic government. Conservative think tanks have been loudly trumpeting the apparent success of contracting out by local governments—especially garbage collection, bus service, hospital administration, and vehicle towing."[169] As state and local governments face financial crises in the 1990s due to increased service demands and decreased revenues, privatization has seemingly, once again, become a policy option.

Regardless of how far the Reagan administration's privatization efforts went, they fell far short of libertarian goals. It is doubtful that all services that the government either controls or regulates will be turned over to the private sector. Whatever the source of these privatization programs, it is clear that it "crosses ideological lines . . . and all the political pressures are pushing toward privatization."[170]

As was discussed in the preceding chapter, one of the primary functions of minor parties in the American political system is that of providing issues and reform ideas for the public and major parties. It is apparent that the idea of privatization stems from the libertarian movement, and that the Republicans have taken this idea as a reasonable solution to the question of how to reduce government size and expenses. It satisfies the Republican's wish to limit the size of government. Yet, to claim without doubt that the libertarians are directly responsible for having this issue placed in the mainstream of political debate cannot be supported without reservations. Just because a minor party agitates for a cause before a major party does, this cannot prove that the latter took up the idea because the former did so first. This contention lacks the needed evidence to prove itself valid. It could be that after the Libertarian Party began to agitate and campaign for privatization, it appeared to be a feasible solution for many problems and thus appealed to conservative elements in the Republican Party. The idea became a part of the Republican agenda after Reagan's 1980 victory. Therefore, it would seem likely that libertarian and conservative thinkers had reached the same conclusion regarding privatization at about the same time.

The Libertarian Party has also supported a tax-credit or tuition voucher system for education for many years. The Republican Party came out in support of such a system in the late 1970s. Again, the originator of this idea cannot be discerned, but the dual support for these alternatives to the present education system does indicate the beginnings of the cooptation of the Libertarian Party by the GOP. Therefore, the libertarians have provided ideas for a major party and, at least on the surface, have seemingly performed the function of issue innovator, issue educator, and a possible provider of ideas for at least one major party.

The next function considered is that of being a pressure valve for a discontented group and therefore being an avenue of legitimate protest within the political system. It almost goes without saying that the party has to some extent fulfilled this function. The party is the culmination of discontented groups who have sought a political means to educate the public about, and eventually implement, their philosophical ideals. It is unknown whether some of these groups, especially the anarchists, would have ever resorted to illegal means to agitate their cause as many did in the 1800s and early 1900s. However, as long as there existed a legitimate avenue of protest through partisan politics, these types of actions may have been averted.

Schattschneider has characterized the American party system as being one of political conflict between many diverse interests.[171] Each major party attracts its own loose constellation of pressure groups, and it is these groups that bargain and compete within the parties to have their interests represented in government. Thus, according to Schattschneider, political conflict is waged by coalitions of inferior interests held together by a dominant interest.[172] These coalitions are the political parties in the United States and the dominant interest is that of capturing governmental power through the election system. Each party's effort in the political struggle (the election process), is primarily to exploit any weaknesses in the opposition while simultaneously attempting to consolidate one's own side.[173] The strategy of the parties is to change the focus of issues, or to substitute one conflict with another. This permits the parties to strengthen their respective position and rebuild for future competition.[174]

Schattschneider's assertion about the nature of the American party system implies that the Libertarian Party has served as an avenue of protest and a pressure valve within the political system. The party is a coalition of interests held together by a dominant interest — desiring that libertarian ideals become prevalent in American thought and or winning elections. The party is an avenue of protest for these interests. By providing this outlet, the party may have given the Republican Party the chance to consolidate its stance against opposition. The more radical elements of the Republican Party have deviated to the newer, more fiscally conservative Libertarian Party. Thus, in conclusion, various groups discontented with the issue stances of the GOP still have had a channel for their views to be expressed in the political system. It can be surmised that the major issues causing this discontent revolved around individual freedoms and economic solutions. The Libertarian Party has served as an avenue of protest and a pressure valve in the American political system, thus fulfilling another function described in the explanatory framework.

In the next section the study examines how well the party performed in representing the voters who support libertarianism in the American electoral system. In conjunction it will be determined whether or not the party ever performed the function as an election spoiler. The section has been divided into the national, state, and local levels. In the subsection on national elections, a description of the campaigns for president will be provided.

Electoral Performance: Presidential Nominations and Election Campaigns

In 1972 the Libertarian Party nominated John Hospers and Theodora Nathan as its first presidential and vice presidential candidates. With a membership largely composed of objectivists and minarchists, the party entered the electoral contest hoping only to establish a basis for victory within a few decades.[175] The campaign was run with the hope that voters would turn to the party because they were tired and disappointed with the two major parties.[176]

The results of the 1972 campaign hardly showed the potential for ultimate electoral success. Its candidates were on the ballot in only two states, receiving a total of 3,671 votes.[177] This poor showing can be partly blamed on the late start that the party had for the election, not starting until June 1972. The only positive result from this effort was that the Hospers/Nathan ticket did get one electoral college vote from a Republican party defector from Virginia. This elector was Roger MacBride.

MacBride's vote for the party in 1972 basically guaranteed his nomination as the party's presidential nominee for the 1976 presidential race. He continued to stress the party's effort to utilize the campaign as a means to educate the public about libertarian programs. By suggesting that the party "offers one of the few nonviolent opportunities" for change, MacBride hoped that the Libertarian Party would increase its voter support and, ultimately, replace one of the two major parties.[178]

The 1976 campaign centered on criticizing the role of government in the economy and society, espousing the benefits of libertarianism, and explaining the differences between the two major parties and the Libertarian Party. MacBride presented the party as an alternative to the big government and big spending Democrats and Republicans. In keeping with libertarian philosophy, MacBride confronted what he believed to be the malignant growth of government and the consequences that this had for the individual. American liberty, as envisioned by the founders, had been curtailed, regulated, and confiscated by the government argued MacBride.[179] The citizenry had lost their freedom without even realizing it through the increased amount of governmental intervention in the social and economic spheres.

MacBride blamed government interference in the market system for problems such as inflation.[180] Subsidies, agricultural price supports, tariffs, licenses, price controls, and "corporate coddling" must be stopped in order to achieve a healthy economy.[181]

In the area of social policy, the campaign focused on the need to limit government to the role of protector of individual rights and freedoms. All victimless crime, sexual conduct, and antiobscenity laws were to be repealed if elected. If there is consent between those individuals involved, there is no crime being committed and the government must stop being a parent and allow each person the right to choose and decide what is in their best interest.[182] After all, people are rational and should be free.

Foreign policy was to be on a noninterventionist scale. A national defense was the only acceptable role for the military. It was to be a volunteer force and utilized only if attacked.

With regard to the two major parties, MacBride argued that there was no real difference in their taxing and spending policies. The Democrats tax and spend in the social sphere; and the Republicans tax and spend on defense.[183] He criticized both parties for utilizing federal money in their campaigns and stated that his party would refuse the money on principle if it was offered to them.[184] In fact, MacBride asked the pointed question of how the major party candidates can complain of high taxes and excessive government spending and yet justify spending millions of FEC money that was collected from individual taxpayers?

The MacBride/Bergland ticket succeeded in significantly increasing the party's ballot status from two states in 1972 to thirty-two states in 1976.[185] Most of these states were in the midwest and western United States. The party was on more ballots than any other minor party. The total vote for the party in 1976 was 173,019; second only to independent candidate Eugene McCarthy. Nevertheless, this showing of the Libertarian Party fell far short of the goal of one million votes.[186] Reflecting on the party's performance in 1976, MacBride commented that the "next obstacle to overcome is to demonstrate that we [the Libertarian Party] can get somewhere, that idealism does not equate with ineffectuality."[187]

At the regular convention in 1979 approximately 2,000 delegates and alternates arrived to vote and nominate the party's 1980 presidential candidate.[188] Two candidates vied for the nomination: Edward Clark and William Hunscher. Clark was nominated on the first ballot with 365 votes to Hunscher's 195, and 6 for None of the Above.[189] For the vice presidential nominee, David Koch received 421 votes, while 62 were cast for None of the Above.[190] Clark had been the party's gubernatorial candidate in California in 1978, and won around 377,960 votes, or 5.5 percent of the votes cast in the state.[191]

Although both Clark and Hunscher expressed opposition to antiabortion laws, the issue was debated at the convention, with some delegates believing it was a crime against the unborn child and others holding that it was coercion against the mother to make her keep the child.[192] This issue created an ethical dilemma at the convention, and was finally settled by putting abortion in the context of a property right which could be exercised at the mother's discretion. The two candidates' approach to the federal deficit was different. Hunscher believed that a balanced budget was a future goal, and could only be achieved after reducing expenditures by the government. Clark placed a balanced budget as an immediate goal and stated that it was a realistic and attainable goal.[193]

David Koch was nominated as the vice presidential candidate to take full advantage of the personal spending limit loophole created by *Buckley v. Valeo* (1976).[194] Koch had pledged a $500,000 contribution if he received the nomination.[195] The influx of Kochian funds into the party was to have an important impact. As one writer commented, "Until Koch opened his wallet, the movement was a ragtag collection of obscure academics, gold bugs, science fiction nuts and cranks, united only by their hatred of the state and their joy of squabbling with one another. His money transformed the Libertarian movement from a doughty band of true believers into a political force that is on the verge of becoming the first party since the Socialists to offer a serious challenge to the 'Replocrat' monopoly."[196] David Koch's contributions enabled the party to run a determined campaign and establish organizations, such as the Cato Institute, to spread the ideas and policies of libertarianism.

The party entered the 1980 campaign with four main goals. First, and most obvious, it hoped that the Clark/Koch ticket would win the election. Second, the party sought to establish their presence in American electoral politics by offering themselves as a legitimate, viable, and reasonable alternative to the major parties. In fact, the party was projecting that if it did not win, then it would at least receive 5 percent of the popular vote, thereby establishing itself as a credible third party.[197]

The third goal of the party for the 1980 election was to get on all fifty state ballots, thus enhancing its potential appeal to both the public and the press.[198] Equally important, the party's presence on all fifty state ballots and a substantial percentage of votes would enable the party to have permanent ballot status in most states. Broad representation on the presidential ballot would allow the party to field a wide range of candidates in the 1982 state and local elections.[199] Thus the real motive behind the party's 1980 campaign may have been to gain inroads into American politics through activity in state and local elections.

The creation of a stable organization was clearly essential to the party's viability as a third major party.[200] Grass root party and campaign organizations in every state would allow a challenge of the two-party dominance in ever-increasing numbers of elections at every level. Furthermore, despite defeat in elections, the party would extend its appeal through education of voters about libertarian goals and programs.[201]

In 1980 the Libertarian Party's ticket of Ed Clark and David Koch was able to achieve its goal of ballot status in all fifty states. In fact, the party was the first minor party to attain this status since the Socialist candidate, Allan Benson, did it in 1916.[202]

Clark and Koch conducted a strenuous campaign, and with a war chest of over $3 million (a great portion of this from Koch himself) the party clearly increased its visibility. The party continued to agitate for its philosophical goals. Clark criticized the two-party system as a device that simply reinforced the dimensions of big government, thus ignoring the need for a fundamental reordering of the political system.[203] Clark and the party offered themselves as a consistent, principled, and rational alternative to major party policies that had resulted in major social and economic problems. Clark charged that voters have been socialized into accepting the Democrats and Republicans as the only two political parties, yet neither party could adequately define the differences between the two since the parties remained in the safe middle ground.[204] Given no meaningful alternatives between the two major parties, voters were opting not to participate, thereby passively rejecting the two major parties. Both parties continue to play political manipulation games by rewarding some groups at the expense of others. They cared little for individual rights, whether economic or social.[205] The policy of government, regardless of the party in power, had ruined the economy beyond any hopes of incremental improvement.[206] The Libertarian Party was to be the essential alternative to this downward spiral.

Clark's campaign constantly compared the two major parties and their policies to the Libertarian Party alternatives. The first point of comparison was government taxation and spending. Clark argued that spending was much too high and programs were wasteful. This was the basic problem with a government-dominated economy, Clark explained. Special interest groups were lobbying to get tax dollars for themselves, and because both major parties were indebted to these groups, they usually got what they wanted.[207] Neither party had the courage to cut taxes or spending.

The libertarian alternative was to cut taxes drastically and to balance the budget by ending deficit spending as well as the government subsidy system.[208] Clark stated that the result of these plans would be to reduce taxes and permit the consumer to spend more in the market. Government intervention via regulations, subsidies, or monetary management only resulted in an increase in inflation, prices, interest rates, and unemployment.[209] By instituting a free-market system, these problems would eventually disappear.

A major issue for the party in the 1980 election was social security. Social security was "nothing but an involuntary, fraudulent pyramid scheme in which government bureaucrats arbitrarily decide how much a citizen is to put into the system and how much they get out of the system."[210] In its place, Clark hoped to utilize alternative tax credits for individual retirement plans, voluntarily chosen by each citizen. Private plans could give better returns since the citizen had direct control over their investments.

The welfare system was to be disbanded. The welfare bureaucracy manipulated benefits in order to control recipient behavior. By eliminating much of the social and defense spending, the budget could be balanced. Less government implied lower spending and less taxes.

Privatization of governmental services was to be the next step of this program. One public service, in particular, that Clark stressed needed to be privatized was education. Clark proposed a detailed tax-credit system to allow parents a choice to which school they could send their children.[211]

(Another idea adopted and later proposed by the Republican Party.) Government-operated schools are centers of indoctrination that were based on coercion and replaced the parent's responsibility with its own. If education was private, parents would be more involved since they were paying directly to the school for their child's education. Again, the right to choose was the focus of Clark's argument. Parents must have the right to select the type of schooling that best suited their children, a choice that would permit the child's individuality to develop.[212] A secondary benefit of the privatization of education was the amount by which government spending, and thus bureaucracy, would also decrease.

In characterizing his own party, Clark stated that it was an alternative movement that stressed liberty as a counter to government's mania for control. It urged the citizen to be responsible for their own actions and to also readily accept the consequences of the same.[213] The libertarian alternative to the major parties was freedom, the right to choose, to accept responsibility, and solve problems on a voluntary basis.[214]

By mid–1980 Clark was admitting that while he did not expect to win the election, he intended to make the party a part of the national political scene.[215] He was selling ideas, hoping to promote the party and put it on a respectable plane of recognition. The presidential election, according to Clark, should have an ethical, moral, and philosophical basis, which the party provided, and not simply be a horse race.[216]

Clark's hope that by pressing forth the libertarian ideas the party could affect the outcome of the election, or at least change the mood of the American voter, was hardly successful. Despite its presence on all fifty ballots, it received 921,299 (1.06 percent) of the popular vote.[217] The total may have been more if one important factor had not been present, John Anderson's independent campaign. Anderson received 5,720,600 votes, of which it is conceivable that some might have gone to the Libertarian Party had he not run. Ed Clark constantly warned that Anderson was not a protest vote against the major parties since Anderson supported the same establishment and system that Carter and Reagan did.[218] Calling Anderson an establishment candidate, Clark noted that Anderson's campaign was a personality rather than an issue-oriented campaign and would soon fade.[219] Anderson was a source of frustration for many ambitious minor parties in that he drew away media attention and eventually votes. The Libertarian Party had hoped to be a serious challenge to the two parties since they offered long-range, institutional alternatives, but instead they had to operate in Anderson's shadow.[220] Despite this major drawback, the 1980 election results made the Libertarian Party the third largest political party in the United States.[221]

The total vote that the party received was too small to retain its ballot status in several states. In 1982 a new Campaign Committee was initiated to help the party maintain its electoral momentum. The committee was to assist in recruiting candidates, provide campaign assistance in state and local endeavors, and, most importantly, get the party back on the ballots in those states where it had lost its status.[222]

By the time that the next regular convention was held, the party was once again ready for a serious attempt at getting its candidate elected president. Approximately seven hundred delegates arrived at the New York City convention, held fourteen months before the November 1984 presidential election.

The nomination of candidates did not go as smoothly as it had in 1980. The race for the nomination was three-way, including Gene Burns, a radio talk show host; David Bergland, the party chairman from 1977–81 and Mac-Bride's running mate in 1976; and, Earl Ravenal, a Georgetown University professor of political science who had been the foreign policy adviser to the party in the previous two campaigns, and who was associated with the Cato Institute.[223] Burns dropped out early because he was disillusioned about the low amount of money the party could muster to mount a credible race, leaving the choice between Ravenal and Bergland.[224]

Bergland was much more doctrinaire than Ravenal in his outlook for the party. Whereas Ravenal promised to mount a campaign that would be aimed at the national media, Bergland argued for a more concentrated effort at building a grass roots party organization and remaining steadfastly loyal to the principles and ideals of the party and libertarianism as a whole.[225]

It took four ballots before a winner was declared. In a close contest, Bergland won with 270 votes to Ravenal's 242 and None of the Above with 24.[226] Ravenal was a pragmatist who was perceived as willing to sway from libertarian philosophy in order to attract more votes. Because of this, Bergland's victory was a win for the libertarian purists who wanted a dedicated ideologue rather than a gradualist as the party's candidate.[227] As a hardliner, Bergland promised to hold strictly to the party's platform and philosophy. He refused to accept the notion that the party would, or should, moderate or gradually initiate its programs in order to attract the support of voters aligned with one of the major parties.[228] In choosing Bergland the convention delegates chose ideological purity over the gradualism and pragmatism first initiated by Clark in the 1980 campaign.[229] This signal would have later implications for the party.

Bergland kept true to his promises throughout his campaign. Rather than promise the reduction and eventual elimination of taxes and social spending, he insisted that they would be ended immediately. The privatization of *all* government services was promised.[230] Bergland stated that based on principle he would refuse any FEC matching money and that he would not appeal to the FCC for equal time provisions as had Clark during the 1980 campaign.[231]

Even with special efforts to maintain or regain ballot status in all fifty states, the party's Bergland/Lewis ticket succeeded in getting on only 38 ballots. It received a total of 228,796 votes nationwide, a 75.2 percent decline in support from 1980.[232] However, the Libertarian Party remained the third largest political party in terms of popular votes and ballot status. Lacking adequate funding, the party was unable to run a large media campaign. In fact, much of the budget had to be diverted from campaign activities to the ballot access area.[233]

Where the 1984 results were disappointing to many, others managed to see victory in the election. Murray Rothbard was one of these supporters. Rothbard found that the party had settled down in 1984 and that the goals it had set (mainly being a major party by 1984) had been overly optimistic and their only result would be voter disillusionment with the party.[234] "The 1976 and 1980 elections were a historical glitch, products of a strictly temporary infusion of funds from the Koch family," Rothbard wrote.[235] He lamented the infusion of Kochian funds into the party because it compromised principle and created disloyal, temporary supporters of the libertarian cause. The Koch funds had produced false hopes, leaving the 1984 election to establish again the core membership of true members in the libertarian movement.[236] This has left the party in a stronger position. It is growing at the grass roots level first, as it should and must. Rothbard praised Bergland for not straying from the principles of the party, even if it meant less voters and media attention.[237]

The nominating convention for the 1988 presidential election would once again be a time of conflict between party pragmatists and purists. Two relatively new party members were seeking the nomination: Russell Means, and former Congressman Ron Paul. Russell Means, an Oglala Sioux, and leader in the American Indian Movement (AIM) is also known for leading the seventy-one-day occupation of Wounded Knee in 1973 to protest the unfair treatment of Native Americans. As such, Means sought the nomination to prove that the entire United States was fast becoming one big reservation.[238] Means stated that it was natural for him to seek the nomination since the Indian belief in individual freedom was reflected in the Libertarian's philosophy and party platform. In fact, Means claimed that the Indian policy plank in the platform—that the government was to honor all treaties and return all lands that rightfully belonged to Indian tribes—was a result of his comments.[239] Means was an appealing possible candidate since he had the name recognition, but questions arose about his dedication to the party and its principles.

Ron Paul was the main contender for the nomination. Paul, a medical doctor who was from the Houston, Texas, area was first elected to the U.S. House of Representatives in 1974 as a Republican. While serving four terms in Congress, Paul stood out from among his peers for his opposition to federal spending. He opposed deficit spending in all areas, was upset with the IRS, its practices, and the outrageous tax system, condemned the Federal Reserve Board for restricting economic freedoms, and lamented over the renewed attacks on personal liberties.[240] Paul exuded a libertarian-like philosophy while serving in the House. In fact, he was the only Republican to vote against the 1981 defense budget, arguing instead for a more noninterventionist and thus less expensive stance for the United States.[241] In 1984 Paul ran for the U.S. Senate and lost. By 1987 he had decided that the Republican Party shared in the blame for deficits, the national debt, and other affronts to individual liberties and he resigned from the party. In February 1987 Paul announced his candidacy for the Libertarian Party's presidential nomination.

Thus, when the party met in Seattle in September 1987 several issues affronted it. Some saw this as an "opportunity for America's most persistent third party of the last two decades, enabling it to reach beyond its usually narrow segment of the electorate."[242] Paul had the political experience and background the party was seeking, yet Means had the name recognition. However, members were a little uneasy that both nominees were new to the party. They expressed concern that "the party was becoming the last refuge of conservatives when it really is not."[243] When the votes were tabulated, Paul won on the first ballot, 196 votes to Means's 120. Jim Lewis, the 1984 vice presidential nominee and a tax resister from Connecticut received 49 and None of the Above garnished 17 votes. Andre Marrou received the vice presidential nomination.

The Paul/Marrou ticket faced an uphill struggle from the very beginning. First of all, as of 1987 the party was only on fifteen ballots. Thus, the first order of business was to regain ballot status. Members kept referring to the 1980 campaign as a measuring stick and hoped the party could duplicate its achievement of being on every ballot. Yet, the party would spend nearly $449,000 and still fall short, getting on forty-six state ballots and on the ballot in the District of Columbia.[244] Secondly, the party was hoping to rejuvenate itself. It had become static since 1984, winning only a few local offices.[245] The campaign issues for the party did not deviate from the libertarian norm. As previously mentioned, Paul ran on a fiscally conservative and socially liberal platform. Arguing that the federal government's primary duty was to protect liberty, Paul stated that if elected, he would abolish the public education system, end social security, welfare, farm subsidies, repeal all victimless crime laws, and lead the United States along a noninterventionist foreign and military policy. His fiscal conservatism would get him support from some Pat Robertson supporters who disliked the economic plans put forth by George Bush.[246] However, Paul and the official party platform did not always agree. The libertarian pro-choice stance on abortion was contrary to Paul's personal belief that abortion was morally wrong.[247] Hence, it might not be any wonder why Paul's campaign focused primarily on foreign policy and the issue of drug legalization.

Paul seemed almost apologetic and his rhetoric at times was self-defeating. He was quoted as saying he knew he had no chance of winning and that getting 2 percent of the vote would be an achievement. He stated that "we're building the Libertarian Party and we're just as interested in the future generations as this election."[248] Paul's hopes would not be fulfilled. The 1988 campaign ended in disappointment for most party members. The Libertarian Party kept its number three status with 432,116 votes or .47 percent (compared to almost 49 million for Bush and almost 42 million votes for Dukakis).[249]

This examination of the presidential campaigns illustrates the fact that in no election since 1972 has the Libertarian Party performed the function of election spoiler or power broker. Its best performance was in 1980, yet it still could not attract more than 1 million votes, thus falling far short of its goals of 5 million votes and permanent ballot status in all fifty states. This is one explanation of the framework that can, at least on the national level, be discounted as not being supported by the evidence. An examination of the party's performance at the state and local levels is needed in order to determine if the election spoiler function might be applicable there.

Electoral Performance: State and Local Elections

When the Libertarian Party entered national politics in November 1972 it also entered state and local contests on a limited scale. The most notable effort at this level was in New York, where the Free Libertarian Party sponsored candidates for U.S. Congress and the state assembly.[250] However, the New York party made little impact on the election. Not until 1974 did the party mount its first serious efforts in subnational elections.[251] The party sponsored 10 candidates in 8 states but only received a total of 103,815 votes, a disappointing beginning.[252] Although most of these campaigns were run with the intentions of gaining a permanent slot on the state ballot, even this goal went substantially unrealized.

By the 1976 elections the party had made some impressive gains at the state and local levels. It now had 55 candidates running in 16 states. These congressional, gubernatorial, legislative, and municipal candidates amassed 181,923 votes. Only 11 of the candidates gained at least 1 percent or more of the vote.[253] Many of these campaigns were intended to stress ideas rather than actually win the contest. For example, in Illinois, the Libertarian candidate for lieutenant governor, Georgia Shields, stated the party's opposition to government-protected labor unions as bargaining agents and thus forfeited any chance of winning their support in the upcoming election.[254] Speaking after the election, Illinois state party chairman Milton Mueller stated it best when he said that "winning an election is not everything; we feel if our candidate can whip up some issues and spark some responses from other candidates, we've done our job."[255]

By 1978 the party was able to offer 39 candidates running for various positions in 18 states. Together they received 542,809 votes.[256] The libertarians had become the third largest party by 1978 and it was the only minor party that could claim to have organizations in all 50 states.[257] However, most of the party's success was generated in 2 states, Alaska and California.

In Alaska, libertarian candidate Dick Randolph was elected to the state legislature on the party's ticket. Speaking in 1980, Republican Lieutenant Governor Terry Miller said that the Libertarian Party was the best organized party in the state of Alaska.[258] It is this organization that enabled libertarian candidate, Ken Fanning, to win election to the legislature in 1980, and another candidate, Andre Marrou, to win in 1984. Marrou won in a three-way race with the major party candidates.[259] Even though the race was close, the Libertarian Party far outspent its opponents: the Republicans, $15,000; the Democrats, $4,000; and the Libertarian Party, $21,600, with over $10,150 spent on television advertising.[260] The efforts of the state party has made it an officially registered party within the state of Alaska.

The 1978 California gubernatorial race had Edward Clark representing the party's hopes of winning the office, or at least gaining permanent ballot status in the state for the 1980 presidential election. Clark's campaign platform included the ideas of education tax credits and the privatization of government services. The party, the "wave of the future" as Clark described it, received approximately 372,939 votes (5.5 percent), easily exceeding the 2 percent necessary to qualify for ballot status in the next election.[261]

Alaska and California were important campaigns for the party because it provided the impetus for future state and local campaigns as well as setting the stage for the 1980 presidential campaign. The party claimed to have around 550 candidates running in 1980 at the state and local levels, including 3 for governor, 14 for the U.S. Senate, and 112 for the U.S. House of Representatives.[262] Yet, even with this increased presence the party could claim only a few local level election victories.

The elections of 1982 were of special interest to the party because Dick Randolph was running for governor of Alaska. After overcoming legal problems due to the Alaska Public Office Commission labeling the party as a political action committee and attempted to limit its contributions, Randolph still managed to finish with 29,067 (14.9 percent) of the vote.[263] This was by far the best showing in any gubernatorial election for the party. Some of the party's other candidates were able to gain 1 percent or more of their state's vote. Among these were: Sam Steiger of Arizona with 36,649 or 5 percent of the vote; Dan Dougherty in California with 81,076 or 1 percent of the vote; Paul Grant got 19,349 or 2 percent of the vote in Colorado; Dan Becan in Nevada got 4,621 or 1.9 percent of the vote, but None of the Above received 6,894 or 2.9 percent; and, Paul J. Cleveland in Oregon received 2.6 percent or 27,394 votes in his race for governor on the Libertarian Party ticket.[264]

In the 1984 elections the party had candidates in thirty-eight states for offices ranging from the U.S. Congress to town councils. The only real success was Andre Marrou to the Alaskan state house. Yet, since the 1984 election the party has contested subnational offices in an average of thirty-five states. Successes have been few, but serious challenges many. For example, in the 1988 races several Libertarian Party candidates garnished over 20 percent of the votes for state legislative seats.[265] However, those few offices captured are usually inconsequential.

It can be ascertained from this review of Libertarian electoral endeavors that at no time has the party played the role of spoiler. Rarely has the party had enough votes to alter the outcome of an election by siphoning enough votes away from one of the two major parties to force a victory for the other. There have been few high visibility offices won by the party in any of the elections. At best, these numerous electoral attempts have provided an avenue of legitimate protest for voters discontented with the two major parties. Additionally, the party can claim some success in communicating its programs and ideas through placement of an increased number of candidates in state and local elections.

In concluding this section, it is clear that the foremost function of the Libertarian Party has been that of issue education. Some of the issues focused upon by the party, especially privatization and an educational tax-voucher system, may have found their way into the present arena of political debate due to the party's agitation. Since the party has provided a legitimate avenue of protest for the more radical elements of the electorate, it may have innocuously supported the Republican Party. By diverting these radical elements into its organization and programs, the Libertarian Party has permitted the Republican Party to remain in the more moderate zone of consensus of American political thought and partisan politics. Finally, despite its initial idealistic goals, the party has not been an election spoiler or a political threat to the dominance of the two major parties. The next section will analyze the framework's third category of explanations as they apply to the Libertarian Party.

The Decline of the Libertarian Party

In this section the third category of explanations found in the framework are analyzed. This category involves the numerous institutional, social, and organizational hurdles and barriers that a minor party must overcome in the political process in order to have any hopes of measurable electoral success.

Institutional Barriers

The institutional barriers to minor party success include the effects of ballot access laws; federal election campaign finance laws; lack of media exposure; the weakening effects that result from the single member district/plurality system, and the structure of the electoral college.

"Public policy in the U.S. does discourage the formation of new parties, to a greater degree than in any other country usually classed as a democracy."[266] As such, since the party's inception in 1972, it has fought an uphill battle for a place on the ballot that peaked in 1980 when it was on all fifty state ballots. The party has challenged ballot laws in many states, not always with success. The party has lost suits in Florida, Arizona, Connecticut, and California among other states.[267] The problem is cyclical in its detrimental effects; since the party has not received high percentages of votes, it is disqualified for ballot status in many states. Then, in order to regain this ballot status, the party must spend thousands of dollars to get back on the ballot. This diverts needed resources away from actual campaigns. A weak campaign implies a low voter percentage and the cycle begins once again. This problem has plagued most minor parties and is not new nor is it limited to the libertarians. Despite its losses the party has won some ballot cases. A 1984 challenge in federal court to Colorado's ballot laws was successful. The Court's decision lowered the needed percentage of votes to remain on the ballot for the 1984 and 1986 elections.[268] Therefore, the party was able to gain status and offer candidates.

The concern over ballot status has caused the party to create a Ballot Access Committee that would oversee the party's attempts at permanent status in all fifty states. Stephen Fielder, chairman of the committee, wanted ballot status in all fifty states by 1988. Critics within the party argued for status in only the more important states so as to conserve funds.[269] Fielder's long-range plan cost was estimated at $600,000. This is more money than the party has ever had in its operating budget.

It almost goes without saying that the party has been hindered by the requirements of federal election campaign laws. Even though the party was a successful coplaintiff in *Buckley v. Valeo* (1976), the contribution limits upheld by the U.S. Supreme Court have hampered the party. The party receives most of its money from individuals. With a limit placed by federal law on the amount, the party has had to seek revenues elsewhere. One manner is the nomination of wealthy candidates and another is the selling of published materials.[270]

The largest problem that the party faces is the lack of matching funds, or at least the unfair competition created by the major parties receiving this money. The party has stated that it would refuse federal campaign funds on principle, even though it has sometimes qualified for funding during the primaries. It has never received enough popular votes to qualify for general election funding. As long as the two major parties receive millions of dollars in federal funds, the Libertarian Party, and other minor parties for that matter, will be at a distinct monetary disadvantage. The effects take on a cyclical nature. The lack of money implies no campaigns and no ballot status in several states, which in turn means less chances of receiving the necessary number of votes in order to qualify for either federal funding or ballot status.

Media coverage is another institutional factor that minor parties must overcome. Nicholas von Hoffman has very clearly stated that the media has the power "to label and determine the sanity of any candidate or party," and because of this power, it can limit those who may listen seriously to that particular party or candidate.[271] By calling a party crazy, out of the mainstream, radical, or strange, the media can effectively deprive that party of a national podium. This has been part of the Libertarian Party's problem. "When libertarian candidates are treated as psychiatric specimens — [they are] only human interest stories given one-shot personality profiles."[272] This type of coverage ignores the party's platform and issue stances.

The lack of in-depth media attention has been one of the major complaints of the party for some time. Without more time devoted to issue ideas, education of the public will be nearly impossible. The party has realized that it must cultivate the media for the purposes of issue education.[273] Another complaint of the party about the media refers to what von Hoffman addressed, that of labeling the libertarians as lunatics or armchair anarchists. The party has had difficulty in ridding itself of the negative-image or novelty-type coverage usually given by the national media. It has also had problems in getting coverage. In a debate with Barry Commoner of the Citizens Party and Ed Clark at the University of Michigan, even though invited, no television and very few newspaper reporters showed up to cover the affair.[274] As mentioned earlier, the League of Women's Voters, the Commission on Presidential Debates, the major party candidates, and the FCC have denied legitimacy to all minor parties by excluding them from the televised presidential debates. Without the proper media exposure, the party cannot generate needed support. Thus far, the party has relied primarily upon its own publications and foundations to detail and explain its issue stances.

Social Barriers

With regard to the social barriers that minor parties must overcome, such as the wasted vote idea, the political socialization process in America, and the general social consensus that two-partyism is desirable, it is not difficult to conceive how the Libertarian Party is hindered by these barriers. Although empirical evidence of causation or association between these three explanations and the decline of a minor party may be hard to ascertain, one can assume with almost complete assurance that they do have a part in limiting the success of these parties. Just like any minor party that developed and failed before 1972, the Libertarian Party has had to combat the almost instinctive endorsement of the dual party system by voters.

The party has attempted to break this instinct by comparing itself to the two major parties and thus offering itself as a true alternative to the usual status quo. It has done this by explaining that its programs, unlike those of the major parties, offer the only real solutions to the problems found in America. These solutions are, for the most part, based upon free-market principles.

Another manner in which the party seems to be trying to overcome these social barriers, especially that of social consensus, is to explain that the party is actually based on a fulfillment of the basic founding principles of the United States. By claiming that it is the embodiment of the Declaration of Independence and the Constitution on a more contemporary scale, the party hopes to remain within the respected and accepted bounds of voter opinion.

Therefore, the party has hurled itself against these barriers, but there is no empirical manner to measure its effect or success. If there is one factor that has the potential to hinder the success of the Libertarian Party the most, it is the organizational and ideological problems in the party itself. The following section will address these problems and other contributing factors leading to the decline of a contemporary minor political party.

Organizational Factors of Decline

Several of the decline explanations have already been covered in other contexts above. Some of them are interrelated and dependent upon one another. These explanations involve the low resource base of minor parties; the lack of committed workers; and the criteria and incentives for becoming a member of the party in the first place. Once again, these explanations have a cyclical effect upon minor political parties. If the party has a high cost of membership, accompanied by low membership incentives, a lack of needed volunteers and workers will ensue—which will be a contributing factor to the party's lack of resources. People will not financially support a party if they cannot readily join it.

The Libertarian Party's membership requirements are not extreme. Signing a pledge of nonviolence and paying an annual membership fee is not a harsh endeavor. In conjunction, as with any American political party, voters can vote for the party, regardless of previous membership. Therefore, party membership in the United States can be transitory, lasting only for election day. The real problem for the Libertarian Party is the decline in the number of dues-paying members. The reasons for this are elusive, but it is most likely due to internal disillusionment and the cooptation of libertarian ideas by the Republican Party.

The party has yet to have any electoral success at the national level, and has had only minimal success at the state and local levels. Supporters are growing impatient waiting for the "wave of the future" to begin. Besides this, some of the issues that could be labeled as libertarian—such as privatization of government services—are appearing on the Republican Party agenda. It is logical that voters who support these issues will vote for a party that has a better chance of being elected and putting these issues into policy; therefore, they vote Republican.

The cyclical effects of nonsupport come into play once again at this point. Voters perceive a minor party as having good ideas but with little chance of winning. If they are given the option of supporting a major party with similar goals and ideas, their support will shift to the major party. When they shift their support there is little sense in remaining a member or joining the minor party. With fewer members in the minor party, obviously the amount of money collected by the party decreases. With a lower operating budget, the party cannot advertise, campaign effectively, nor challenge and initiate ballot status petition drives. It can no longer compete on a respectable and reasonable scale with the major parties, and so eventually declines into obscurity.

The final three explanations regarding the decline of a minor political party are the most pertinent for the Libertarian Party. These explanations are interrelated, and have some striking similarities with the history of other doctrinal minor parties. The next section examines the explanations of ideological extremism, fission within the party, and fusion of the minor party with one of the major parties.

Ideology and Decline

Like many minor parties before it, the Libertarian Party suffers from its doctrinal stance regarding political, social, and economic issues. Its unwavering attention to principle has caused the party to be labeled as nothing more than an eccentric blend of conservatism and liberalism. Rather than call the libertarian ideology extreme (since it does include several principles found in more acceptable ideological stances), it is more correct to say that the libertarian ideology suffers from various shortcomings. It is these shortcomings that have, or will, contribute to the decline of the party. It causes the party to be perceived by the public as cranky, amusing, and an intellectual curiosity rather than a true political movement and or party within the United States.[275]

According to Jerome Tuccille, the primary shortcoming of the party's ideology is that the party has been hopelessly utopian in its outlook and policy programs.[276] Tuccille's main criticism of the party, and a problem with many minor parties, is that they have rejected any attempt to solve problems in a realistic and practical manner.[277] Many government programs are slated for abolition by the party, yet the party does not offer any credible alternative other than quoting free-market theories. In other words, the party has failed to create a constructive plan of transition from the present system to the libertarian version. The party calls for the end to social security, welfare, and other social programs with no explanation of how it would handle the social and political consequences of such actions.

Tuccille states that since the party members are "not content to generate realistic programs designed to control the excesses of growing federal power, libertarians have insisted on their purity and refused to work for anything less than a fantasy land straight out of the pages of *Atlas Shrugged.*"[278] By refusing to accept more pragmatic approaches toward various issues, the party has reduced its appeal as a realistic political alternative to the major parties. The party offers slogans rather than viable solutions and thus the party remains an intellectual exercise or a provocative fringe movement, not a serious political alternative as it has hoped.[279]

This poses an ideological dilemma. Should the party remain unwaveringly dedicated to the principles of libertarianism regardless of the electoral consequences, or should it adopt a more tapered and pragmatic approach toward American politics? This split over the appropriate approach has affected the membership of the party, especially after the 1980, 1984, and 1988 presidential campaigns. It has divided the party into two factions, consisting of the more pragmatic members and those who want doctrinal purity over all else. Each faction has a different concept of the party's role within the political system. The pragmatists, or gradualists, believe that some ideas may have to be compromised in order to achieve electoral inroads into the system and the libertarian victory can be achieved gradually through elections. The purists, among them Rothbard and the anarcho-capitalists, believe that any compromise on policy is a betrayal to the founding principles and philosophy of the party and therefore should be opposed at all costs.

The Libertarian Party has been plagued by a division that developed in the ranks of the party between the more extreme doctrinal elements, the purists, and the more pragmatic moderate group, the gradualists.[280] The purists oppose all state functions and call for a complete and immediate cessation of the state and its activities.[281] They condemn any hint of gradualism in libertarian theory or practice, regardless of the cost in support from the electorate. Compromise, according to the purist faction, would undercut the overriding goal of the movement itself.[282] Gradualism, as Rothbard argues, contradicts and postpones the inevitable victory of liberty, a victory so essential that it justifies the speediest, most efficacious means possible for its achievement.[283]

The gradualist libertarians, which include Ed Clark, John Hospers, and the minarchists, adhere to the same libertarian principles as the purists but are willing to accommodate intraparty differences and reach compromises through the political process in order to achieve libertarian goals. Moderate libertarians sometimes appear almost indistinguishable from more traditional political conservatives.[284] Both support the Constitution, a national defense, a cut in social programs and spending, economic freedom, and both oppose the left, but they differ on the amount of individual liberty that should be permitted, with libertarians placing almost no limits on this freedom.

The debate between the purist and gradualist factions of the party has become more profound since the 1980 election. Ed Clark represented the gradualist interests of the party in his 1980 campaign. He argued that the only way that the party could grow was gradually, with the support of educational programs, so as not to frighten away potential voter support.[285] Only in this manner can the party hope to grow into the third major party. In short, if the party is believed to be too radical, or too ideologically extreme, voters will avoid supporting it. This has been the problem with many doctrinal parties, and one that the gradualist libertarians are hoping to avoid.

The course of pragmatism and gradualism as the basis for party political activity was set after Alicia Clark was elected as the party's national chair in 1981. The vote was by no means lopsided in her favor. Alicia Clark was opposed by John Mason, a purist. Clark won on the third ballot, 273 to 228 votes with the anarchists casting 35 votes for None of the Above.[286] Once in office, she placed an emphasis on a gradual, phased-in approach toward libertarian program goals.[287] Changes were to be made from within the system in an incremental manner.

Party members that stress ideological purity over electoral power as the chief goal of the party continue to support a more radical direction for the party. They were critical of the 1980 campaign. One action, in particular, infuriated this doctrinal faction. Ed Clark was refused airtime on NBC, and he sued under FEC rules in the FCC. His action was condemned by the doctrinaire elements as being unlibertarian by invoking the state's coercive power on a private corporation.[288] A libertarian candidate that decries government interference in the election process should not employ the same system he has condemned. Ed Clark, therefore, was charged with watering down and threatening the basic philosophical stances of the party.

Purists believed the party was threatened not only by the Republican Party, but also by Reagan's rhetoric, a rhetoric with libertarian overtones but without libertarian substance. By allowing such meaningless rhetoric to go unchallenged, the ideological integrity of the libertarian movement would be destroyed or weakened. Ed Clark's campaign was perceived by purists as failing to clearly distinguish Reagan and Republican positions from the principles of the Libertarian Party.

The Bergland campaign of 1984, although less successful in terms of ballots and votes, was actually hailed as a victory for the party by the purists. Rothbard, as mentioned earlier, stated that the 1984 election was the one in which the party had finally settled in. The 1980 election reflected nothing but an infusion of Koch's funds into the party. It caused, according to Rothbard, a momentary excitement of believing that the party was stronger than it was in reality.[289] Now that the funds had dried up, the party was in a healthier state since only the true and dedicated libertarian supporters remained in the party.

The Bergland/Lewis ticket of 1984 represented a purist victory. Bergland himself was a purist and promised to never deviate from principle in his campaign by currying favor with the media or electorate.[290] Although the purists hoped that the internal factionalism with the gradualists had ended, leaving only the true libertarians in the party, Rothbard had cautioned that ideological revolutions and wars against the state, represented in the Libertarian Party, are slow and long struggles.[291] Only the most loyal and unwavering supporters can be counted on for help. The party is designed to educate, recruit, and eventually win elections whereas the major parties only focus on winning.[292] Regardless of how many losses are suffered by the party, one needs a healthy realism to realize that there are no quick victories in a philosophical movement such as this. Rothbard and the purist faction believe that when the party places its entire interest on winning elections, disregarding the consequences for the principles of the party, the movement will cease to be effective.

As was the case for the socialists, the libertarians must decide on their role in American politics. The socialists were faced with the dilemma of whether they were a political party, a pressure group, a political forum, or a revolutionary sect.[293] The libertarians must make a similar decision about their party. Both the gradualists and purists have different conceptualizations of the party and the path for the future. The gradualists seem to have centered on being a political party in the more traditional pattern of American pragmatic politics. The purists, on the other hand, envision the party as being a revolutionary sect, a vanguard of a new philosophical movement in the United States.

There are strong indications that this quarrel between the two groups within the party has taken its toll and caused defections to other parties. In

November 1985 Dick Randolph announced he was leaving the Libertarian Party and joining the Republican Party. Randolph stated that the Libertarian Party was "in shambles, and it continues on both the national and state scene in a descending position. It's declining, not gaining members and is at a very low ebb of activity."[294] Randolph placed the most blame for this decline on the Republican Party's cooptation of the libertarian message.[295] (It should be noted that Randolph lost a bid for the governor's office on the libertarian ticket in 1982, and this defect may be the result of his disillusionment with the party.) Reactions to the Randolph defection were mixed. Andre Marrou condemned Randolph for compromising himself on issues in order to fit into the GOP mold. Others reacted with confusion, shock, and disdain. Overall, the defection was a blow to the morale of the party.

Even more important, as of 1987, a substantial number of Libertarian Party members were seeking to form a coalition with the Republican Party. Former members of the Libertarian Party Radical Caucus have been encouraging a mass exodus from the party into the GOP. The group has renamed itself the Libertarian Republic Organizing Committee (LROC).[296] The LROC had two basic goals: the first was to work with sympathetic GOP organizations; and the second was to convince libertarians to join the Republican Party and support those GOP candidates who espouse libertarian ideals.[297] The full impact of the action of the LROC cannot be fully measured, but it does demonstrate that the party has had significant internal strife, factionalism, and disillusionment that, if not resolved, will eventually cause the party to splinter.

Still another piece of evidence that the party has had internal difficulties is that many libertarians have sought nomination for office through major party primaries. Libertarians in Washington, Michigan, and Arkansas, among other states, ran as Republicans and Democrats because the Libertarian Party could not, or did not qualify for the ballot in that state. Some of these candidates have even received support from one of the major parties. For example, De Anne Pullar was helped by the GOP with filing fees and campaign assistance in her effort to win election to the Washington state house.[298] Pullar states that her action was justified for, as a Libertarian Party candidate, "we can educate, educate, educate, but it will take ten years to get anywhere."[299]

Other libertarians are also using the major party avenue because the party has lost ballot status in many states. This is the case in Michigan where four libertarians ran in both major party primaries, although none won nomination. One libertarian candidate did, however, receive 35 percent of the vote in his race.[300] In Arkansas the state chair, Alan Lindsay, ran in the Democratic Party's primary for the U.S. Congress and received 22,694 votes, or 21.9 percent.[301] By utilizing a technique used by LaRouche supporters in the 1986 elections, these libertarian candidates are hoping to achieve some electoral success through a different route. They are impatient with the educate and wait process used by the party thus far. Continued evidence of fusion with the major parties, particularly the GOP, will exacerbate existing strains on the unity of ranks within the Libertarian Party.

The three explanations of ideological extremism, fission, and fusion are interrelated and cumulative in their explanatory power. Ideological problems create disillusioned party members and less support from the electorate. In order to counter this, some members want pragmatic compromises in order to keep the party viable. This has generated reaction from other members who seek doctrinal purity at all costs. Eventually, as can already be observed, members begin dropping out of the party altogether, or join other parties. This can leave the original party in a depleted state, both in numbers and contribution levels. The final result is a much smaller, more dogmatic and doctrinaire Libertarian Party, one that will not and or cannot adequately compete in the American electoral system.

The purist faction has yet to fully control the party. The NatCom is divided among the two factions. Since the purists were victorious in their nomination of the doctrinaire Bergland in 1984, the 1988 convention may have been the deciding event in determining the future of the party. Since the pragmatists succeeded in having one of their number nominated — Ron Paul — the party had another chance to survive. The purist faction still may leave the party out of protest. The end result for the party could possibly be a decrease in size and effectiveness after the 1991 convention.

In the next and final chapter the outlook for the Libertarian Party will be discussed. Already the debate between the purists and pragmatists has erupted, mainly over the issue of the party accepting federal matching funds. Thus, the future course of the party will be evaluated along with some recommendations on how the party may improve its chances in upcoming presidential elections.

4

Conclusion

Freedom, your freedom, your children's freedom is the issue; there is no dearer commodity on earth. We are convinced that freedom is the cure and government is the problem. We are the only alternative to the bankruptcy of the Republicans and Democrats. We know there's been no two-party system and hasn't been for decades, there's only been one party and one philosophical trend masquerading under two labels.

— Dick Randolph, 1978
Former LP State Legislator, Alaska
Statement made at National LP
Convention, New York City, 1938

The Americanization of democracy has not kept democracy true to the Jeffersonian ideal. Instead, it has resulted in the anathema of democracy: a system in which two parties tightly control the status quo, refusing entrance to others wishing to participate in the electoral process. This monopolization of the American political process has stifled the free-market exchange of ideas and prevented their expansion, thereby robbing the voters of the democratic right of free choice. It is little wonder, then, that voter turnout is low, major party platforms are very similar, and minor party inroads are dead ends.

In this final chapter the discussion will turn toward an evaluation of the American electoral system and its impact upon minor political parties. The main viewpoint put forth here is that democracy is not being served under the present system. In this light the chapter will take a last look at the Libertarian Party. The party's problems and possible solutions will be delineated in relation to upcoming presidential elections.

Status Quo Democracy

The American political system has evolved slowly to its present stage. Evolution occurred in the past when the system allowed and welcomed

113

parties to form and dissolve according to the opinions of the populace. The system's present condition works contrary to the ideals of democracy. The two major parties have attempted to establish a system whereby the natural ebb and flow of political parties and ideas is halted, thus stopping the evolutionary process of political development and permitting political stagnation. What remains is a maintenance of the status quo via a variety of structures. As such, today's political scene is best characterized as a status quo democracy rather than any version of Jeffersonian, Madisonian, Hamiltonian, or Jacksonian democracy.

As the American electoral system has changed over time, outside opponents have been systematically excluded. Some authors believe that the last real effort to restore America's democratic premises faded with the decline of the Populist Party in the late 1800s and early 1900s.[1] Although from time to time arguments appear about reforming the system, most if not all of these are focused entirely upon intangibles. Few reformers have mentioned that one way to improve the system, to increase voter turnout, or to make candidates more responsible to their campaign promises may be to simply allow more than two political options at the ballot box.

These "reformers," concerned with the influence of wealth, set up public financing of national and some state elections. While "reforming" the system to guarantee democracy, however, they ignored the very foundations upon which the system was based. Lost are the ideals of free and open political competition, the free exchange of political ideas and the freedom to choose from among the top candidates for any office. While claiming that keeping the two-party status quo is essential for sustaining American democracy, the reformers have effectively shut out third party opposition. They have reinforced this opinion with strict ballot access laws and other legal maneuvers. Meanwhile, the media has aided in the furtherance of this so-called democracy by becoming self-appointed "guardians" of the two-party status quo.

Media coverage, as mentioned previously, has almost always excluded alternative party candidacies, except as human interest stories. These stories are usually done in such a way that the candidates are viewed more as curiosities than real contenders with serious political ideas. Besides this, the League of Women Voters and the Commission on Presidential Debates have always ignored minor party candidates, no matter how formidable they may have been. It is ironic that the League has made its power to exclude minor parties from the presidential debates a key in its defense for maintaining control of the debate process. It is illogical that the very essence of democracy—the freedom of speech—can be protected by denying this right to plausible party candidates.

Rather than reforming the system to guarantee the foundations of democracy, most argue in favor of closing the system and preserving the two-party monopoly of access and power. From anti-fusion laws passed to prevent a Populist-Democrat alliance from defeating the Republicans in the late 1800s, to the idea that American voters will become confused if they have more than two choices for any office, to recent efforts at keeping alternative candidates off ballots and out of presidential debates, the system has become firmly entrenched in the status quo. The result has been that no strong opposition to the two parties has occurred since Wallace's AIP in 1968.

Yet, voter turnout continues to decline and both parties become more ideocentric in their campaign positions. Apathy is not always to blame for this low turnout. As one study suggests, citizens do not vote because they feel powerless and do not believe they can "change the status quo."[2] In addition, voters are dissatisfied with the present system. They are, as one author points out, tired of the phony, symbolic issues that have dominated politics for decades and want real solutions. The voters "believe that the purpose of politics is to solve problems and resolve disputes."[3] What has happened is that the two major parties protect themselves and maintain the status quo by introducing phony issues to cloud the electoral choices and turn public attention away from real concerns toward manufactured issues which best suit their moderate platforms. For example, while most Americans worry about crime, especially those crimes that affect them the most (i.e., burglary, robbery, and auto theft), the two major parties devote their attention to a debate of the death penalty and the early release of Willie Horton.

Both conservatives and liberals are guilty of this political misdirection. Whereas conservatives support the free market system with limited governmental intervention *and* the traditional values of work, family, and community, they are strangely silent when these two pillars collide.[4] Instead of attempting to solve the dilemma, they turn to symbolic politics in order to divert attention away from the real issues. Liberals are also quiet when their support for individual rights and freedoms clashes with the values of the welfare state. As such, both groups turn to the phony issues and debates during election time (i.e., the pledge of allegiance, volunteerism, being a member of the ACLU, or being pro-business). Salient issues are rarely addressed in the carefully planned and rehearsed major party debates. Campaigns have become moral warfare with the Republicans blaming individual irresponsibility, flight from family life, sexual permissiveness, and the lack of a work ethic and the Democrats blaming greed, racism, and intolerance for America's social and economic problems.[5] Neither party actually addresses real issues or solutions. As a result, Americans are "rebelling against a politics of false choices" and want politics turned back to its basics.[6]

Therefore, the time may be right for a party that can offer this choice. However, as politicians, media, and political experts continue to decry the

lack of voter interest, their recommendations still revolve around improv-
ing the situation for the major parties (i.e., such as more public financing
of campaigns or more televised debates). Few, if any, have ever argued for
a diversity in political representation through expansion of the party system
so those with new ideas can participate.

In order to break the two-party stranglehold on the system, a strong
and serious alternative party is needed. The Libertarian Party served as a
case study in Chapter 3 because it was considered to be the most capable
of breaking the status quo. However, at its present rate, the party no longer
appears to be the answer to the problem. In the next section the possible
challenges to the status quo from various ideological perspectives will be
undertaken.

Challenging the Status Quo

The future of American minor political parties and their abilities to
challenge the present major party status quo democracy is bleak. Regardless
of the ideological focus a minor party takes, breaking through the status quo
will remain a major undertaking which many will not survive.

A minor political party with a leftist orientation will not possess an appeal wide enough to seriously challenge the two major parties. In order to
make any inroad, this type of party would have to appeal to the usually
noninvolved segments of the electorate (i.e., the poor and minorities).[7] A
prime example of this argument would be recent calls by the National
Organization for Women (NOW) to form a third party in order to press
feminist issues to the forefront of the political agenda.

In 1989 and 1990 NOW's Commission for Responsible Democracy set
about exploring the possibility of forming an alternative to the two major
parties. NOW was frustrated with the lack of substantial support in both major parties for a pro-choice stance on abortion, among other issues. Yet, this
lack of support is not quite true. The Democrats have been pro-choice,
although it could be viewed as lukewarm support. The Republicans, on the
other hand, have allowed exceptions to their antiabortion stance. The
Democratic Party has also traditionally taken up the feminist banner
whenever possible. Unlike the Free Soil or Progressive parties, NOW has
not faced a situation in which the two major parties could be charged with
completely ignoring its issue concerns. with ignoring their issue concerns.
As such, if NOW did form a new party, the Democrats would suffer the
negative consequences, not the Republicans.[8]

The idea or threat of NOW forming a new party has brought out every
"entrenched warrior for the status quo."[9] With the system's present structure, it is inconceivable that NOW could ever seriously challenge the present

two party status quo. The leaders of NOW have countered this criticism by stating that they are not seeking the formation of a "women's party," but a new political movement for the numerous alienated voters who are upset with the present political situation.[10] They are, in one writer's opinion, suggesting a movement for democracy rather than simply protecting the status quo.[11]

Many political analysts see NOW's efforts as wasted energy. Others in the abortion rights movement believe that NOW's seeking a third party alternative will possibly break up the pro-choice coalition by diverting attention from the main goal. Still others are concerned that these recent tribulations within the feminist movement may further strain existing relationships by causing a deepening rift between older radical elements and the younger, more moderate members.[12] Overall, NOW faces an uphill battle. It must overcome internal differences and problems. Furthermore, its support base is narrow, especially if it constructs its base around a single issue such as abortion. There already exists an antiabortion party, the Right-to-Life Party. They become the focus of Republican interests only when they constitute the votes needed for victory. At best, NOW could hope for the same type of attention from the Democrats. Overall, a leftist party with a narrow appeal and limited political agenda will not provide a salient challenge to the status quo.

A minor political party with a moderate political agenda does not seem to be the answer either. John Anderson's efforts demonstrated how a centrist party would fit into the two-party competition—at a low third place finish. Because the two major parties actively seek the moderate voter through their vague platform stances and social consensual appeals, any party hoping to break the major parties' monopoly of power by appealing to this segment of the voting population will also fail. Unless one of the two major parties veered noticeably to the far left or right, any moderate minor party will have a difficult time challenging the status quo democracy.

This leads the discussion to the possibility that a right-wing or conservative party may offer a profound attack upon the status quo. The Libertarian Party serves as the best example in this case. The Libertarian Party faces a tougher challenge than any other minor party because of its ideological stances. As the Republican Party becomes more and more associated with conservative causes, any party that espouses similar views will have a difficult time gathering support. Since most voters viewed George Bush as more conservative than themselves during the 1988 election, a minor party that favors less government involvement in the economy and drastic cuts in domestic programs will not likely have a wide base of support.[13]

As discussed earlier, some conservatives were disaffected from the Bush candidacy because it failed to stress social issues such as school prayer and antiabortion. However, the economy was a primary concern in 1988 (as it probably will be for the 1992 elections) and Bush's stance carried the conservative vote. The Libertarian Party must compete for the same conservative-economic supporters as the GOP, but with institutional and structural handicaps that the GOP does not have to consider.

The Libertarian Party: At the Crossroads

The Libertarian Party has yet to be a serious threat to the continuing status quo of the two major parties. However, it has provided an ideological challenge through its agitation and its offering of alternatives to the status quo programs of the Democrats and Republicans.[14] The Libertarian Party has offered many dissatisfied voters a utopian version of the principles upon which the American republic is based.

During the 1980s, the Libertarian Party seemed to be at the front of an emerging ideological movement. As a result, some of its ideas have become accepted in American society. This may eventually dissolve the party by robbing it of its purpose and platform. As success has held the seeds of failure for many minor parties before it, the libertarians will face a similar dilemma because its issues are being absorbed into the political and social agendas of the major parties. Although this means the party will fade away, it will have succeeded by having its platform issues accepted into the mainstream of American politics.

Much of the problem with having its issues accepted and thus removing the party's purpose can be attributed to the party's emphasis on issue education. The libertarians are not breaking away from the role of an educational group, and because of this, they will be viewed as political agitators rather than serious competition for the major parties. This stereotype will result in fewer votes and less media attention. More importantly, the strong focus on issue education implies that the party suffers from a lack of definition and direction. The libertarians cannot seem to decide whether they are a political party, an interest group, an agitational association, or merely a discussion group. Although the libertarians did begin their history as a party, it has since declined to the role of an agitational association that occasionally stirs the political waters. Rothbard's exhortations claiming that the 1984 presidential election defeat was in reality a victory in disguise brings to mind the question of what role the party actually plays and just what is its proper place in the American electoral process. Without a clear direction and goal, the libertarians will never rise above their few successes.

Additionally, the party must move forward. Using the 1980 election as a yardstick to measure later electoral endeavors keeps the party and its members from facing the real challenge: the future of the party itself. There is internal questioning of the party's purpose and direction. The Libertarian Republican Organizing Committee (LROC) is still arguing that libertarians would be better served by joining the Republican Party rather than continuing their third party efforts. LROC members believe that the conservative movement is in disarray and the libertarians are now in the best position to push the GOP past its rhetoric and actually redirect it back to its roots of individual rights.[15] Eric Garris, director of the LROC, states that the "third party approach has been tried now through five presidential elections, and partisans of the Libertarian Party need to come to grips with the failure of this strategy. As difficult as libertarian political ideas are to sell, they are not nearly as unsalable as the third party strategy itself."[16] Garris urges that members of the Libertarian Party realize that if they are to get any of their ideas across to the American electorate, they must work from within the status quo. He continues by stating that "marketing the ideas of individual liberty in a third party package makes them appear to be what they are not: exotic, removed from the problems of ordinary people, and completely out of the mainstream of American politics."[17] Whereas Garris and the LROC believe that libertarians can achieve success, at least on a philosophical scale, from within the ranks of the GOP, others argue that it would be better for libertarians to consider allying themselves with the Democrats.

Proponents of this stance explain that a libertarian–liberal Democrat venture would allow a better chance of issue success. They point out that the Republicans have given lip service to libertarian concerns for a long time, but have continually acted to the contrary. An example would be their condemnation of big government while calling for more government regulation of social morals. The advocation of free-market economics, laissez-faire social tolerance, the right to privacy, a strict separation of the church and state, concern for human rights, and a noninterventionist foreign policy by the liberal Democrats is much more in line with libertarian goals.[18] Richard Dennis warns that the Republicans have become the party of social populism due to its calls for mandatory AIDS and drug testing, pledge of allegiance, a school prayer amendment, and antiabortion among other issues.[19] If carried to the extreme, those opposed to a libertarian–Republican alliance worry that the Republican philosophy could lead to a new version of statism. Therefore, since liberals and libertarians have parallel views of individuals, their freedom, and ability to reason, it is better that those libertarians dissatisfied with the third party approach consider supporting the Democrats rather than Republicans.

It appears that the Libertarian Party is truly at the crossroads of its history. When the party's members consider leaving it to join one of the two major parties, it is a clear signal that the party must reevaluate itself in order to maintain its political survival. Thus, the Libertarian Party is faced with several dilemmas as it enters the 1990s. In order to succeed and survive, the party must enter the mainstream of American politics, even if it means compromising some of its principles. The party's unwavering dedication to certain philosophical dictates only serves to alienate it from an electorate searching for a party with issue solutions.

Final Evaluation: 1992 and Beyond

Undoubtedly, a large part of the Libertarian Party's political impotency stems from its internal squabbles over purity and pragmatism. However, it is this rift that most challenges the party as it approaches the final elections of the twentieth century. Uncompromising support of a philosophy is fine; however, the political costs of doing so are beginning to wear on the party. The party has failed to adapt its platform to the changing moods of the electorate. As it stands now, the party's platform is not distinct enough to set it apart from the two major parties in some areas (i.e., free market economics or social toleration), while it is too radical for the average voter in others (i.e., drug legalization and ending welfare and defense) to adequately reflect the social consensus. One issue, in particular, has arisen that may eventually set the cast for the party's future. This issue is that of the Libertarian Party applying for and accepting federal matching funds in the 1992 presidential election cycle.

As candidates began to actively seek the party's nomination, the taking of federal money became a hotly debated topic. On the one side, the purists refused to compromise the founding principles of the party and did not want the party to accept federal money. Instead, they proposed another election that would build the party, that would get the libertarian message out to the public, rather than raising the standard of competition. The purists risk the eventual failure of the party due to their doctrinal zeal.

On the other hand, the pragmatists wanted to accept the election funds. They believed that this would permit a more thorough and far-reaching campaign, a boost the party surely needs. As donations become more scarce and membership rolls fluctuate, in addition to the increasing costs of ballot access and campaigns, federal matching funds could keep the party afloat. It might even put the party into the political mainstream rather than having it remain on the fringes of obscurity. The pragmatists justified taking the money in an abstract manner, but as everyone surely realizes: politics operates on money and cannot always be clear.

Andre Marrou, the former Alaskan state representative, best typifies the pragmatist camp in this debate. He sought the party's nomination with the platform promise of taking the FEC money. In his campaign newsletter, Marrou stated that "it is a moral imperative that we reclaim looted tax money and use it to defend ourselves. If we truly believe that our money is ours, and if we truly believe in the justice of self-defense, then we must reclaim our money and defend ourselves. A serious commitment to our principles demands it."[19] Therefore, taking the federal money justified by claiming that it is really tax dollars wrongfully paid to the government in the first place.

Marrou wanted to use the money to further the libertarian message via a massive advertising campaign. He hoped that it would bring in over 100,000 new members and thus break the 1 million vote barrier in the November 1992 election. He hoped to raise $1 million before the convention in order to qualify for approximately $700,000 in matching funds.[20] With this, Marrou wanted to match or even better the party's benchmark election of 1980.

Dick Boddie, an African-American lawyer from California opposed Marrou for the 1992 nomination and represented the purist faction of the Libertarian Party. His platform, as well as Marrou's, was typical of the Libertarian Party. It included the planks of ending welfare, privatizing education, reemphasizing the Bill of Rights, abolishing taxes, repealing the Sixteenth Amendment to the Constitution, and reducing the size of all governments. As such, his goals for the party were familiar: get more members into the party, enhance local growth, procure national and international exposure, and gain substantial financial support for the party.[21] These last two goals were to be achieved, however, without federal matching funds.

Boddie's campaign advertisements stated that "if you believe that taking 'matching funds' as a Libertarian is not only a bad idea, that we should be working to abolish the FEC instead, and that soliciting subsidies from the government is wrong (notwithstanding the fact that taking matching funds is arguably in violation of the principles of those in the Libertarian Party who are opposed), then put your money where your principles are."[22] In lieu of matching funds for advertising, as Marrou promised, Boddie wanted to expand voter awareness and education through the sale and distribution of audio and video tapes, by appearing on the talk show circuit, and getting more coverage in each of the medias. However, he failed to explain where the money for this awareness and education campaign is to come from. It is somewhat naive to believe that, without enough campaign money, any candidate will be known well enough to be invited onto any show in a serious capacity.

David Nolan sums up the pragmatist position when he points out that those in opposition to taking the federal funds are doing so *only* on principle. Everyone uses government services that have been paid for through tax dollars, so why not use them for the election?[23] There are no reasonable alternatives. Denying the use of federal matching funds may be satisfying emotionally and spiritually, but it is not in touch with true politics. As long as all candidates are not treated equally, the pragmatists argue that it is only fair to use some of the government's money to work to change the system. The huge costs of ballot access are a direct result of government inequity; therefore as Nolan points out, the party should use the FEC money as a reimbursement of the costs it takes to qualify to compete against the status quo.[24] In other words, permitting "real democracy" to operate.

Yet, the purists continue their philosophical opposition to the whole idea of taking matching funds. Some even sound pessimistic by stating that even if the party received the money for ballot access, the states would simply readjust their laws to keep the Libertarian Party off their ballots.[25] Even if the party was on all fifty ballots, the purists argue, would this really increase the number of votes received? Hence, the purists argue for a rejection of government as a whole so that no one can accuse the party of political hypocrisy.[26] The Libertarian Party's past successes can be far better measured by the number and quality of ideas it has put forth rather than by anything else.

As the Libertarian Party reaches the end of its second decade, these internal debates should be secondary to the party's primary goal: that of winning elections. The internal grappling over the interpretation of the party's founding principles should be subsiding rather than becoming more common. It will only serve to distract the membership, turn away prospective members, and further weaken the entire party.

The 1992 presidential nomination convention ended with Marrou being selected as the party's hopeful on the first ballot. Marrou won 257 votes, Boddie got 155, two last-minute entries into the race, Hans G. Schroeder and David H. Raaflaub, received 15 and 6 votes respectively, and the traditional "None of the Above" garnished 20 delegate votes. Boddie was placed on the vice presidential ballot by his supporters, yet he was still unsuccessful, narrowly losing to Dr. Nancy Lord, 223 votes to 185. "None of the Above" received six votes and two other candidates received three votes. Lord had run for mayor of Washington, D.C. in 1990 and placed fourth on a ballot of eleven names.[27]

As such, the purist Boddie has now stated that he would like to run for the U.S. Senate from the state of California and will be actively campaigning soon. The entire federal matching funds issue is now moot since Marrou failed to qualify for them. However, it did serve to point out the difference between the two major contenders for the nomination, as well as some basic differences as to which way the Libertarian Party is headed. If Marrou keeps to the pragmatist route, then the party may continue to be a serious challenger of the status quo.

Finally, Ron Paul stated at the convention that he was thinking of running in the Republican primaries against George Bush. This is not a defection, but rather a way to popularize libertarian ideals in the GOP and hopefully get members of the Republican Party to leave and join the Libertarian Party. Overall, Paul pointed out that he was considering this move as an education effort to strengthen the appeal of the libertarian philosophy.[28]

Neither nominee had the charisma needed to unify the two factions within the party. They were not the celebrity candidates like Theodore Roosevelt or George Wallace and, as such, until the Libertarian Party realizes that American politics is based more on personalities than on philosophies, it will always have a difficult time at the ballot box. Instead of appealing to intellectuals with their own brand of phony issues, the party must start appealing to the average voter with good, sound issue solutions that are easily understood and supported. If the party continues to offer radical alternatives to the status quo put forth by the two major parties, its support will remain limited.

The Libertarian Party must become more pragmatic, accept the federal matching funds, get elected, and then implement its plans and ideas for change. Constantly serving as a political martyr—willing to accept defeat as long as their ideas get out—will not sustain the party for much longer. It is time to compete and the only way to do it is by using the political devices established by the two major parties to ensure status quo democracy. It is time to change the status quo.

Appendix A: Required Petition Signatures for Ballot Access

	State	1930	1976	1986	1988
1	AL	0	5,000	11,286	5,000
2	AK	—	2,650	2,132	2,068
3	AZ	198	11,041	20,518	8,670
4	AR	0	38,213	26,597	0
5	CA	12,125	642,350	806,432	128,340
5	CO	300	5,000	500	5,000
6	CT	1,514	14,093	10,839	14,910
7	DE	750	—	140	142
8	FL	1,675	120,000	167,237	56,318
10	GA	0	109,000	27,324	25,759
11	HI	—	3,500	4,190	3,493
12	ID	250	1,500	8,223	8,224
13	IL	1,000	25,000	25,000	25,000
14	IN	7,047	10,500	35,040	30,950
15	IA	500	—	1,000	1,000
16	KS	0	2,500	15,266	2,500
17	KY	100	1,000	5,000	5,000
18	LA	1,000	15,000	109,143	0
19	ME	1,000	10,920	23,012	4,000
20	MD	2,000	55,000	71,366	10,000
21	MA	1,000	37,095–51,932	41,006	33,682
22	MI	100	17,674–70,696	19,963	16,313
23	MN	2,000	2,000	2,000	2,000
24	MS	0	10,000	0	1,000

State		1930	1976	1986	1988
25	MO	0	15,000–20,000	21,083	21,083
26	MT	0	9,199	13,329	13,329
27	NE	750	4,600	5,480	2,500
28	NV	1,606	4,600	13,532	7,717
29	NH	1,000	1,000	3,000	3,000
30	NJ	800	800	800	800
31	NM	0	0	2,537	500
32	NY	12,000	20,000	20,000	20,000
33	NC	10,000	10,000	44,535	44,535
34	ND	300	300	1,000	4,000
35	OH	24,740	29,877	45,476	5,000
36	OK	5,000	40,243	62,243	37,671
37	OR	14,680	37,660	60,175	36,695
38	PA	6,354	45,000	36,721	51,578
39	RI	500	500	1,000	25,568
40	SC	0	10,000	10,000	10,000
41	SD	7,775	2,783–8,346	6,960	2,945
42	TN	0	26,018	30,974	275
43	TX	0	16,548	31,909	34,424
44	UT	500	500	300	300
45	VT	1,292	1,409	1,000	1,000
46	VA	250	10,000	12,693	12,963
47	WA	25	100	188	188
48	WV	6,460	7,700	7,044	7,358
49	WI	1,000	40,000	2,000	2,000
50	WY	100	6,347	8,000	8,000
Totals**		127,741	1,510,431*	1,875,734	1,478,138

—*Denotes unavailable data*
*Uses averages of those states with a range of petition signatures
***Does not reflect exact numerical total because some states only provide approximate ballot figures.*

Sources: "Disenfranchising the Franchise," *Libertarian Party News,* May/June 1986, p. 5; Paul H. Blackman, *Third Party President?* (Washington, D.C.: Heritage Foundation, 1976), Appendix 1, pp. 76–106; and *Ballot Access News,* August 1988, p. 3.

Appendix B:
Statement of Principles
of the Libertarian Party

We, the members of the Libertarian Party, challenge the cult of the omnipotent state and defend the rights of the individual.

We hold that all individuals have the right to exercise sole dominion over their own lives, and have the right to live in whatever manner they choose, so long as they do not forcibly interfere with the equal right of others to live in whatever manner they choose.

Governments throughout history have regularly operated on the opposite principle, that the State has the right to dispose of the lives of individuals and the fruits of their labor. Even within the United States, all political parties other than our own grant to government the right to regulate the lives of individuals and seize the fruits of their labor without their consent.

We, on the contrary, deny the right of any government to do these things, and hold that where governments exist, they must not violate the rights of any individual; namely (1) the right to life — accordingly we support prohibition of the initiation of physical force against others; (2) the right to liberty of speech and action — accordingly we oppose all attempts by government to abridge the freedom of speech and press, as well as government censorship in any form; and (3) the right to property — accordingly we oppose all government interference with private property, such as confiscation, nationalization, and eminent domain, and support the prohibition of robbery, trespass, fraud, and misrepresentation.

Since governments, when instituted, must not violate individual rights, we oppose all interference by government in the areas of voluntary and contractual relations among individuals. People should not be forced to sacrifice their lives and property for the benefit of others. They should be left free by government to deal with one another as free traders; and the resultant economic system, the only one compatible with the protection of individual rights, is the free market.

Source: Libertarian Party Headquarters (Houston, Texas), 1984.

Chapter Notes

Chapter 1: Introduction

[1]Clinton L. Rossiter, *Parties and Politics in America*, p. 3.

[2]Since 1855 there have been 35 senators and 314 representatives in the U.S. Congress from minor parties (Eugene J. McCarthy, "Third Party May Be a Real Force," *New York Times Magazine*, p. 13).

[3]Alain Gagnon, "Third Parties: A Theoretical Framework," *American Review of Canadian Studies* 11:38.

[4]Frederick E. Haynes, *Social Politics in the United States*, p. 157.

[5]William B. Hesseltine, *Third Party Movements in the United States*, p. 5.

[6]Edward Pendleton Herring, *The Politics of Democracy*, p. 179.

[7]Charles E. Merriam and Harold Foote Gosnell, *The American Party System*, p. 59.

[8]Herring, *The Politics of Democracy*, p. 181.

[9]Hesseltine, *Third Party Movements*, p. 13.

[10]V. O. Key, Jr., *Politics, Parties and Pressure Groups*, p. 243; Hesseltine, *Third Party Movements*, p. 14.

[11]Steven J. Rosenstone, Ray L. Behr, and Edward H. Lazarus, *Third Parties in America*, p. 216.

[12]Walter Dean Burnham, *Critical Elections and the Mainsprings of American Politics*, pp. 27–28.

[13]John F. Freie, "Minor Parties in Realigning Eras," *American Politics Quarterly* 10:49.

[14]Burnham, *Critical Elections*, p. 27.

[15]Rosenstone et al., *Third Parties in America*, p. 215.

[16]Herring, *The Politics of Democracy*, p. 179.

[17]Rosenstone et al., *Third Parties in America*, p. 222.

[18]Frederick E. Haynes, *Third Party Movements Since the Civil War*, p. 1.

[19]Wallace received 13.45 percent of the popular vote and 46 electoral college votes in the 1968 election (Rosenstone et al., *Third Parties in America*, p. 234).

[20]Rhodes Cook, "Third Parties: A Struggle for Attention," *Congressional Quarterly*, 34:2,971.

[21]Leslie Bell, "Constraints on Electoral Success of Minor Political Parties in the United States," *Political Studies* 25:106.

[22]John D. Hicks, "The Third Party Tradition in American Politics," *Mississippi Valley Historical Review* 20:26.

[23]Federal Election Commission, *Presidential Candidate Index*.

[24]E. E. Schattschneider, *Party Government*, p. 61; William Goodman, *The Two-Party System in the United States*, p. 49. This point of view will be discussed in more detail in chapter 2.

[25]Neil A. McDonald, *The Study of Political Parties,* pp. 4, 77.

[26]William J. Crotty, "Political Parties Research," in *Approaches to the Study of Political science,* eds. Nelson W. Polsby, Robert A. Dentler, and Paul A. Smith, p. 269.

[27]Ibid., p. 278; and David Braybrooke, "An Illustrative Miniature Axiomatic System," in *Politics and Social Life,* eds. Michael Haas and Henry S. Kariel, pp. 128, 130. Some of the works surveyed were by Duverger, Downs, Truman, Herring, and Key.

[28]Crotty, "Political Parties Research"; and Braybrooke, "An Illustrative Miniature," p. 130.

[29]Braybrooke, "An Illustrative Miniature," p. 120. The two consensus-lists were composed of axioms, or propositions regarding the two major parties. Braybrooke explains that the purpose of the axiomatic system was to make the relations between the axioms and consensus-lists clearer, and readily admitted that the system had a limited scope but could be expanded in the future (pp. 121–22).

[30]Crotty, "Political Parties Research," p. 279. Stephen Wasby concurred in 1970 that there are advantages in collecting inventories of propositions in that it helps in the development of theories. He notes that a propositional inventory is not the equivalent of a theory since the propositions are not fully related to one another. An inventory is used only to classify generalizations, assumptions, or explanations so that a clearer understanding of a subject can be attained (Stephen L. Wasby, *Political Science: The Discipline and Its Dimensions,* p. 72).

[31]Kenneth Janda, *Political Parties: A Cross-National Survey,* p. xi. Janda characterized his study as an "encyclopedic compendium of facts about the world's political parties" (p. xii).

[32]Ibid., p. 136.

[33]Ibid.

[34]Ibid., p. 160.

[35]McDonald, *The Study of Political Parties,* p. 4.

[36]A similar approach was used by Alain Gagnon, "Third Parties." Gagnon hoped to provide the beginnings of a theoretical framework in order to explain the formation, durability, and failure of Canadian third parties. The framework consisted of five interrelated factors which were related to various phases of Canadian third party efforts. These factors were compared to the American political system and minor parties. Gagnon's goal was to organize the information on third parties, rather than actually test any specific theory.

[37]There are several examples of studies that focus on a single minor party. Among these are Peter H. Argersinger, *Populism and Politics;* John D. Hicks, *The Populist Revolt;* David A. Shannon, *The Socialist Party of America;* William Z. Foster, *History of the Communist Party of the United States;* Lowell K. Dyson, *Red Harvest;* Irving Howe and Lewis Coser, *The American Communist Party;* Emile B. Ader, *The Dixiecrat Movement;* Amos R. Pinchot, *History of the Progressive Party, 1912–1916;* and George Thayer, *The Farther Shores of Politics.* One exception to the usual descriptive focus of one-party works is a study by Maurice Pinard, *The Rise of a Third Party,* which utilizes election and survey data to analyze the economic, political, social, and psychological factors behind the emergence of a new third party, the Social Credit Party of the early 1960s in Canada. Pinard's hypothesis that one-party dominance and social and political unrest will inspire third party efforts in Canada's provinces is tested and found to be supported by the data.

[38]Janet B. Johnson and Richard A. Joslyn, *Political Science Research Methods,* p. 113.

39Ibid., p. 112; Wasby, *Political Science*, p. 158; and Michael Haas and Theodore L. Becker, "The Behavioral Revolution and After," in Haas and Kariel, *Politics and Social Life*, p. 492. In their explanation of the need for a multimethodological approach, Haas and Becker state that the primary purpose of a case study is to aid in developing concepts and propositions for further research.

40Jay D. White, "On the Growth of Knowledge in Public Administration," *Public Administration Review* 46:16. Positive research involves the development of testable laws that demonstrate causal relationships among variables and uses empirical methods and models. Critical research wants to bring awareness to unconscious determinants of beliefs in a philosophical sense (p. 16).

41Ibid., pp. 16, 18. See also Brian Fay, *Social Theory and Political Practice*. Fay states that one task for the interpretive social scientist is to discover sets of rules for a given class of actions, to make these rules explicit, and then relate them to other rules in society (p. 76).

42George Friedman and Gary McDowell, "The Libertarian Movement in America," *Journal of Contemporary Studies* 6:49.

43Ibid., p. 53.

44Ibid.

45Ibid.

46Wasby, *Political Science*, p. 72.

47Ibid.

48Braybrooke, "An Illustrative Miniature," p. 120. Braybrooke continues by stating that an axiomatic system "makes the logical picture of the whole subject a great deal clearer. Indeed it gives us a picture. We might ask for a better likeness, but it could hardly be said that there was a picture before" (p. 129).

49Janda, *Political Parties*, p. 160.

50Wasby, *Political Science*, p. 158.

Chapter 2: The Nature and Definitions of Minor Political Parties

1V. O. Key, Jr., *Politics, Parties and Pressure Groups*, p. 207–8; John A. Crittenden, *Parties and Elections in the United States*, p. 19.

2John A. Crittenden, *Parties and Elections*, p. 5.

3Samuel J. Eldersveld, *Political Parties: A Behavioral Analysis*, p. 4.

4E. E. Schattschneider, *Party Government*, pp. 4, 12.

5Neil A. McDonald, *The Study of Political Parties*, p. 5.

6William Goodman, *The Two-Party System in the United States*, p. 6.

7Kay Lawson, *Political Parties and Democracy in the United States*, p. 18.

8Ibid.; and Allan P. Sindler, *Political Parties in the U.S.*, pp. 9–12.

9Martin P. Wattenberg, *The Decline of American Political Parties*, pp. 1–2; Frank J. Sorauf, *Political Parties in the American System*, p. 10; McDonald, *The Study of Political Parties*, pp. 23–25; and, Schattschneider, *Party Government*, p. 50.

10Richard S. Katz, *A Theory of Parties and Electoral Systems*, p. 4.

11Austin Ranney and Willmoore Kendall, *Democracy and the American Party System*, p. 422.

12Goodman, *The Two-Party System*, p. 74.

13Ibid.

14Paul H. Blackman, *Third Party President?*, p. 18.

15Ibid.

[16]Ibid., p. 19.

[17]Ibid., p. 32.

[18]Federal Election Commission, *Federal Election Campaign Laws*, 9002.7. This definition is primarily for the purpose of determining the amount of matching funds a minor party may receive from the FEC election fund.

[19]Goodman, *The Two-Party System*, p. 136.

[20]Ibid., p. 350.

[21]Key, *Politics, Parties and Pressure Groups*, p. 208.

[22]Sorauf, *Political Parties*, p. 5.

[23]Ibid., p. 61.

[24]Clinton L. Rossiter, *Parties and Politics in America*, p. 7.

[25]Schattschneider, *Party Government*, p. 35.

[26]Ibid., p. 61.

[27]Ibid., p. 63.

[28]Goodman, *The Two-Party System*, p. 49.

[29]Ibid. Goodman continues and argues that minor parties are not even in the same category as the major ones and they cannot be properly called political parties at all.

[30]McDonald, *The Study of Political Parties*, p. 31.

[31]Ibid.

[32]Ibid., p. 32.

[33]Rossiter, *Parties and Politics*, pp. 4–5.

[34]Key, *Politics, Parties and Pressure Groups*, p. 236.

[35]Ibid., p. 237; and Murray S. Stedman and Susan W. Stedman, *Discontent at the Polls*, p. 4.

[36]Key, *Politics, Parties and Pressure Groups*, pp. 237–38; Rhodes Cook, "Alternate Party Candidates May Have Substantial Impact on 1980 Presidential Election," *Congressional Quarterly* 38:3,148–49.

[37]Key, *Politics, Parties and Pressure Groups*, p. 241.

[38]John J. Gargan, "Conservative Success in Liberal New York: Some Determinants of Conservative Party Support," in *The Future of Political Parties*, eds. Louis Maisel and Paul M. Sacks, p. 185. Gargan's study utilizes aggregate data analysis to examine why the Conservative Party tends to be supported in New York State and how the party operates within the state during elections.

[39]Judson L. James, *American Political Parties: Potential and Performance*, p. 49.

[40]Ibid.; and Gargan, "Conservative Success in Liberal New York," p. 186.

[41]Gargan, "Conservative Success in Liberal New York," p. 169.

[42]Ibid., p. 174.

[43]Ibid., p. 183.

[44]Ibid., p. 185.

[45]Ibid.

[46]Malcolm E. Jewell and David M. Olsen, *American State Political Parties and Elections*, p. 37.

[47]Ibid.

[48]Rossiter, *Parties and Politics*, p. 4; and Frank Smallwood, *The Other Candidates: Third Parties in Presidential Elections*, pp. 20–21.

[49]Smallwood, *The Other Candidates*, pp. 22–23. Both the Dixiecrats and the AIP opposed the Democratic Party's stance on civil rights issues and programs. Thurmond's group of supporters were to shift their allegiance back to the Republicans after the election (p. 22).

[50]Leslie Bell, "Constraints on Electoral Success of Minor Political Parties in the United States," *Political Studies* 25:107.

[51]Smallwood, *The Other Candidates,* p. 20.

[52]Rossiter, *Parties and Politics,* p. 5.

[53]Daniel A. Mazmanian, *Third Parties in Presidential Elections,* p. 27. Mazmanian determined the significance of a minor party in terms of voter appeal. Using this criterion, he has determined 10 minor parties to be more significant than the others. These were the Anti-Masons (1932); Free Soil Party (1848); the American Party (1856); the Breckinridge Democrats and the Constitutional Party (1860); the Populists (1892); Bull-Moose Progressives and Socialist parties (1912); the La Follette Progressives (1924); and Wallace's American Independent Party (1968) (p. 5).

[54]Ibid., pp. 136–37.

[55]Ibid., p. 137.

[56]Ibid., p. 7.

[57]Ibid., p. 11.

[58]Ibid., p. 15.

[59]Ibid., pp. 136–37. Mazmanian also stated that the political crisis of 1968 was unique. By 1976 a minor party forming out of political crisis did not appear feasible anymore since the U.S. was now suffering a "crisis of confidence" due to Watergate, economic disarray, and a general sense of unease in the middle class. The result was an increase in the number of independent voters, not the formation of a new minor party. There were no issues of crisis proportions in the 1976 elections. See Mazmanian, "1976: A Third Party Year?" *Nation,* pp. 201–4.

[60]Frederick E. Haynes, *Third Party Movements Since the Civil War,* p. 156.

[61]Walter Dean Burnham, *Critical Elections and the Mainsprings of American Politics,* p. 10.

[62]James A. Woodburn, *Political Parties and Party Problems in the United States,* pp. 65, 64.

[63]Steven J. Rosenstone, Ray L. Behr, and Edward H. Lazarus, *Third Parties in America,* chart on p. 231; and Woodburn, *Political Parties and Party Problems,* p. 65.

[64]Rosenstone et al., *Third Parties in America,* chart on p. 231.

[65]Woodburn, *Political Parties and Party Problems,* pp. 74–75.

[66]Ibid., p. 91.

[67]Joseph C. Harsch, "Third Parties: Wild Cards in Politics," *Christian Science Monitor,* 16 January 1986, p. 15.

[68]Rosenstone et al., *Third Parties in America,* p. 134; and Stedman and Stedman, *Discontent at the Polls,* pp. 32–33.

[69]Rosenstone et al., *Third Parties in America,* p. 134; and Robert A. Dahl, ed., *Political Oppositions in Western Democracies,* pp. 52–53.

[70]Haynes, *Third Party Movements,* p. 159.

[71]Stedman and Stedman, *Discontent at the Polls,* p. 32. This work is a good, but slightly outdated, account of the Farmer-Labor parties and their performance at both the state and national levels.

[72]Ibid.

[73]Ibid., p. 39; and Jewell and Olsen, *American State Political Parties,* p. 37.

[74]Stedman and Stedman, *Discontent at the Polls,* p. 39.

[75]Ibid., p. 83. In a separate study, Rosenstone et al., *Third Parties in America,* claim that voters do abandon the major parties in periods of agricultural adversity due to long-term changes in farm prices (p. 165).

[76]Ranney and Kendall, *Democracy and the American Party System,* p. 431.

[77]Ibid.

[78]Stedman and Stedman, *Discontent at the Polls,* p. 96. In many states the Green-

backs had fused with Labor parties and won several mayoral elections; see James
L. Sundquist, *Dynamics of the Party System,* p. 113.

   [79]Woodburn, *Political Parties and Party Problems,* p. 147.

   [80]Ibid., pp. 148–49; and Haynes, *Third Party Movements,* p. 163.

   [81]Ranney and Kendall, *Democracy and the American Party System,* p. 433. The
electoral college votes came from Colorado, Idaho, Kansas, and Nevada.

   [82]Crittenden, *Parties and Elections,* p. 114.

   [83]Mazmanian, *Third Parties in Presidential Elections,* p. 137.

   [84]Ibid.

   [85]Ibid., p. 126.

   [86]Ibid., pp. 126, 138; and Smallwood, *The Other Candidates,* p. 13.

   [87]Key, *Politics, Parties and Pressure Groups,* p. 243.

   [88]Eugene J. McCarthy, "Third Party May be Real Force in 1972," *New York Times
Magazine,* p. 6.

   [89]Gargan, "Conservative Success in Liberal New York," p. 165.

   [90]William H. Riker, "The Number of Political Parties," *Comparative Politics* 9:98.

   [91]Rosenstone et al., *Third Parties in America,* p. 163.

   [92]Ibid., p. 164.

   [93]Ibid., pp. 119–21.

   [94]Smallwood, *The Other Candidates,* p. 24.

   [95]Key, *Politics, Parties and Pressure Groups,* p. 245. Other examples were the
Socialist Party centered around Eugene Debs and the Farmer-Labor Party around
La Follette (p. 245).

   [96]Smallwood, *The Other Candidates,* p. 24.

   [97]Nelson W. Polsby and Aaron Wildavsky, *Presidential Elections,* p. 9.

   [98]Rosenstone et al., *Third Parties in America,* pp. 170–71.

   [99]Ranney and Kendall, *Democracy and the American Party System,* p. 424.

   [100]Goodman, *The Two-Party System,* p. 49.

   [101]Smallwood, *The Other Candidates,* p. 20; and C. A. M. Ewing, *Presidential Elections,* pp. 122–23. The Socialist Party hoped to have the transition toward socialism
on a more gradual or evolutionary basis rather than through revolutionary tactics.
The Communist Party would also split from the Socialist Party in 1919 over doctrinal
disputes (William B. Hesseltine, *The Rise and Fall of Third Parties,* pp. 39, 90).

   [102]Mazmanian, *Third Parties in Presidential Elections,* pp. 27–28.

   [103]Ranney and Kendall, *Democracy and the American Party System,* p. 454; Key,
Politics and Pressure Groups, p. 244; Stedman and Stedman, *Discontent at the Polls,*
p. 168; Smallwood, *The Other Candidates,* p. 26; and Haynes, *Third Party Movements,* p. 154.

   [104]Rossiter, *Parties and Politics,* pp. 61–62.

   [105]Charles E. Merriam and Harold Foote Gosnell, *The American Party System,* p. 59.

   [106]Howard P. Nash, *Third Parties in American Politics,* p. vi.

   [107]Merriam and Gosnell, *The American Party System,* p. 59.

   [108]Ibid., p. 60; Donald B. Johnson, *National Party Platforms: Volume I, 1840–1956,*
p. 52.

   [109]Dahl, *Political Oppositions in Western Democracies,* p. 67.

   [110]Ranney and Kendall, *Democracy and the American Party System,* p. 454.

   [111]Edward Pendleton Herring, *The Politics of Democracy,* p. 189.

   [112]Ibid.

   [113]Ranney and Kendall, *Democracy and the American Party System,* p. 454;
Rosenstone et al., *Third Parties in America,* p. 8; Haynes, *Third Party Movements,*
p. 3; and Hesseltine, *The Rise and Fall of Third Parties,* p. 10. Hesseltine has claimed

that minor parties have stimulated the lethargic and timid major parties into action and adoption of new ideas and reforms (p. 10).

[114]Mazmanian, *Third Parties in Presidential Elections*, pp. 471, 479.

[115]Ewing, *Presidential Elections*, p. 109.

[116]Ibid., p. 108.

[117]Johnson, *National Party Platforms, Volume I*, p. 96.

[118]Ibid., pp. 304–24.

[119]Ibid., p. 375.

[120]Ibid., pp. 420–25.

[121]Ranney and Kendall, *Democracy and the American Party System*, p. 454; Herring, *The Politics of Democracy*, p. 181; and Stedman and Stedman, *Discontent at the Polls*, pp. 29–30.

[122]Ranney and Kendall, *Discontent at the Polls*, pp. 29–30.

[123]Mazmanian, *Third Parties in Presidential Elections*, p. 81.

[124]George Will, "Is a Third Party Necessary?" *Newsweek*, p. 88.

[125]Ranney and Kendall, *Democracy and the American Party System*, p. 455.

[126]Frederick E. Haynes, *Social Politics in the United States*, p. 152.

[127]Rossiter, *Parties and Politics*, p. 48.

[128]Haynes, *Third Party Movements*, pp. 4, 470. Haynes notes the Greenback, Labor, and Populist parties of the late nineteenth century as prime examples of this agitational role in American politics.

[129]Woodburn, *Political Parties and Party Problems*, p. 243.

[130]Goodman, *The Two-Party System*, p. 49.

[131]Ranney and Kendall, *Democracy and the American Party System*, p. 455; Nash, *Third Parties in American Politics*, p. v; Key, *Politics, Parties and Pressure Groups*, p. 244; Lawson, *Political Parties and Democracy*, p. 49; and William B. Hesseltine, *Third Party Movements in the United States*, p. 13.

[132]Key, *Politics, Parties and Pressure Groups*, p. 244.

[133]James Ceaser, *Reforming the Reforms*, p. 89. Ceaser continues this line of argument by stating that this minor party option strengthens the case for the legitimacy of a party governed representative nominating system (p. 89).

[134]Lawson, *Political Parties and Democracy*, pp. 49, 50.

[135]Ceaser, *Reforming the Reforms*, p. 101.

[136]John S. Saloma, III, and Frederick H. Sontag, *Parties: The Real Opportunity for Effective Citizen Politics*, p. 72.

[137]Ibid.

[138]Lawson, *Political Parties and Democracy*, p. 49–50.

[139]Ranney and Kendall, *Democracy and the American Party System*, p. 458.

[140]Ibid.

[141]Smallwood, *The Other Candidates*, p. 26.

[142]Ibid.; Mazmanian, *Third Parties in Presidential Elections*, p. 68; and Lawson, *Political Parties and Democracy*, p. 55.

[143]Ewing, *Presidential Elections*, p. 109.

[144]Ibid., p. 133.

[145]Mazmanian, *Third Parties in Presidential Elections*, p. 69.

[146]John D. Hicks, "The Third Party Tradition in American Politics," *Mississippi Valley Historical Review* 20:26.

[147]Key, *Politics, Parties and Pressure Groups*, p. 245. Roscoe Drummond notes that in examining major party splintering, "third parties can only be election spoilers, but not winners." (Roscoe Drummond, "Point of View: Fractured Parties," *Christian Science Monitor*, 26 March 1975, p. 5.)

[148]Mazmanian, *Third Parties in Presidential Elections*, pp. 70, 71.

[149]Ewing, *Presidential Elections*, p. 133.

[150]Ibid., p. 73.

[151]Ibid., p. 133.

[152]Key, *Politics, Parties and Pressure Groups*, p. 245.

[153]James, *American Political Parties*, p. 49.

[154]Jewell and Olsen, *American State Political Parties*, p. 37.

[155]Ibid., p. 38.

[156]Burnham, *Critical Elections*, p. 8.

[157]Ibid., p. 6.

[158]Ibid., p. 7.

[159]Ibid.

[160]Ibid., p. 10.

[161]Key, *Politics, Parties and Pressure groups*, p. 286; and James, *American Political Parties*, p. 49.

[162]Mazmanian, *Third Parties in Presidential Elections*, p. 139.

[163]Burnham, *Critical Elections*, p. 28.

[164]Ibid., pp. 28–29; and James, *American Political Parties*, p. 50.

[165]Burnham, *Critical Elections*, pp. 28–29.

[166]Ibid., p. 30. The Anti-Mason Party focused on political democratization; the Free Soil Party agitated the cause of abolitionism; Populism represented the strife between urban and rural interests and sectionalism; and the Progressives represented welfare liberalism against laissez-faire economics in the 1920s (p. 30).

[167]John F. Freie, "Minor Parties in Realigning Eras," *American Politics Quarterly* 10:51.

[168]Ibid., p. 53. The Populists obtained over 62 percent of its vote in 1892 from the West; the Progressives in 1924 had 70 percent of its vote come from the Northwest and West; and in 1968 the AIP received 52 percent of its vote from the South.

[169]Ibid., pp. 56, 57.

[170]Ibid.

[171]Ibid., p. 61.

[172]Rossiter, *Parties and Politics*, pp. 3, 4.

[173]Ibid., p. 61.

[174]Blackman, *Third Party President?* p. 2.

[175]Ibid., p. 3. The minor party that probably has borne the brunt of most of these restrictions has been the U.S. Communist Party (see Sorauf, *Political Parties in the American System*, p. 34).

[176]Schattschneider, *Party Government*, p. 105.

[177]Hesseltine, *The Rise and Fall of Third Parties*, p. 100; Mazmanian, *Third Parties in Presidential Elections*, p. 98; Goodman, *The Two-Party System*, p. 74; and Smallwood, *The Other Candidates*, p. 10.

[178]Stedman and Stedman, *Discontent at the Polls*, p. 125.

[179]Key, *Politics, Parties and Pressure Groups*, p. 552.

[180]Rosenstone et al., *Third Parties in America*, p. 19.

[181]"Minor Political Parties and Their Candidates," *Congressional Digest* 55:232; "Your Other Choices for White House," *U.S. News and World Report*, p. 30; and Herbert E. Alexander, *Financing the 1980 Election*, p. 350.

[182]Rosenstone et al., *Third Parties in America*, pp. 20, 21.

[183]Blackman, *Third Party President?* pp. 32–33.

[184]Ibid., p. 32.

[185]"Ballot Access—Disenfranchising the Franchise," *Libertarian Party News*, May/June 1986, p. 5; and Blackman, *Third Party President?* p. 34.

[186]Blackman, *Third Party President?* pp. 35, 36. Such states are California (at least 5 percent but not more than 6 percent); Wisconsin (a minimum of 5,000 but not more than 6,000 signatures); and Massachusetts (a range of 2 to 2.8 percent) (p. 36).

[187]Ibid., p. 38. About one-third of the states forbid voters from signing more than one party ballot petition (p. 39).

[188]Ibid., p. 45.

[189]Ibid., p. 77.

[190]See ibid., pp. 76–106.

[191]"What About That Third Party?" *Washington Post,* 29 March 1980, p. A-12.

[192]Blackman, *Third Party President?* p. 47.

[193]Ibid., pp. 3, 4.

[194]Ibid., p. 4.

[195]*Williams v. Rhodes,* pp. 7, 8. Also see Frank J. Sorauf, *Party Politics in America,* pp. 52, 53.

[196]*Williams v. Rhodes,* p. 11. The SLP had been a party in Ohio since the end of the nineteenth century but ended in the state in 1948 when the new ballot laws were instituted.

[197]Ibid. Justice Douglas in a concurring opinion states that the Ohio laws force a third party, in order to qualify, to "first erect elaborate political machinery, and then rest it upon the ranks of those who have proved both unwilling and unable to vote" since convention delegates had to prove that they did not vote in any primary for the previous four years (p. 13).

[198]Ibid., p. 14.

[199]Smallwood, *The Other Candidates,* pp. 250–53.

[200]*American Party of Texas v. Bob Bullock, Secretary of State of Texas.*

[201]Ibid., p. 26.

[202]*Jenness v. Fortson,* p. 1,970.

[203]Ibid., p. 1,974; Blackman, *Third Party President?* p. 5.

[204]*Jenness v. Fortson,* p. 1,975.

[205]Blackman, *Third Party President?* p. 4.

[206]*Munro v. Socialist Workers Party,* p. 540. In a 7–2 decision, the Court ruled that the state of Washington may limit ballot access to avoid voter confusion, ballot overcrowding, or frivolous candidacies without violating the First and Fourteenth amendments. Yet the level of limitation that would be deemed reasonable was never defined by the Court. This was Justice Marshall's main reason for dissent.

[207]Blackman, *Third Party President?* p. 6.

[208]*Munro v. Socialist Workers Party,* p. 540.

[209]Bell, "Constraints on Electoral Success," p. 105.

[210]*Munro v. Socialist Workers Party,* p. 544.

[211]Key, *Politics, Parties and Pressure Groups,* p. 218.

[212]Rosenstone et al., *Third Parties in America,* p. 16; Smallwood, *The Other Candidates,* p. 10; and Rossiter, *Parties and Politics,* p. 9. Rossiter goes so far as to note that the single-member system is the death of third parties in the U.S. (p. 9).

[213]Rosenstone et al., *Third Parties in America,* p. 16; and Sorauf, *Party Politics in America,* p. 35.

[214]Rossiter, *Parties and Politics,* p. 9.

[215]Ibid.

[216]Rosenstone et al., *Third Parties in America,* p. 18. Duverger's law that the simple majority/single ballot system favors the two-party system was retested and found to be indirectly supported in a study by Riker ("The Number of Political Parties," p. 93).

[217]Schattschneider, *Party Government*, p. 83.

[218]James, *American Political Parties*, p. 52.

[219]Rosenstone et al., *Third Parties in America*, p. 26.

[220]Alexander, *1980 Election*, p. 346; and Federal Election Commission, *Federal Election Campaign Laws*, 9004(a)(2)(A), p. 63.

[221]Ibid.

[222]Herbert E. Alexander, *Financing Politics*, p. 95; Federal Election Commission, *Federal Election Campaign Laws*, 9004(a)(2)(B), p. 64; Rosenstone et al., *Third Parties in America*, p. 26; and Nelson W. Polsby, *Consequences of Party Reform*, p. 83.

[223]Polsby and Wildavsky, *Presidential Elections*, p. 64.

[224]"Presidential Results Analyzed," *Libertarian Party News*, November 1984/February 1985, p. 7.

[225]Richard L. Berke, "Minor Candidate Gets U.S. Funds," *New York Times*, 29 January, p. I-1.

[226]Alexander, *1980 Election*, p. 115.

[227]Ibid. Other minor party spending, in comparison, for 1980 was: Libertarian, $3,320,678; Citizens, $1,140,171; Socialist Workers, $526,000; Communist, $316,275; Socialist, $39,000; and the American Independent, Conservative, Constitution, Freedom, Labor, Peace and Freedom, People's Capitalist, People's National, U.S. Labor (LaRouche), U.S. Congress, and the Worker's World spent a total of only $228,000 (p. 116).

[228]Alexander, *1980 Election*, p. 115. This increased amount for 1980 could be partially attributed to the Libertarian Party spending $3.3 million in its presidential campaign (p. 116).

[229]Samuel J. Eldersveld, *Political Parties in American Society*, p. 321; and Alexander, *Financing Politics*, p. 22.

[230]Alexander, *Financing Politics*, p. 35.

[231]Ibid., pp. 35–36, 95. The Court gave a *percuriam* decision in which Justice Stevens abstained.

[232]Smallwood, *The Other Candidates*, p. 173. The total amount spent by the party was $3.5 million.

[233]"Libertarians: The Third Non-Party," *Economist*, p. 24.

[234]Herbert E. Alexander, *Financing the 1972 Election*, p. 313.

[235]Polsby, *Party Reform*, p. 84.

[236]Ernest Evans, "Covering Third Parties," *Christian Science Monitor*, 20 October 1988, p. 14.

[237]Ibid.

[238]Smallwood, *The Other Candidates*, p. 267. In 1959 broadcast time in the form of newscasts, interviews, and documentaries were excluded from section 315(a) equal time requirements (p. 267).

[239]Polsby and Wildavsky, *Presidential Elections*, p. 80. For a larger discussion of free media time, although a bit outdated, see Delmer D. Dunn, *Financing Presidential Campaigns*. Dunn examines the question and consequences of waiving the equal time doctrine (section 315a), the amount of time by office and party, and the value of political debates.

[240]Polsby and Wildavsky, *Presidential Elections*, p. 269.

[241]Ibid., p. 270; and Alexander, *1980 Election*, p. 353.

[242]Smallwood, *The Other Candidates*, p. 270; and Alexander, *1980 Election*, p. 353. Anderson did appear in a September televised debate with Ronald Reagan.

[243]Alexander, *1980 Election*, p. 354. However, Polsby and Wildavsky note that

Anderson steadily lost ground after being excluded from debating the major party candidates at Carter's insistence (*Presidential Elections*, p. 80).

[244]Alexander, *1980 Election*, p. 353.

[245]Ibid.

[246]David K. Walter, "We're a Third Party!" *Christian Science Monitor*, 27 February 1987, p. 15; and see also Richard Winger, "Why Voters' Options Seem So Few," *Wall Street Journal*, 2 November 1988, A-20.

[247]James, *American Political Parties*, p. 51.

[248]Woodburn, *Political Parties and Party Problems*, p. 525.

[249]Rosenstone et al., *Third Parties in America*, p. 44.

[250]Ibid.; and Smallwood, *The Other Candidates*, p. 9. Smallwood explains that 1924 Progressive candidate Robert La Follette lost hundreds of thousands of votes when the major parties used this type of strategy (p. 9).

[251]Rosenstone et al., *Third Parties in America*, p. 46.

[252]Everett Carl Ladd, Jr., *American Political Parties*, p. 46.

[253]Rosenstone et al., *Third Parties in America*, p. 46.

[254]Smallwood, *The Other Candidates*, p. 8.

[255]Sindler, *Political Parties in the U.S.*, p. 56; Haynes, *Social Politics*, p. 154; Rossiter, *Parties and Politics*, p. 8; and also see Eldersveld, *Behavioral Analysis*, pp 492–501 for an expanded explanation about political consensus in the American Electorate.

[256]Schattschneider, *The Semi-Sovereign People*, p. 57.

[257]Smallwood, *The Other Candidates*, p. 5.

[258]Rosenstone et al., *Third Parties in America*, pp. 46–47.

[259]Lawson, *Political Parties and Democracy*, p. 46.

[260]Rosenstone et al., *Third Parties in America*, p. 30.

[261]Ibid.

[262]Ranney and Kendall, *Democracy and the American Party System*, p. 453.

[263]Eugene E. Methvin, "Lyndon LaRouche's Raid on Democracy," *Reader's Digest*, p. 90.

[264]"LaRouche Followers Linked to Fraud Probe," *Knoxville News-Sentinel*, 30 March 1986, p. A-5. Also see Philip Shenon, "Ten Close Associates of LaRouche Charged with Fraud, Conspiracy," *Chattanooga Times*, 7 October 1986, p. A-7. It is interesting to note that when the author of this work was doing research in 1984 on various minor parties, he was contacted several times by LaRouche's NDPC. Several high-pressure phone calls were received, each explaining the great need for LaRouche to be in office and they all ended with a plea for contributions, and or a $500 loan on a major credit card that would be paid back, in full, after the campaign was completed.

[265]Methvin, "Lyndon LaRouche's Raid on Democracy," p. 93; "LaRouche Followers," *Knoxville News-Sentinel*, 30 March 1986, p. A-5. (Some estimates put the total closer to $1 to $30 million in fraudulent loans; see *New York Times*, 19 February 1987, p. 11.)

[266]Mike Royko, "Debt Is No Big Deal for Lyndon's Crowd," *Knoxville News-Sentinel*, 4 April 1986, p. A-14.

[267]Eldersveld, *Political Parties*, p. 40.

[268]Ranney and Kendall, *Democracy and the American Party System*, p. 452.

[269]Communist Party, U.S.A., *Constitution of the Communist Party*, pp. 28, 32 (Article VI, Section 4, and Article VIII, Sections 1, 2).

[270]Harvey Klehr, *Communist Cadre*, p. 4.

[271]Ibid., pp. 83–85.

[272]Ibid., p. 83.

[273]Ibid.

[274]Ibid., p. 49. Klehr's study notes that in these two periods, 19 party leaders in 1928–29 and 22 party leaders in 1957–59 were expelled or left the party due to ideological differences (p. 88).

[275]Ibid., p. 90.

[276]Ibid., p. 23.

[277]Ibid., p. 85. Klehr points out that between 1948 and the mid–1950s the federal government under the auspices of the Smith Act indicted and tried over 100 party leaders, effectively hampering its actions in America (p. 90).

[278]James Lewis Canfield, *A Case of Third Party Activism*, p. 1; and see also Robert H. Salisbury, "An Exchange Theory of Interest Groups," *Midwest Journal of Political Science* 13:15.

[279]Ibid., p. 8.

[280]Ibid., p. 11.

[281]Ibid., p. 12.

[282]Ibid.

[283]Herring, *The Politics of Democracy*, p. 182; and Sorauf, *Party Politics in America*, p. 34.

[284]Sorauf, *Party Politics in America*, p. 34.

[285]Herring, *The Politics of Democracy*, p. 183.

[286]Katz, *A Theory of Parties*, p. 4.

[287]Jean Blondel, *Political Parties*, p. 67.

[288]Everett Carl Ladd, Jr., "The American Idea of Nation," *Christian Science Monitor*, 30 September 1985, p. 16.

[289]Seymour M. Lipset and Earl Raab, *The Politics of Unreason*, p. 428.

[290]Ibid., p. 429.

[291]Ibid.

[292]George Thayer, *The Farther Shores of Politics*, p. 24.

[293]Ibid., p. 50.

[294]Ibid., pp. 34–39. Smith was pro–Nazi during the war.

[295]Lipset and Raab, *The Politics of Unreason*, p. 168.

[296]Ibid., pp. 168–69.

[297]Ibid., p. 170.

[298]Ibid., pp. 170–71.

[299]Ibid., p. 177.

[300]Ibid., p. 171. The postmaster general had banned Coughlin's magazine, *Social Justice*, from the mail as seditious and the attorney general urged the archbishop to silence Coughlin (p. 171).

[301]Peter H. Argersinger, "An Upset in the Land of Lincoln," *U.S. News and World Report*, p. 8; "LaRouched in Illinois," *Newsweek*, p. 22; and Andrew H. Malcolm, "Two Conservative Extremists Upset Democrats in the Illinois Primary," *New York Times*, 20 March 1986, p. I-1. In an ironic twist of fate, Adlai Stevenson had to run for the office of governor on a third party ticket. Stevenson's new party, the Illinois Solidarity Party, had to meet the petition requirements for ballot status and had to overcome many of the barriers already discussed in this chapter.

[302]David Gelman, Mark Miller, et al., "Lyndon LaRouche: Beyond the Fringe," *Newsweek*, 7 April 1986, p. 39.

[303]"LaRouched in Illinois," *Newsweek*, p. 22.

[304]Methvin, "Lyndon LaRouche's Raid on Democracy," p. 93; and Gelman, Miller, et al., "Lyndon LaRouche: Beyond the Fringe," *Newsweek*, p. 39.

[305]"Conservative Blasts 'Idiots' of the World," *Knoxville Journal*, 10 April 1986, p. A-7.

[306]Dahl, *Political Oppositions in Western Democracies*, p. 35.

[307]Ibid.

[308]Ibid., p. 61.

[309]Ibid.

[310]Ibid., p. 66.

[311]Stedman and Stedman, *Discontent at the Polls*, pp. 108, 109.

[312]Haynes, *Third Party Movements*, p. 4.

[313]Stedman and Stedman, *Discontent at the Polls*, p. 111.

[314]Goodman, *The Two-Party System*, p. 49; and Rosenstone et al., *Third Parties in America*, p. 43.

[315]Rosenstone et al., *Third Parties in America*, p. 44.

[316]Ibid., p. 43.

[317]Mazmanian, *Third Parties in Presidential Elections*, p. 143.

[318]Hicks, "The Third Party Tradition in American Politics," p. 26.

[319]Peter H. Argersinger, "A Place on the Ballot: Fusion Politics and Antifusion Laws," *American Historical Review* 85:288.

[320]Ibid.

[321]Sundquist, *Dynamics of the Party System*, p. 114.

[322]Argersinger, "A Place on the Ballot," p. 288.

[323]Ibid., p. 290.

[324]Ibid., pp. 291–96. Argersinger explains that the Republican Party used antifusion laws to guarantee their ascendancy into offices. The Republicans feared that a fusion party would surely defeat them. For a much deeper look into the Populist-Democratic fusion party, see Sundquist, *Dynamics of the Party System*, pp. 134–69.

[325]Argersinger, "A Place on the Ballot," p. 297. Sundquist notes that the Bryan Democratic Party was in fact Populist in everything but name (Sundquist, *Dynamics of the Party System*, p. 153).

[326]Argersinger, "A Place on the Ballot," p. 300.

Chapter 3: The Libertarian Party

[1]Mark Paul, "Seducing the Left: The Third Party That Wants You," *Mother Jones*, p. 62.

[2]Jerome Tuccille, *Radical Libertarianism*, p. 2.

[3]John Hospers, *Libertarianism*, p. 10.

[4]Tibor R. Machan, *Human Rights and Human Liberties*, p. 51. Machan argues that rights are natural and are the equivalent of moral principles that must be followed.

[5]Tibor R. Machan, "Libertarianism and Conservatives," *Modern Age* 24:21.

[6]John Hospers, "Conservatives and Libertarians," *Modern Age* 25:372.

[7]Hospers, *Libertarianism*, p. 14.

[8]Ibid., p. 16.

[9]Murray N. Rothbard, *The Ethics of Liberty*, pp. 24, 35.

[10]Hospers, *Libertarianism*, p. 22.

[11]Ibid., pp. 50, 51. Hospers notes that property rights are only second to the rights to life (p. 62).

[12]Ibid., p. 117.

[13]Ibid., p. 115.

[14]Ibid., p. 107.

[15]Ibid., pp. 105, 224.

[16]Ibid., pp. 128–29.

[17]Ibid., pp. 216, 219.

[18]Rothbard, *The Ethics of Liberty*, p. 162.

[19]Ibid.

[20]Ibid., pp. 169, 170.

[21]Hospers, *Libertarianism*, p. 15.

[22]David Bergland, *Libertarianism in One Lesson*, p. 2.

[23]Murray N. Rothbard, "Myth and Truth About Libertarianism," *Modern Age* 24:9.

[24]Ibid.

[25]Ibid., p. 10.

[26]Ibid.

[27]Ibid., p. 12.

[28]Ibid., p. 14.

[29]Ibid., p. 13.

[30]Ibid.

[31]Rothbard, *The Ethics of Liberty*, p. 21.

[32]Bergland, *Libertarianism in One Lesson*, p. 4.

[33]Rothbard, *The Ethics of Liberty*, p. 253.

[34]Dante Germino, "Traditionalism and Libertarianism: Two Views," *Modern Age* 26:51; and Robert Nisbet, "Conservatives and Libertarians: Uneasy Cousins," *Modern Age* 24:3.

[35]Russell Kirk, "Libertarians: The Chirping Sectaries," *Modern Age* 25:345.

[36]Ibid., pp. 347–49.

[37]J. W. Woelfel, "We're Not Rational Animals: A Liberal Reply to Libertarianism," *Christian Century*, pp. 1, 100.

[38]Douglas Den Uyl and Douglas B. Rasmussen, "The Philosophical Importance of Ayn Rand," *Modern Age* 27:68.

[39]Ibid., p. 67.

[40]George Friedman and Gary L. McDowell, "The Libertarian Movement in America," *Journal of Contemporary Studies* 6:57. However, it is interesting to note that Rand spurned the party as a "random collection of emotional hippies of the right to seek to play at politics without philosophy" (Wallace Turner, "Major Libertarian Candidate Opposes Party Stand on Abortion," *New York Times*, 4 September 1987, p. I-10).

[41]Friedman and McDowell, "The Libertarian Movement in America," p. 57; and Uyl and Rasmussen, "The Philosophical Importance of Ayn Rand," p. 68.

[42]Uyl and Rasmussen, "The Philosophical Importance of Ayn Rand," p. 68.

[43]Friedman and McDowell, "The Libertarian Movement in America," p. 57.

[44]Ibid., p. 58.

[45]Ibid., p. 55.

[46]Ibid., pp. 54–55.

[47]Ibid., p. 55.

[48]Friedrich A. Hayek, *Economic Freedom and Representative Government*, p. 8.

[49]Ibid., p. 13.

[50]Ibid., pp. 10, 12, 17, 19.

[51]Friedman and McDowell, "The Libertarian Movement in America," p. 56.

[52]Hayek, *Economic Freedom*, p. 14.

[53]Ibid., p. 11.

[54]Hospers, *Libertarianism*, p. 81. This point was explained in an earlier section of this chapter.

55Ibid., pp. 50, 51.

56Ibid., p. 419.

57Ibid., p. 420; and "Has the Libertarian Movement Gone Kooky?" *National Review*, p. 973.

58Hospers, *Libertarianism*, p. 420.

59Ibid., p. 241.

60Ibid., pp. 62, 299.

61Rothbard, *The Ethics of Liberty*, p. 229.

62Robert Nozick, *Anarchy, State, and Utopia*, p. ix.

63Ibid., p. 149.

64Rothbard, *The Ethics of Liberty*, pp. 30–31, 55–56.

65Ibid., p. 30.

66Ibid., p. 113.

67Ibid., pp. 113–16.

68Ibid., pp. 97–102.

69Ibid.

70Stephen L. Newman, *Liberalism at Wits' End: The Libertarian Revolt Against the State*, p. 43.

71Rothbard, *The Ethics of Liberty*, pp. 51, 77.

72Ibid., p. 162. See also Murray N. Rothbard, *For a New Liberty: The Libertarian Manifesto*, pp. 45–69.

73Rothbard, *The Ethics of Liberty*, p. 170.

74Ibid., p. 169.

75Ibid.

76Rothbard, *The Libertarian Manifesto*, p. 23.

77Tibor R. Machan, "Libertarianism and Conservatives: Further Considerations," *Modern Age* 26:21.

78Friedman and McDowell, "The Libertarian Movement in America," pp. 48–49.

79Ibid., p. 48.

80Tuccille, *Radical Libertarianism*, pp. 7, 10.

81Ibid., p. 10; and Friedman and McDowell, "The Libertarian Movement in America," p. 49.

82Newman, *Liberalism at Wits' End*, p. 21.

83Ibid., pp. 19, 21. Newman explains that the libertarians are the heirs of the antistatist tradition handed down by Paine, Thoreau, Nock, and others (p. 24). These themes of antistatism and individualism can be observed in the party's Statement of Principles in Appendix B.

84Bergland, *Libertarianism in One Lesson*, p. 5.

85Ibid.

86Peter de Rosa, "Where They Stand," *Journal of Libertarian Studies* 3:393, 394.

87Newman, *Liberalism at Wits' End*, p. 28; Carl Polsgrove, "In Pursuit of Liberty," *Progressive* 42:38, 39; and Kenneth L. Woodward, "Every Man for Himself," *Newsweek*, p. 91.

88Newman, *Liberalism at Wits' End*, p. 29; and John Judis, "Libertarianism: Where the Left Meets the Right," *Progressive* 44:36.

89Newman, *Liberalism at Wits' End*, p. 29.

90Bergland, *Libertarianism in One Lesson*, p. 5.

91Ibid.

92Ibid. The Statement of Principles is in Appendix B.

93Newman, *Liberalism at Wits' End*, p. 30. The effects of the anarcho-capitalists, the more radical fringe of the party, will be discussed in more detail shortly.

[94]Roger L. MacBride, *A New Dawn for America: The Libertarian Challenge*, p. 96.

[95]Daniel Mazmanian, *Third Parties in Presidential Elections*, pp. 27, 136–37.

[96]Paul K. Conkin and David Burner, *A History of Recent America*, p. 648.

[97]Ibid.

[98]James L. Sundquist, *Dynamics of the Party System*, p. 381. George Wallace and the AIP ran again in the 1972 presidential election. The AIP's efforts were dampened after Wallace was shot on 15 May 1972 while on the campaign trail (Conkin and Burner, *A History of Recent America*, p. 661).

[99]Sundquist, *Dynamics of the Party System*, p. 383.

[100]Ibid., p. 390.

[101]Ibid., p. 374.

[102]Ibid., pp. 369, 394.

[103]Ibid., p. 382.

[104]Conkin and Burner, *A History of Recent America*, p. 652.

[105]Ibid., p. 659.

[106]Ibid.

[107]Ibid, p. 660.

[108]The party was only on 2 ballots and received only 3,600 votes. It did receive, however, 1 electoral college vote.

[109]Elisabeth Bumiller, "Third Partying," *Washington Post*, 22 January 1980, p. B-1; Nicholas von Hoffman, "Libertarians Put Focus on Freedom," *Chicago Tribune*, 28 October 1974, p. II-4; and Gladwin Hill, "Libertarians, Foes of Big Government," *New York Times*, 10 September 1979, p. II-10.

[110]K. Woodward, "Every Man for Himself," p. 91.

[111]Ibid.

[112]Newman, *Liberalism at Wits' End*, p. 9.

[113]Ibid., p. 10.

[114]Polsgrove, "In Pursuit of Liberty," p. 39.

[115]Ibid., p. 38.

[116]Carey McWilliams, "Second Thoughts," *Nation*, p. 358.

[117]Ibid.

[118]David A. Shannon, *The Socialist Party of America* (Chicago: Quadrangle, 1967), pp. 1–4.

[119]Libertarian Party, *Libertarian Party Bylaws and Convention Rules*.

[120]"Membership Form," *Libertarian Party News*, November 1984/February 1985, p. 29.

[121]Mike Holmes, "Is the LP in Trouble? Part II," *American Libertarian*, October 1986, 1:6; Joseph W. Dehn III, "LP Membership Figures Reveal Distorted Growth," *Libertarian Party News*, January/February 1989, p. 3; and "LP Membership," *Libertarian Party News*, March 1991, p. 1.

[122]"Party Membership: What's in It for Me?" *Libertarian Party News*, Spring 1986, p. 3.

[123]Ibid.

[124]Ibid.

[125]De Rosa, "Where They Stand," p. 391.

[126]Sampson O. Onwumere, "The Libertarian Party of America and Presidential Elections," Dissertation, p. 105.

[127]Libertarian Party, *Bylaws*, Article 6, p. 1.

[128]Ibid., Article 6, Sec. 5.

[129]Ibid., Article 6, Sec. 6.

[130]"State Party Rejuvenation," *Libertarian Party News*, May/June 1986, p. 9.

[131]Libertarian Party, *Bylaws,* Article 8, Sec. 1(d), p. 2.

[132]Ibid., Article 8, Sec. 7.

[133]Ibid., Article 8, Sec. 10.

[134]Friedman and McDowell, "The Libertarian Movement in America," p. 53.

[135]Ibid.

[136]Alicia G. Clark, "From the Chair," *Libertarian Party News,* March/April 1982, p. 2.

[137]Ibid.

[138]Libertarian Party, *Bylaws,* Article 9, Sec. 1.

[139]Ibid., Article 9, Sec. 2.

[140]"Financial Status," *Libertarian Party News,* May/June 1986, p. 9. This is the most recent and complete data available.

[141]Ibid. The 1986 data is the most recent information available.

[142]Federal Election Commission, "Report on Financial Activity 1983–1984; Presidential Pre-Nomination Campaigns," Table A-4.

[143]Ibid., Table A-3.

[144]"1984 LP Financial Results," *Libertarian Party News,* March/April 1985, p. 5.

[145]Libertarian Party, *Bylaws,* Articles 11, 12, pp. 4, 5.

[146]Ibid., Article 11, Sec. 4.

[147]Ibid., Rule 11, p. 8.

[148]Clark, "From the Chair," *Libertarian Party News,* March/April 1982, p. 2.

[149]Donald Johnson, *National Party Platforms: Volume II,* p. 946.

[150]Ibid.; and Donald B. Johnson, *National Party Platforms: 1980 Supplement,* p. 87.

[151]Johnson, *National Party Platforms: Volume II,* p. 947.

[152]Ibid., p. 948; and Johnson, *1980 Supplement,* p. 88.

[153]Libertarian Party, *1984 Platform of the Libertarian Party,* Sec. 21, p. 4.

[154]Ibid.

[155]"Libertarians Tell Conflict on Abortions," *Los Angeles Times,* 19 February 1979, p. II- 5.

[156]Libertarian Party, *1984 Platform,* Sec. 20, p. 4.

[157]Ibid., Sec. 1, p. 4.

[158]These ideas run fairly consistently from the 1972 to the 1988 platforms, although the actual wording varies somewhat.

[159]Johnson, *National Party Platforms: Volume II,* pp. 823, 950; Johnson, *1980 Supplement,* p. 92; and Libertarian Party, *1984 Platform,* p. 5. The language is the same from the 1976 to the 1984 platforms.

[160]Johnson, *National Party Platforms: Volume II,* p, 950; Johnson, *1980 Supplement,* p. 93; Libertarian Party, *1984 Platform,* p. 5; and "The Libertarian Party Platform in Brief," *Libertarian Party News,* Special Research Edition, 1988, pp. 6–7.

[161]Johnson, *National Party Platforms: Volume II,* p. 951.

[162]Ibid., pp. 951–52.

[163]Ibid., p. 953.

[164]Judis, "Libertarianism," p. 38.

[165]MacBride, *A New Dawn for America,* pp. 22, 23.

[166]Ibid., p. 37.

[167]Edward E. Clark, *A New Beginning,* p. 2.

[168]Tom Morganthau and Rich Thomas, "For Sale: Uncle Sam," *Newsweek,* p. 18.

[169]Walter Shapiro and Rich Thomas, "Getting Ready for a Federal Fire Sale," *Newsweek,* p. 44.

[170]Monroe W. Karmin, Richard Alm, et al., "Hanging a 'For Sale' Sign on Government," *U.S. News and World Report,* p. 19.

[171]E. E. Schattschneider, *The Semi-Sovereign People*, pp. 27, 57.

[172]Ibid., pp. 57, 69.

[173]Ibid., pp. 69–70.

[174]Ibid., p. 74.

[175]Barry Klazura, "Libertarians: Idealists in a Real World," *Chicago Tribune*, 26 August 1972, p. I-10.

[176]Ibid.

[177]Rhodes Cook, "Third Parties: A Struggle for Attention," *Congressional Quarterly*, p. 2,973.

[178]MacBride, *A New Dawn for America*, p. 96; and Cook, "Third Parties: A Struggle for Attention," p. 2,974.

[179]MacBride, *A New Dawn for America*, pp. 5, 9.

[180]Ibid., p. 23.

[181]Ibid., pp. 37, 50–55.

[182]Ibid., pp. 79–84.

[183]Nicholas von Hoffman, "Third Party Gets Silent Treatment," *Chicago Tribune*, 29 November 1975, p. N1-10.

[184]Linda Charlton, "Libertarian Candidate Would Burn Federal Check Providing Campaign Aid," *New York Times*, 19 August 1976, p. I-19.

[185]Cook, "Third Parties: A Struggle for Attention," p. 2,972.

[186]Rhodes Cook, "Third Parties Face Obstacles to Prominence," *Congressional Quarterly* 37:2,004.

[187]Cook, "Third Parties: A Struggle for Attention," p. 2,974.

[188]"Libertarian Party Target: Government," *Christian Science Monitor*, 19 July 1977, p. 22.

[189]Mark Stevens, "Libertarians Set Realistic '80 Goals," *Christian Science Monitor*, 10 September 1979, p. 6.

[190]David Larsen, "Clark Nominated to Head Libertarian Ticket in '80," *Los Angeles Times*, 9 September 1979, p. I-10.

[191]Frank Smallwood, *The Other Candidates*, p. 173; and "Libertarians Map Election Strategy," *Los Angeles Times*, 18 February 1979, p. I-38.

[192]"Libertarians Tell Conflict on Abortions," *Los Angeles Times*, p. II-5.

[193]"Libertarian Candidates Split on Budget Balancing," *Los Angeles Times*, 17 February 1979, p. I-25.

[194]Cook, "Third Parties Face Obstacles," p. 2,004.

[195]Smallwood, *The Other Candidates*, p. 173.

[196]Paul, "Seducing the Left, pp. 47, 48.

[197]Roger Smith, "A Credible Third Party Is Goal of Libertarians," *Los Angeles Times*, 6 September 1980, p. I-1.

[198]David Axelrod, "Ed Clark: Left, Right, No Middle," *Chicago Tribune*, 28 October 1980, p. I-1.

[199]Cook, "Third Parties Face Obstacles," p. 2,003.

[200]Ibid., p. 2,005.

[201]"Libertarians Map Election Strategy," *Los Angeles Times*, p. I-38.

[202]Cook, "Alternate Party Candidates," p. 3,143. Cook goes on to state that the Libertarian Party had clearly emerged as the most potent minor party in the 1980 election (p. 3,144).

[203]"Libertarian Party Candidate Says U.S. Needs Alternative," *Los Angeles Times*, 2 July 1980, p. I-20.

[204]Clark, *A New Beginning*, p. 4.

[205]Ibid., p. 5–6.

[206]Ibid., p. 6.

[207]Ibid., pp. 10, 11.

[208]Ibid., pp. 12, 14.

[209]Ibid., pp. 22, 25. Clark stated that the only way to halt inflation was to balance the budget. If inflation stopped, unemployment would also decrease (pp. 25, 28).

[210]Ibid., pp. 74, 75.

[211]Ibid., p. 68; and Jack Mabley, "Libertarian Offers Challenging Ideas," *Chicago Tribune*, 25 March 1980, p. I-4.

[212]Clark, *A New Beginning*, pp. 66, 69.

[213]Ibid., pp. 100, 104, 106.

[214]Ibid., p. 129.

[215]"Libertarian Party Candidate Says U.S. Needs Alternative," *Los Angeles Times*, p. I-20.

[216]Megan Rosenfeld, "Candidate Clark: Carrying His Banner High," *Washington Post*, 2 November 1980, p. H-1.

[217]Smallwood, *The Other Candidates*, p. 285. In comparison, Barry Commoner and the Citizens Party received 254,264 votes on 30 ballots; Andrew Pulley and the Socialist Workers Party on 29 ballots received 49,118 votes; Benjamin Bubor and the Prohibitionist Party, 9 ballots and 8,202 votes; Deirdre Griswold and the Workers World Party, 12 ballots and 13,300 votes; and Percy Greaves, the American Party on 7 ballots with 6,647 botes. See Cook, "Alternative Party Candidates," p. 3,146, for the ballot status of minor parties in 1980; and "Presidential Results Analyzed," *Libertarian Party News*, November 1984/February 1985, p. 7.

[218]Robert Scheer, "Libertarian Clark Vows to Create Third-Party System," *Los Angeles Times*, 18 October 1980, p. I-30.

[219]Bill Peterson, "Libertarian Clark Says He's the Real Alternative," *Washington Post*, 1 July 1980, p. A-2.

[220]Cook, "Alternative Party Candidates," p. 3,143.

[221]Jack Germond and Jules Whitcover, "Ed Clark and His Party Won Their Objective," *Chicago Tribune*, 2 January 1981, p. 3-40. Anderson was an independent candidate and thus, did not qualify as a political party candidate.

[222]"Campaign '82," *Libertarian Party News*, January/February 1982, pp. 1, 4.

[223]R. Brookhiser, "Saving the UOS," *National Review*, p. 1,274.

[224]Ann Groer, "Libertarian Lark," *New Republic*, 3 October 1983, p. 16.

[225]Brookhiser, "Saving the UOS," p. 1,297.

[226]Ibid., p. 1,274.

[227]Groer, "Libertarian Lark," p. 16.

[228]T. R. Reid, "Libertarians Pick Candidate for President," *Washington Post*, 4 September 1983, p. A-17.

[229]Ibid., p. A-18.

[230]Keith Love, "Libertarian's Bergland Stresses Differences with Traditional Parties," *Los Angeles Times*, 29 September 1984, p. I-14.

[231]Groer, "Libertarian Lark," p. 16. Obviously, the idea of doing this would mean a confirmation and endorsement of governmental intervention in the elections and broadcast media.

[232]"Presidential Results Analyzed," *Libertarian Party News*, November 1984/February 1985, p. 7. For comparison: Citizens Party—72,141; Populist—66,171; Socialist Workers—24,677; Communist—36,375; Workers World—17,968; Prohibition—4,238; and American—13,148.

[233]"1984 LP Financial Results," *Libertarian Party News*, March/April 1985, p. 4.

[234]Murray N. Rothbard, "The Consolidation Election," *Libertarian Party News*, November 1984/February 1985, p. 22.

[235]Ibid.

[236]Ibid.

[237]Ibid.

[238]"Russell Means Runs for President as Libertarian," *New York Times*, 31 May 1987, p. I-11.

[239]Ibid.

[240]Alan W. Bock, "Radical Views, Conservative Style," *Reason* 20:35–38.

[241]Ibid., p. 36.

[242]Ibid., p. 35.

[243]Wallace Turner, "Libertarians Pick Ex-Congressman in '88 Bid," *New York Times*, 6 September 1987, p. I-35.

[244]Bock, "Radical Views, Conservative Style," p. 38.

[245]Tom W. Ferguson, "Libertarians Look to Restart the Engine," *Wall Street Journal*, 27 August 1987, p. A-22.

[246]Wayne King, "Some Republicans Back Foe of Bush," *New York Times*, 10 August 1988, p. I-14. It is interesting that Robertson supporters in Michigan would oppose Bush by backing Paul based on his conservative fiscal planks, yet whether they would have also backed him knowing the Libertarian Party's social planks is questionable.

[247]Wallace Turner, "Major Libertarian Candidate Opposes Party Stand on Abortion," *New York Times*, 4 September 1987, p. I-10; and Bock, "Radical Views, Conservative Style," p. 38.

[248]Andrew Rosenthal, "Now for a Real Underdog: Ron Paul, Libertarian, for President," *New York Times*, 17 October 1988, p. I-16.

[249]Other minor parties were also disappointed in the results. The New Alliance Party's Lenora Fulani, the only minor party on all fifty-one ballots and recipient of federal matching funds, received 217,219 votes. Some other results: David Duke, Populist Party 47,047; Eugene McCarthy, Consumer Party 30,905; James Griffin, American Independent 27,818; Lyndon LaRouche, National Economic 25,542; William A. Marra, Right to Life Party 20,504; Edward Winn, Workers League 18,662; and James Mac Warren, Socialist Workers 15,604.

[250]Alfonso Narvaez, "A Party Is Formed by 'Libertarians'," *New York Times*, 6 July 1972, p. 24. The New York Libertarian Party took the name, Free Libertarian Party, so as to not be confused with the New York Liberal Party (see E. J. Dionne, Jr., "Libertarian's Candidate for 1980 in New York," *New York Times*, 26 November 1979, p. IV-8).

[251]De Rosa, "Where They Stand," p. 397.

[252]Ibid., p. 368.

[253]Ibid., p. 399. Only two candidates broke the 1 percent level in the 1974 elections.

[254]Jack Mabley, "Third Party May Plant Some Seeds," *Chicago Tribune*, 4 October 1976, p. I-4.

[255]William Griffin, "Run for Fun—Or Get Slated as Libertarian," *Chicago Tribune*, 6 July 1977, p. III-7.

[256]De Rosa, "Where They Stand," p. 400.

[257]Ibid.

[258]Jay Mathews, "From Fringe to Mainstream," *Washington Post*, 7 November 1981, p. A-2.

[259]"Marrou Gains State House," *Libertarian Party News*, November 1984/February

1985, p. 1. Fanning lost his seat due to state district reapportionment in 1982; and Randolph did not run for reelection in 1982 so as to run for governor.

[260]Ibid., pp. 1, 4.

[261]Al Martinez, "No Groundswell Yet for Wave of Future," *Los Angeles Times,* 25 October 1978, p. II-1; and Bill Billiter, "Libertarian Gets 5% of Vote," *Los Angeles Times,* 9 November 1978, Sec. II, p. II-24. Also see "Libertarians Map Election Strategy," *Los Angeles Times,* p. I-38.

[262]Cook, "Alternative Party candidates," p. 3,144.

[263]Steve DeLiso, "Randolph Campaign: All Systems Go," *Libertarian Party News,* January/February 1982, p. 4; and Thomas E. Mann and Norman J. Ornstein, *The American Elections of 1982,* p. 175. This defeat is the most likely cause behind Randolph's defection to the GOP in late 1985.

[264]"1984 LP Vote Totals," *Libertarian Party News,* November 1984/February 1985, pp. 13–14. This is a list of all known candidates, the office they sought, and the percentage of votes they received. In only a very few cases did the party's candidate receive more than 10 percent of the vote. Data for the 1986 elections was unavailable.

[265]Steve Dasbach, "Campaign '88 Highlights," *Libertarian Party News,* November/December 1988, pp. 6–7. The Libertarian Party had a total of 91 candidates running in 1988 and together they garnished 447,822 votes. In 1990, 47 party members ran for Congress and received a total of 380,892 votes ("1990 Vote Increase," *Libertarian Party news,* May 1991, p. 2).

[266]Richard Winger, "Why Voters' Options Seem So Few," *Wall Street Journal,* 2 November 1988, p. A-20.

[267]The details of these suits can be found in "State Ballot Restriction Upheld by High Court," *New York Times,* 2 October 1984, p. I-22; "Libertarian Party Loses Bid to Be on Connecticut Ballot," *New York Times,* 2 November 1984, p. II-7; and Leo C. Walinsky, "Vote Suit Lost by Libertarians," *Los Angeles Times,* 14 March 1979, p. I-28.

[268]"Major Victory in Colorado Ballot Case," *Libertarian Party News,* January/February 1984, pp. 1, 12. According to Richard Winger, a new party seeking ballot status in every state would need over 1.6 million signatures, whereas the major parties needed only 25,500 total to qualify in *all* states ("Why Voters' Options Seem So Few," *Wall Street Journal,* 2 November 1988, p. A-20).

[269]Mark Lisheron, "Ballot Access Dominates NatCom Meeting," *Libertarian Party News,* May/June 1986, p. 8.

[270]Libertarians are associated with several publications that espouse the goals and ideas of the party and movement. Publications such as *Inquiry, Reason, Libertarian Forum,* the *Journal of Libertarian Studies,* and the *Cato Journal* indirectly support the party and its efforts by keeping libertarian ideas circulating in society. There are also many libertarian foundations and think tanks that further the libertarian cause. Foremost among these is the Cato Institute, formed in 1977. The institute's focus on Jeffersonian democracy, minarchism, and the free-market system provides a philosophical base for a steady stream of publications and issue-papers on several topics. Overall, the Cato Institute is the center for the intellectual side of the libertarian movement in America.

[271]Nicholas von Hoffman, "Lunacy of Press Puts Libertarians in Restraints," *Chicago Tribune,* 23 February 1980, p. I-10.

[272]Ibid.

[273]Alicia G. Clark, "Issue Campaigns Can Keep Libertarians Active in 1983," *Libertarian Party News,* January/February 1983, p. 2.

[274]T. R. Reid, "A Rare-Ideas Night as Two Candidates for President Debate," *Washington Post*, 4 August 1980, p. A-5.

[275]Jerome Tuccille, "The Failure of Libertarianism," *National Review*, p. 489.

[276]Ibid. It should be noted that Tuccille was the party's unsuccessful New York gubernatorial candidate in 1974 and ran not necessarily to win but to achieve permanent ballot status for the New York Free Libertarian Party (Woodward, "Every Man for Himself," *Newsweek*, p. 91).

[277]Tuccille, "The Failure of Libertarianism," *National Review*, p. 489.

[278]Ibid.

[279]Ibid., p. 511.

[280]This problem has historical precedence. The Socialist Party split when the Trotskyites became disillusioned with the party's path. Their party, the Socialist Workers Party, formed in the 1930s. The whole process resulted in political impotence and financial difficulties for both parties (Shannon, *The Socialist Party of America*, pp. 252–53).

[281]Friedman and McDowell, "The Libertarian Movement in America," p. 59.

[282]Rothbard, *The Ethics of Liberty*, p. 255.

[283]Ibid.

[284]Friedman and McDowell, "The Libertarian Movement in America," p. 60.

[285]T. R. Reid, "Libertarians, with Eye on Voters, Debate Needs to Be More Radical," *Washington Post*, 30 August 1981, p. A-8.

[286]T. R. Reid, "Libertarians Elect Alicia Clark as National Chair," *Washington Post*, 31 August 1981, p. A-2.

[287]Ibid. Also see Maura Dolan, "Libertarians Meet Again in Spite of Themselves," *Los Angeles Times*, 16 February 1982, p. I-3.

[288]T. R. Reid, "Libertarians, with Eye on Voters," *Washington, Post*, 30 August 1981, p. A-8.

[289]Rothbard, "The Consolidation Election," *Libertarian Party News*, November 1984/February 1985, p. 22.

[290]Ibid.

[291]Ibid., pp. 32, 33.

[292]Ibid., p. 33.

[293]Shannon, *The Socialist Party of America*, p. 258.

[294]"Randolph Defects," *Libertarian Party News*, November/December 1985, p. 1.

[295]Ibid.

[296]"LROC Stirs Interest, Controversy," *American Libertarian*, October 1986, 1:1.

[297]Ibid.

[298]"Libertarians Run in Major Party Races," *American Libertarian*, October 1986, 1:1.

[299]Ibid. The GOP may also be pleased to have some libertarians within its ranks so as to escape being bogged down and dominated by the fundamental Christian right.

[300]Ibid., p. 2.

[301]Ibid.

Chapter 4: Conclusion

[1]Lawrence Goodwin, *The Populist Movement*, p. 315.

[2]Peter A. Brown. "Study Says Voters Feel Powerless to Change Things," *Commercial Appeal*, 5 June 1991, p. A-2. The study was conducted by the Kettering Foundation.

[3]E. J. Dionne, Jr., "Voter Beware: Americans Tired of Politics as Usual," *Commercial Appeal,* 26 May 1991, p. B-4.

[4]Ibid. An example would be the conservative support of family and work, but the need of government support for childcare, job training, and housing that will allow these values to grow.

[5]Ibid.

[6]Ibid.

[7]Paul R. Abramson, John H. Aldrich, and David W. Rohde, *Change and Continuity in the 1988 Elections,* pp. 296–97.

[8]Ross K. Baker, "Women's Splinter Party Would Stymie Friends," *Los Angeles Times,* 27 July 1989, p. II-7.

[9]Melinda V. McLain, "Third Party Sought by Women," *Los Angeles Times,* 30 July 1989, p. V-5.

[10]Ibid.

[11]Ibid.

[12]David Shribman, "NOW Chief's Crusade for Women's Party Favored by Republican," *Wall Street Journal,* 5 September 1989, p. A-20.

[13]Abramson et al., *Change and Continuity in the 1988 Elections,* p. 296.

[14]Stephen L. Newman, *Liberalism at Wits' End,* pp. 16–17.

[15]Eric Garris, "Libertarians Belong in the GOP," *Reason* 20:27.

[16]Ibid.

[17]Ibid., p. 28.

[18]Richard Dennis, "Libertarian Is an L-Word, Too," *Reason* 20:29.

[19]Ibid.

[20]"Marrou for President," Newsletter mailed in January 1991. What Marrou's argument fails to note is that the money is *voluntarily* collected through the $1 check-off on income tax forms.

[21]Ibid.

[21]"Campaign Ad." *Libertarian Party News,* June 1991, pp. 3, 8.

[22]Dick Boddie, "Boddie Outlines Campaign Goals, Tactics," *Libertarian Party News,* June 1991, p. 8.

[23]David F. Nolan and Steven Alexander, "Matching Funds—Clashing Opinions," *Libertarian Party News,* July/August 1989, p. 14.

[24]Ibid.

[25]Ibid.

[26]Ibid.

[27]Jim Hankey, "It's Marrou/Lord in 1992," *Libertarian Party News,* October 1991, pp. 1, 4.

[28]Randy Langhenry, "Paul Testing GOP Waters," *Libertarian Party News,* October 1991, pp. 1, 4.

Bibliography

General Works

Abramson, Paul R., John H. Aldrich, and David W. Rohde. *Change and Continuity in the 1988 Elections*. Washington, D.C.: Congressional Quarterly, 1990.

Agar, Herbert. *The Price of Union*. Boston: Houghton Mifflin, 1960.

Alexander, Herbert E. *Financing Politics: Money, Elections and Political Reform*. Washington, D.C.: Congressional Quarterly, 1976.

_____. *Financing the 1972 Election*. Lexington, Mass.: D.C. Heath and Co., 1976.

_____. *Financing the 1980 Election* Lexington, Mass: D.C. Heath and Co., 1983.

Asher, Herbert. *Presidential Elections and American Politics*. Homewood, Ill.: Dorsey, 1976.

Bernhard, Winfred E., ed. *Political Parties in American History*. New York: Putnam, 1974.

Binkley, Wilfred. *American Political Parties: Their Natural History*. New York: Alfred A. Knopf, 1962.

Blondel, Jean. *Political Parties: A Genuine Case for Discontent?* London: Wildwood House, 1978.

Bone, Hugh Alvin. *American Politics and the Party System*. New York: McGraw-Hill, 1971.

Brock, William R. *Parties and Political Conscience: American Dilemmas 1840–1850*. Millwood, N.Y.: KTO, 1979.

Burnham, Walter Dean. *Critical Elections and the Mainsprings of American Politics*. New York: W. W. Norton, 1970.

Castles, Francis G., ed. *The Impact of Parties: Politics and Policies in Democratic Capitalist States*. Beverly Hills, Calif.: Sage, 1982.

Ceaser, James. *Reforming the Reforms: A Critical Analysis of the Presidential Selection Process*. Cambridge, Mass.: Ballinger, 1982.

Chambers, William Nisbet. *Political Parties in a New Nation: The American Experience, 1776–1809*. New York: Oxford University Press, 1963.

Charles, Joseph. *The Origins of the American Party System*. New York: Harper & Row, 1956.

Conkin, Paul K., and David Burner. *A History of Recent America*. New York: Thomas Y. Crowell, 1974.

Conway, M. Margaret. *Political Participation in the United States*. Washington, D.C.: Congressional Quarterly, 1985.

Cook, Rhodes, and Elizabeth Wehr. *Profiles of American Political Parties*. Washington, D.C.: Congressional Quarterly, 1975.

Crittenden, John A. *Parties and Elections in the United States*. Englewood Cliffs, N.J.: Prentice-Hall, 1982.

153

Crowe, Beryl L., and Charles G. Mayo, eds.*American Political Parties: A Systematic Perspective*. New York: Harper & Row, 1967.

Dahl, Robert A., ed. *Political Oppositions in Western Democracies*. New Haven, Conn.: Yale University Press, 1966.

Diamond, Martin. *The Electoral College and the American Idea of Democracy*. Washington, D.C.: American Enterprise Institute, 1977.

Douglas, Paul H. *The Coming of a New Party*. New York: McGraw-Hill, 1932.

Downs, Anthony. *An Economic Theory of Democracy*. New York: Harper, 1957.

Dunn, Delmer D. *Financing Presidential Campaigns*. Washington, D.C.: Brookings Institution, 1972.

Duverger, Maurice. *Political Parties, Their Organization and Activity in the Modern State*. New York: John Wiley and Sons, 1959.

Eldersveld, Samuel J. *Political Parties: A Behavioral Analysis*. Chicago: Rand McNally, 1964.

_____. *Political Parties in American Society*. New York: Basic Books, 1982.

Epstein, Leon D. *Political Parties in Western Democracies*. New York: Praeger, 1967.

Ewing, C. A. M. *Presidential Elections*. Norman: University of Oklahoma Press, 1940.

Fenton, John H. *People and Parties in Politics*. Glenview, Ill.: Scott, Foresman, 1966.

Fiorina, Morris. *Retrospective Voting in American National Elections*. New Haven, Conn.: Yale University Press, 1981.

Goldwin, Robert A., ed. *Political Parties, U.S.A.* Chicago: Rand McNally, 1964.

Goodman, William. *The Two-Party System in the United States*. New York: Van Nostrand, 1956.

Greenstein, Fred I. *The American Party System and the American People*. Englewood Cliffs, N.J.: Prentice-Hall, 1970.

Greer, Thomas H. *American Social Reform Movements: Their Pattern Since 1865*. Englewood Cliffs, N.J.: Prentice-Hall, 1949.

Haas, Michael, and Henry S. Kariel, eds. *Politics and Social Life*. Scranton, Penn.: Chandler, 1970.

Haynes, Frederick E. *Social Politics in the United States*. New York: AMS Press, 1970.

Herring, Edward Pendleton. *The Politics of Democracy: American Parties in Action*. New York: Holt, Rinehart and Winston, 1940.

Huckshom, Robert J. *Political Parties in America*. Monterey, Calif.: Brooks, Cole, 1984.

James, Judson L. *American Political Parties: Potential and Performance*. New York: Pegasus, 1969.

Janda, Kenneth. *Political Parties: A Cross-National Survey*. New York: Free Press, 1980.

Jewell, Malcolm E., and David M. Olsen. *American State Political Parties and Elections*. Homewood, Ill.: Dorsey, 1982.

Johnson, Donald B. *National Party Platforms: Volume I, 1840–1956*. Urbana: University of Illinois Press, 1978.

_____. *National Party Platforms: Volume II, 1960–1976*. Urbana: University of Illinois Press, 1978.

_____. *National Party Platforms: 1980 Supplement*. Urbana: University of Illinois Press, 1982.

Katz, Richard S. *A Theory of Parties and Electoral Systems*. Baltimore: Johns Hopkins University Press, 1980.

Key, V. 0., Jr. *Politics, Parties and Pressure Groups*. New York: Thomas Y. Crowell, 1964.

_____. *Southern Politics in State and Nation*. New York: Alfred A. Knopf, 1949.

Kolbe, Richard L. *American Political Parties: An Uncertain Future*. New York: Harper & Row, 1985.

Ladd, Everett Carl, Jr. *American Political Parties: Social Change and Political Response*. New York: W. W. Norton, 1970.

_____. *Where Have All the Voters Gone? The Fracturing of America's Political Parties*. New York: W. W. Norton, 1978.

_____, and Charles D. Hadley. *Transformations of the American Party System: Political Coalitions from the New Deal to the 1970's*. New York: W. W. Norton, 1975.

Lawson, Kay. *Political Parties and Democracy in the United States*. New York: Charles Scribner's Sons, 1968.

Leiserson, Avery. *Parties and Politics, An Institutional and Behavioral Approach*. New York: Alfred A. Knopf, 1958.

Lipset, Seymour M. *Political Man*. Garden City: Doubleday, 1960.

_____, and Earl Raab. *The Politics of Unreason: Right-Wing Extremism in America, 1790 1977*. New York: Harper & Row, 1978.

Lubell, Samuel. *The Future of American Politics*. Garden City, N.Y.: Doubleday, 1956.

McCormick, Richard L., ed. *Political Parties and the Modern States*. New Brunswick, N.J.: Rutgers University Press, 1984.

Maisel, Louis, and Paul M. Sacks, eds. *The Future of Political Parties*. Beverly Hills, Calif.: Sage, 1975.

Mann, Thomas E., and Norman J. Ornstein. *The American Elections of 1982*. Washington, D.C.: American Enterprise Institute, 1983.

Mayhew, David R. *Placing Parties in American Politics: Organization, Election Settings, and Government Activity in the Twentieth Century*. Princeton, N.J.: Princeton University Press, 1986.

Merriam, Charles E., and Harold Foote Gosnell. *The American Party System: An Introduction to the Study of Political Parties in the United States*. New York: Macmillan, 1949.

Michels, Robert. *Political Parties: A Sociological Study of the Oligarchial Tendencies of Modern Democracies*. New York: Hearst's International Library, 1915.

Milner, Andrew J., ed. *Comparative Political Parties: Selected Readings*. New York: Thomas Y. Crowell, 1969.

Neuborne, Burt, and Arthur Eisenberg. *The Rights of Candidates and Voters*. New York: Avon, 1980.

Odegard, Peter H. *American Politics: A Study in Political Dynamics*. New York: Harper, 1947.

Ogden, Daniel M., Jr., and Arthur L. Peterson. *Electing the President*. San Francisco: Chandler, 1968.

Owens, John R., and P. J. Staudenraus, eds. *The American Party System: A Book of Readings*. New York: Macmillan, 1965.

Polakoff, Keith I. *Political Parties in American History*. New York: Random House, 1981.

Polsby, Nelson W. *Consequences of Party Reform*. New York: Oxford University Press, 1983.

_____, Robert A. Dentler, and Paul A. Smith, eds. *Politics and Social Life: An Introduction to Political Behavior*. Boston: Houghton Mifflin, 1963.

_____, and Aaron Wildavsky. *Presidential Elections: Strategies of American Electoral Politics*. New York: Charles Scribner's Sons, 1984.

Pomper, Gerald M. *Voter's Choice: Varieties of American Electoral Behavior*. New York: Dodd, Mead, 1975.

Price, David E. *Bringing Back the Parties*. Washington, D.C.: Congressional Quarterly, 1984.

Rae, Douglas W. *The Political Consequences of Electoral Laws*. New Haven, Conn.: Yale University Press, 1971.

Ranney, Austin, and Willmoore Kendall. *Democracy and the American Party System*. New York: Harcourt, Brace, 1956.

Roseboom, Eugene H. *A Short History of Presidential Elections*. New York: Collier, 1967.

Rossiter, Clinton L. *Parties and Politics in America*. Ithaca, N.Y.: Cornell University Press, 1960.

Sait, Edward McChesney. *American Parties and Elections*. New York: D. Appleton Century, 1942.

Salmore, Stephen A., and Barbara G. Salmore. *Candidates, Parties and Campaigns: Electoral Politics in America*. Washington, D.C.: Congressional Quarterly, 1985.

Saloma, John S., III, and Frederick H. Sontag. *Parties: The Real Opportunity for Effective Citizen Politics*. New York: Alfred A. Knopf, 1972.

Schattschneider, E. E. *Party Government*. New York: Farrar and Rinehart, 1942.

_____. *The Semi-Sovereign People: A Realist's View of Democracy in America*. New York: Holt, Rinehart and Winston, 1960.

Schlesinger, Arthur M., and Fred L. Israel, eds. *History of American Presidential Elections, 1789–1968*. New York: McGraw-Hill, 1971.

Scott, Ruth K., and Ronald J. Hrebenar. *Parties in Crisis: Party Politics in America*. New York: John Wiley and Sons, 1979.

Sindler, Allan P. *Political Parties in the U.S.* New York: St. Martin's, 1966.

Sorauf, Frank J. *Party Politics in America*. Boston: Little, Brown, 1984.

_____. *Political Parties in the American System*. Boston: Little, Brown, 1964.

Sundquist, James L. *Dynamics of the Party System*. Washington, D.C.: Brookings Institution, 1973.

Wattenberg, Martin P. *The Decline of American Political Parties 1952–1980*. Cambridge, Mass.: Harvard University Press, 1984.

Woodburn, James A. *Political Parties and Party Problems in the United States*. New York: Putnam, 1924.

Minor Party Works

Ader, Emile B. *The Dixiecrat Movement: Its Role in Third-Party Politics*. Washington, D.C.: Public Affairs, 1955.

Argersinger, Peter H. *Populism and Politics: William Alfred Peffer and the People's Party*. Lexington: University Press of Kentucky, 1974.

Arnold, Stanley. *I Ran Against Jimmy Carter*. New York: Manor Books, 1979.

Blackman, Paul H. *Third Party Presidents? An Analysis of State Election Laws*. Washington, D.C.: Heritage Foundation, 1976.

Canfield, James Lewis. *A Case of Third Party Activism: The George Wallace Campaign Worker and the American Independent Party*. New York: University Press of America, 1984.

Duncan-Clark, S. J. *The Progressive Movement.* Boston: Small, Maynard, 1913.

Durden, Robert F. *The Climax of Populism: The Election of 1896.* Lexington: University of Kentucky Press, 1965.

Dyson, Lowell K. *Red Harvest: The Communist Party and American Farmers.* Lincoln: University of Nebraska Press, 1982.

Fine, Nathan. *Labor and Farmer Parties in the United States, 1828–1928.* New York: Russell and Russell, 1961.

Foster, William Z. *History of the Communist Party of the United States.* New York: International, 1952.

Goodwin, Lawrence. *The Populist Movement: A Short History of the Agrarian Revolt in America.* New York: Oxford University Press, 1978.

Hackney, Sheldon, ed. *Populism: The Critical Issues.* Boston: Little, Brown, 1971.

Haynes, Frederick E. *Third Party Movements Since the Civil War; With Special Reference to Iowa: A Study in Social Politics.* New York: Russell and Russell, 1966.

Hesseltine, William Best. *The Rise and Fall of Third Parties, from Anti-Masonry to Wallace.* Washington, D.C.: Public Affairs, 1948.

————. *Third Party Movements in the United States.* New York: Van Nostrand, 1962.

Hicks, John D. *The Populist Revolt: A History of the Farmer's Alliance and the People's Party.* Lincoln: University of Nebraska Press, 1961.

Howe, Irving, and Lewis Coser. *The American Communist Party: A Critical History, 1919–1957.* Boston: Beacon, 1957.

Johnsen, Julia E. *Should the Communist Party Be Outlawed?.* New York: H. W. Wilson, 1949.

King, Dennis. *Lyndon LaRouche and the New American Fascism.* Garden City, N.Y.: Doubleday, 1989.

Klehr, Harvey. *Communist Cadre: The Social Background of the American Communist Party Elite.* Stanford, Calif.: Hoover Institution, 1978.

Major, Reginald. *A Panther Is a Black Cat: A Study in Depth of the Black Panther Party—Its Origins, Its Goals, Its Struggle for Survival.* New York: William Morrow, 1971.

Mazmanian, Daniel A. *Third Parties in Presidential Elections.* Washington, D.C.: Brookings Institution, 1974.

Nash, Howard P. *Third Parties in American Politics.* Washington, D.C.: Public Affairs, 1959.

Pinard, Maurice. *The Rise of a Third Party: A Study in Crisis Politics.* Englewood Cliffs, N.J.: Prentice-Hall, 1971.

Pinchot, Amos R. *History of the Progressive Party, 1912–1916.* New York: New York University Press, 1958.

Rosenstone, Steven J., Ray L. Behr, and Edward H. Lazarus. *Third Parties in America: Citizen Response to Major Party Failure.* Princeton, N.J.: Princeton University Press, 1984.

Shannon, David A. *The Socialist Party of America: A History.* Chicago: Quadrangle, 1967.

Smallwood, Frank. *The Other Candidates: Third Parties in Presidential Elections.* Hanover: University Press of New England, 1983.

Stedman, Murray S., and Susan W. Stedman. *Discontent at the Polls: A Study of Farmer and Labor Parties, 1827–1948.* New York: Columbia University Press, 1950.

Thayer, George. *The Farther Shores of Politics: The American Political Fringe Today.* New York: Simon and Schuster, 1967.

Walton, Hanes. *Black Political Parties: An Historical and Political Analysis.* New
    York: Free Press, 1972.
_____. *The Negro in Third Party Politics.* Philadelphia: Dorance, 1969.
Youngdale, James M. *Third Party Footprints.* Los Angeles: Ross Enterprises, 1984.

Methodology

Bernstein, Richard J. *The Restructuring of Social and Political Theory.* San Diego,
    Calif.: Harcourt Brace Jovanovich, 1976.
Crotty, William J. *Approaches to the Study of Party Organization.* Boston: Allyn and
    Bacon, 1968.
Easton, David. *A Framework for Political Analysis.* Englewood Cliffs, N.J.: Prentice-
    Hall, 1965.
_____, ed. *Varieties of Political Theory.* Englewood Cliffs, N.J.: Prentice-Hall,
    1966.
Fay, Brian. *Social Theory and Political Practice.* New York: Holmes and Meier, 1976.
Haas, Michael, and Henry S. Kariel. *Approaches to the Study of Political Science.*
    Scranton, Penn.: Chandler, 1970.
Johnson, Janet Buttolph, and Richard A. Joslyn. *Political Science Research Methods.*
    Washington, D.C.: Congressional Quarterly, 1986.
McDonald, Neil A. *The Study of Political Parties.* Garden City, N.Y.: Doubleday, 1955.
Neumann, Sigmund, ed. *Modern Political Parties: Approaches to Comparative
    Politics.* Chicago: University of Chicago Press, 1956.
Polsby, Nelson W., Robert A. Dentler, and Paul A. Smith, eds. *Approaches to the
    Study of Political Science.* Boston: Houghton Mifflin, 1970.
Popper, Karl R. *Conjectures and Refutations: The Growth of Scientific Knowledge.*
    London: Routledge and Kegan Paul, 1963.
_____. *The Logic of Scientific Discovery.* New York: Basic Books, 1959.
Wasby, Stephen L. *Political Science—The Discipline and Its Dimensions.* New York:
    Charles Scribner's Sons, 1970.

Libertarianism

Barry, Norman P. *Hayek's Social and Economic Philosophy.* London: Macmillan, 1979.
Bergland, David. *Libertarianism in One Lesson.* Costa Mesa, Calif.: Orpheus, 1984.
Carey, George W., ed. *Freedom and Virtue: The Conservative-Libertarian Debate.*
    Lanham, Md.: University Press of America, 1984.
Clark, Edward E. *A New Beginning.* Aurora, Cal.: Caroline House, 1980.
Gray, John. *Hayek on Liberty.* New York: Blackwell, 1984.
Hayek, Friedrich A. *Economic Freedom and Representative Government.* London:
    Institute of Economic Affairs, 1973.
Hazlitt, Henry. *Economics in One Lesson.* New York: Harper & Row, 1946.
_____. *Man Versus the Welfare State.* New Rochelle: Arlington House, 1968.
Hospers, John. *Libertarianism: A Political Philosophy for Tomorrow.* Santa Barbara,
    Calif.: Reason, 1971.
Lewis, Jim, and Jim Peron. *Liberty Reclaimed: A New Look at American Politics.*
    Houston: Libertarian Party, 1984.
MacBride, Roger L. *A New Dawn for America: The Libertarian Challenge.* Ottowa,
    Ill.: Green Hill, 1976.

Machan, Tibor R. *Human Rights and Human Liberties: A Radical Reconsideration of the American Political Tradition.* Chicago: Nelson-Hall, 1975.

_____, ed. *The Libertarian Alternative.* Chicago: Nelson-Hall, 1974.

Newman, Stephen L. *Liberalism at Wits' End: The Libertarian Revolt Against the Modern State.* Ithaca, N.Y.: Cornell University Press, 1984.

Nock, Albert Jay. *Our Enemy the State.* New York: Free Life Editions, 1973.

Nozick, Robert. *Anarchy, State, and Utopia.* New York: Basic Books, 1974.

Rand, Ayn. *Capitalism: The Unknown Ideal.* New York: Signet, 1966.

Read, Leonard Edward. *Elements of Libertarian Leadership: Notes on the Theory, Methods and Practice of Freedom.* New York: Foundation for Economic Education, 1962.

Rothbard, Murray N. *The Ethics of Liberty.* Atlantic Highlands, N.J.: Humanities, 1982.

_____. *For a New Liberty: The Libertarian Manifesto.* New York: Collier, 1978.

_____. *Man, Economy and State: A Treatise on Economic Principles.* New York: D. Van Nostrand, 1962.

Taylor, Michael. *Community, Anarchy and Liberty.* New York: Cambridge University Press, 1982.

Tuccille, Jerome. *Radical Libertarianism: A Right-Wing Alternative.* Indianapolis: Bobbs-Merrill, 1970.

Reference Works

ABC-Clio Information Services. *The American Electorate: A Historical Bibliography.* Santa Barbara, Calif.: ABC-Clio Information Services, 1984.

Rockwood, D. Stephen. *American Third Parties Since the Civil War: An Annotated Bibliography.* New York: Garland, 1985.

Wymar, Lubomyr R. *American Political Parties: A Selective Guide to Parties and Movements of the Twentieth Century.* Littleton, Colo.: Libraries Unlimited, 1969.

Party Publications

African People's Socialist Party. *A New Beginning: The Road to Black Freedom and Socialism.* Oakland, Calif.: Burning Spear, 1982.

Burt, William D. *Local Problems: Libertarian Solutions.* Washington, D.C.: Libertarian National Party Headquarters, 1979.

Communist Party, U.S.A. *Constitution of the Communist Party of the United States of America.* New York: Communist Party, U.S.A., 1983.

LaRouche, Lyndon H. *The Independent Democrats' 1984 Platform: Five Crises Facing the Next President.* New York: Independent Democrats, 1984.

Libertarian Party. *Brief History of the Libertarian Party.* Washington, D.C.: Libertarian Party National Headquarters, 1981.

_____. *Clark for President: A Report on the 1980 Libertarian Presidential Campaign.* Washington, D.C.: Libertarian Party National Headquarters, 1981.

_____. *Libertarian Party Bylaws and Convention Rules.* Houston: Libertarian Party National Headquarters, 1984.

_____. *1984 Platform of the Libertarian Party.* Houston: Libertarian Party National Headquarters, 1985.

_____. *Questions and Answers About the Libertarian Party*. Houston: Libertarian Party National Headquarters, n.d.

Andre Marrou, "Campaign Newsletter." Mailed January 1991.

Socialist Worker's Party. *A Revolutionary Strategy for the '70s*. New York: Pathfinder, 1971.

Dissertation

Onwumere, Sampson Onuigbo. "The Libertarian Party of America and Presidential Elections: An Analysis of a New Political Party Struggling to Capture Political Power and Authority." Dissertation, Howard University, 1978.

Periodical Articles

Adamony, David, and George Agree. "Election Campaign Financing: The 1974 Reforms." *P.S. Quarterly* 90 (Summer 1975): 201–21.

Argersinger, Peter H. "A Place on the Ballot: Fusion Politics and Antifusion Laws." *American Historical Review* 85 (April 1980): 287–306.

_____. "An Upset in the Land of Lincoln." *U.S. News and World Report*, 31 March 1986, p. 8.

Baker, James N. "The Greens of Vermont." *Newsweek*, 27 February 1989, p. 33.

Barnes, Peter. "Starting A Fourth Party." *New Republic*, 24 July 1971, pp. 19–21.

Bayte, H. "Prospectus for a New Party; Opportunity for an Activist Anti-Corporate Party." *Progressive* 38 (July 1974): 13- 18.

Bell, Leslie. "Constraints on Electoral Success of Minor Political Parties in the United States." *Political Studies* 25 (1977): 103–9.

Berns, Walter. "The Need for Public Authority." *Modern Age* 24 (Winter 1980): 16–20.

Bock, Alan W. "Radical Views, Conservative Style." *Reason* 20 (November 1988): 35–38.

Brookhiser, R. "None of the Above." *National Review*, 31 October 1980, pp. 1324–25.

_____. "Saving the UOS (Bergland Wins Nomination)." *National Review*, 14 October 1983, pp. 1,274ff.

Burnham, Walter Dean. "Revitalization and Decay: Looking Toward the Third Century of American Electoral Politics." *Journal of Politics* 38 (August 1976): 146–72.

Carey, George W. "Conservatives and Libertarians View Fusionism: Its Origins, Possibilities and Problems." *Modern Age* 26 (Winter 1982): 8–18.

Ceaser, James W. "Political Parties and Presidential Ambition." *Journal of Politics* 40 (1978): 708–39.

Clark, Edward E. "Candidate Who Promises to Sell Dulles Airport (Libertarian Platform)." *Fortune*, 6 October 1980, pp. 111–12ff.

"Communist in America." *Newsweek*, 27 February 1984, p. 9.

Cook, Rhodes. "Alternate Party Candidates May Have Substantial Impact on 1980 Presidential Election." *Congressional Quarterly* 38 (18 October 1980): 3,143–49.

_____. "Third Parties: A Struggle for Attention." *Congressional Quarterly* 34 (16 October 1976): 2,971–76.

_____. "Third Parties Face Obstacles to Prominence." *Congressional Quarterly* 37 (15 September 1979): 2,003–5.

Crane, Edward H. "America's Third Largest Party: Success." *Reason* 9 (1977): 15–18.

Dennis, Richard. "Libertarian Is an L-Word, Too." *Reason* 20 (March 1989): 28–30.

Downs, Anthony. "Up and Down with Ecology—the 'Issue-Attention Cycle'." *Public Interest* (Summer 1972): 38–50.

East, John P. "The American Conservative Movement of the 1980's: Are Traditional and Libertarian Dimensions Compatible?" *Modern Age* 24 (Winter 1980): 34–38.

Einsiedel, E. F., and M. Jane Bibbie. "The Newsmagazines and Minority Candidates: Campaign '76." *Journalism Quarterly* 56 (Spring 1979): 102–5.

Freie, John F. "Minor Parties in Realigning Eras." *American Politics Quarterly* 10 (January 1982): 47–63.

Friedman, George, and Gary L. McDowell. "The Libertarian Movement in America." *Journal of Contemporary Studies* 6 (Summer 1983): 47-64.

Gagnon, Alain. "Third Parties: A Theoretical Framework." *American Review of Canadian Studies* 11 (Spring 1981): 37–63.

Garris, Eric. "Libertarians Belong in the GOP." *Reason* 20 (March 1989): 27–28.

Gelman, David, Mark Miller, et al. "Lyndon LaRouche: Beyond the Fringe." *Newsweek*, 17 April 1986, pp. 38–42.

Germino, Dante. "Traditionalism and Libertarianism: Two Views." *Modern Age* 26 (Winter 1982): 49–56.

Greenfield, Meg. "The Lone-Wolf Candidates." *Newsweek*, 12 December 1983, p. 116.

Groer, Ann. "Libertarian Lark." *New Republic*, 3 October 1983, p. 16.

Haag, E. Van Den. "Libertarians and Conservatives." *National Review*, 8 June 1979, pp. 725–27ff.

Hammond, J. L. "Minor Parties and Electoral Realignments." *American Politics Quarterly* 4 (1976): 63–65.

Harrington, Michael. "Radical Strategy: Don't Form a Fourth Party; Form a New First Party." *New York Times Magazine*, 13 September 1970, pp. 28–29ff.

Hart, Benjamin. "In the Pursuit of Happiness: Will the Libertarian Party Survive 1984?" *Policy Review* (Summer 1984): 56–58.

"Has the Libertarian Movement Gone Kooky? A Spirited Exchange." *National Review*, 3 August 1979, pp. 967–969ff.

Hicks, John D. "The Third Party Tradition in American Politics." *Mississippi Valley Historical Review* 20 (June 1933): 3–28.

Hoffman, Nicholas von. "Bucking the System." *New Republic*, 19 April 1980, pp. 12–15.

_____. "Vote for Ed Clark." *New Republic*, 30 August 1980, pp. 11–14.

Hospers, John. "Conservatives and Libertarians: Differences of Theory and Strategy." *Modern Age* 25 (Fall 1981): 369–80.

"How Those Libertarians Pay the Bills." *New York*, 3 November 1980, pp. 18ff.

Jackovich, K. G. "Ed Clark is the Libertarian Party's Headstrong Candidate for the White House." *People*, 22 September 1980, pp. 36–37.

Jacobson, Gary C. "Practical Consequences of Campaign Finance Reform: An Incumbent Protection Act?" *Public Policy* 24 (1976): 1–32.

Judis, John. "Libertarianism: Where the Left Meets the Right." *Progressive* 44 (September 1980): 36–38.

Karmin, Monroe W., Richard Alm, et al. "Hanging a 'For Sale' Sign on Government." *U.S. News and World Report*, 13 January 1986, pp. 18–19.

Kelly, John Lawrence. "John J. Crittenden and the Constitutional Union Party."
    Filson Club Historical Quarterly 48 (1974): 265-76.
Kirk, Russell. "Libertarians: The Chirping Sectaries." *Modern Age* 25 (Fall 1981):
    345-51.
Kirkpatrick, Samuel A., William Lyons, and Michael R. Fitzgerald. "Candidates,
    Parties, and Issues in the American Electorate: Two Decades of Change."
    American Politics Quarterly 3 (1975): 247-83.
Lader, Lawrence. "The Wallace Campaign of 1948." *American Heritage* 28 (1976):
    42-51.
"The 'LaRouche Democrats'." *Newsweek*, 16 April 1984, p. 31.
"LaRouched in Illinois." *Newsweek*, 31 March 1986, p. 22.
Leiserson, Avery. "The Place of Parties in the Study of Politics." *American Political
    Science Review* 51 (December 1957): 945-54.
"Libertarian and Bourgeoisie Freedoms." *National Review*, 5 December 1975, pp.
    1,338-39.
"Libertarian Lark." *New Republic*, 3 October 1983, pp. 15-17.
"Libertarians Off and Running for '88." *Reason* 19 (December 1987): 14-15.
"Libertarians: The Third Non-Party." *Economist*, 20 October 1984, p. 24.
"The Lindsay Idea: Third Party." *New Republic*, 3 October 1970, pp. 5-6.
Lovin, Hugh T. "The Persistence of Third Party Dreams in the American Labor
    Movement, 1930-1938." *Mid-America* 58 (1976): 141-57.
McCarthy, Eugene J. "Third Party May Be a Real Force in 1972." *New York Times
    Magazine*, 7 June 1970, pp. 6ff.
"McCarthy's Call for a Third Party." *New Republic*, 20 June 1970, pp. 5-6.
Machan, Tibor R. "Libertarianism and Conservatives." *Modern Age* 24 (Winter
    1980): 21-33.
————. "Libertarianism and Conservatives: Further Considerations." *Modern
    Age* 26 (Winter 1982): 39-48.
McWilliams, Carey. "Second Thoughts: Libertarian Party." *Nation*, 20 October
    1979, p. 358.
Mazmanian, Daniel A. "Minor Parties and Electoral Reforms—Two Separate
    Issues." *Forensic Quarterly* 48 (1974): 487-93.
————. "1976: A Third Party Year?" *Nation*, 13 September 1975, pp. 201-4.
Methvin, Eugene H. "Lyndon LaRouche's Raid on Democracy." *Reader's Digest*,
    August 1986, pp. 90-94.
"Minor Parties: Widest Choice in Years for Voters." *U.S. News and World Report*,
    12 July 1976, p. 23.
"Minor Political Parties and Their Candidates." *Congressional Digest* 55 (October
    1976): 232.
Morganthau, Tom, and Rich Thomas. "For Sale: Uncle Sam." *Newsweek*, 30 December
    1985, p. 18.
Nelson, Michael. "New Libertarians: Stripping Government of Its Powers." *Saturday
    Review*, 1 March 1980, pp. 21-24.
Newell, P. "Judith Jones: Libertarian for Mayor." *Encore*, October 1981, p. 10.
Nisbet, Robert. "Conservatives and Libertarians: Uneasy Cousins." *Modern Age* 24
    (Winter 1980): 2-8.
Nolan, David. F. "Is the Party Over?" *Reason* 20 (March 1989): 30-31.
O'Conner, Colleen, and Bob Cohn. "A Baby Boomers' Think Tank," *Newsweek*, 1
    September 1986, p. 22.
Paul, Mark. "Seducing the Left: The Third Party that Wants You." *Mother Jones*, May
    1980, pp. 47-49ff.

Polsgrove, Carl. "In Pursuit of Liberty: Libertarian Party." *Progressive* 42 (January 1978): 38–40.

Posner, M. "Marching to a Different Drummer." *MacLeans*, 15 September 1980, pp. 37–38.

"Real Third Party." *Economist*, 27 September 1980, p. 34.

Rieman, J. H. "Fallacy of Libertarian Capitalism." *Ethics* 92 (October 1981): 85–95.

Riker, William H. "The Number of Political Parties: A Reexamination of Duverger's Law." *Comparative Politics* 9 (October 1976): 93-106.

Rosa, Peter de. "Where They Stand: The Libertarian Party and Its Competition, 1968–1978." *Journal of Libertarian Studies* 3 (Winter 1979): 391–403.

Rothbard, Murray N. "Frank S. Meyer: The Fusionist as Libertarian Manqué." *Modern Age* 25 (Fall 1981): 352–63.

_____. "Myth and Truth About Libertarianism." *Modern Age* 24 (Winter 1980): 9–15.

Royce, E. Scott. "America's Third Largest Party: Failure!" *Reason* 9 (August 1977): 19–23.

Salisbury, Robert H. "An Exchange Theory of Interest Groups." *Midwest Journal of Political Science* 13 (February 1969): 15.

Scott, Marvin. "Why John Anderson Won't Give Up." *Parade Magazine*, 12 June 1983, pp. 16–17ff.

Shapiro, Walter, and Rich Thomas. "Getting Ready for a Federal Fire Sale." *Newsweek*, 10 February 1976. p. 44.

Shortridge, Ray M. "Voting for Minor Parties in the Antebellum Midwest." *Indiana Magazine of History* 74 (1978): 117–34.

Smith, Harold T. "The Know-Nothings in Arkansas." *Arkansas Historical Quarterly* 34 (1975): 291–303.

"Third Parties: How Much Impact in November?" *U.S. News and World Report*, 13 September 1976, p. 17.

"Third Parties: Politics of Hope; Libertarian Party." *Newsweek*, 17 September 1979, p. 44.

Tuccille, Jerome. "The Failure of Libertarianism." *National Review*, 29 April 1977, pp. 489–490ff.

Uyl, Douglas Den, and Douglas B. Rasmussen. "The Philosophical Importance of Ayn Rand." *Modern Age* 27 (Winter 1982): 67–69.

Wallace, Henry A. "California and the New Party." *New Republic*, 12 January 1948, pp. 13–14.

_____. "Third Parties and the American Tradition." *New Republic*, 19 January 1948, pp. 12–14.

Ward, Andrew. "The Libertarian Party." *Atlantic*, November 1976, pp. 26–33.

White, Jay D. "On the Growth of Knowledge in Public Administration." *Public Administration Review* 46 (January-February 1986): 15–24.

Will, George F. "Capital Issues: Support for a Conservative Third Party." *National Review*, 9 May 1975, p. 498.

_____. "Is a Third Party Necessary?" *Newsweek*, 23 May 1983, p. 88.

Winkler, Karen J. "Questioning the Science in Social Science, Scholars Signal a 'Turn to Interpretation'." *Chronicle of Higher Education*, 26 June 1985, pp. 5–6.

Woelfel, J. W. "We're Not Rational Animals: A Liberal Reply to Libertarianism." *Christian Century*, 7 November 1973, pp. 1,096–1,100.

Woodward, Kenneth L. "Every Man for Himself." *Newsweek*, 11 November 1974, p. 91.

"Your Other Choices for White House." *U.S. News and World Report*, 5 November 1984, p. 30.

Federal Election Commission Reports

"Disclosure Series, No. 1: Presidential Pre-Nomination Receipts and Expenditures, 1976 Campaign." September 1976.

"F.E.C. Survey Lists 14 Presidential Candidates on General Election Ballots." Press Release, 30 October 1976.

Federal Election Campaign Laws. Washington, D.C.: Government Printing Office, 1984.

Presidential Candidate Index. Washington, D.C.: n.p., 1984.

"Report on Financial Activity 1983–1984; Presidential Pre-Nomination Campaigns." Washington, D.C., November 1984, Table A-4.

"Reports on Financial Activity 1979–1980: Final Report—Presidential Pre-Nomination Campaigns." October 1981.

"Seventeen States Report Unofficial Votes for Minor Presidential Candidates in 1984 Election." Press Release, 5 December 1984.

"Votes Cast." Press Release, 31 December 1980.

Newspaper Articles (Chronologically by Newspaper)

Chicago Tribune

Klazura, Barry J. "Libertarians: Idealists in a Real World." 26 August 1972, Sec. I, p. 10, col. 3.

Hoffman, Nicholas von. "Second Takes on the Elections." 16 November 1973, Sec. I, p. 22, col. 3.

"A Three-party System?" Editorial. 30 June 1974, Sec. II, p. 4, col. 1.

Hoffman, Nicholas von. "Libertarians Put Focus on Freedom." 28 October 1974, Sec. 2, p. 4, col. 1.

"Supreme Court Eases Way for Minor Parties to Place on Ballots." 18 November 1975, Sec. 2, p. 6, col. 2.

Hoffman, Nicholas von. "Third Party Gets Silent Treatment." 29 November 1975, Sec. Nl, p. 10, col. 5.

"Libertarian Party Leader Assails Lack of Freedom." 7 December 1975, Sec. 1, p. 39, col. 1.

Mabley, Jack. "Third Party May Plant Some Seeds." 4 October 1976, Sec. 1, p. 4, col. 1.

Griffin, William. "Run for Fun—Or Get Slated as Libertarian." 6 July 1977, Sec. 3, p. 7, col. 1.

Thimmesch, Nick. "Libertarians May Be Mad, but How They Pep Up Politics!" 5 September 1977, Sec. 5, p. 2, col. 3.

Elsasser, Glen. "Justices Agree to Hear Illinois Ballot Law Case." 25 April 1978, Sec. 1, p. 2, col. 3.

Hoffman, Nicholas von. "Lunacy of Press Puts Libertarian in Restraints." 23 February 1980, Sec. 1, p. 10, col. 5.

Mabley, Jack. "Libertarian Offers Challenging Ideas." 25 March 1980, Sec. 1, p. 4, col. 1C.

Raspberry, William. "There's No Room for a Third Party." 22 May 1980, Sec. 3, p. 4, col. 1.

Paris, Alexander P. "Why I'm Supporting Ed Clark." 23 October 1980, Sec. 3, p. 3, col. 3.

Axelrod, David. "Ed Clark: Left, Right, No Middle." 28 October 1980, Sec. 1, p. 1, col. 4.

Reich, Peter. "Followup: Roger MacBride." 3 November 1980, Sec. 1, p. 16, col. 2P.

"Libertarian Party Fails to Win a Single Race." 6 November 1980, Sec. 1, p. 14, col. 1.

Germond, Jack, and Jules Whitcover. "Ed Clark and His Party Won Their Objective." 2 January 1981, Sec. 3, p. 4, col. 6.

Clark, Edward. "Reagan No Champion of Free Enterprise." 24 April 1981, Sec. 1, p. 20, col. 1.

"A Man Without a Party." 22 June 1983, Sec. 1, p. 14, col. 1.

Cohen, Laurie. "Options Trader Turns to Game of Politics." 7 May 1984, Sec. CT-3, p. 5, col. 1.

Lentz, Philip. "Anti-Percy Conservatives Will Endorse Libertarian." 21 September 1984, Sec. Ct-2, p. 1, col. 3.

"Percy Calls Faction of GOP Backing Libertarian 'Kooky'." 22 September 1984, Sec. CT-1, p. 5, col. 1.

Christian Science Monitor

Favre, George H. "'Mavericks' for '72? Third-Party Challenge Shapes." 9 November 1970, pp. 1, 3.

Drummond, Roscoe. "Point of View: Fractured Parties." 26 March 1975, p. 5.

Sitomer, Curtis J. "Libertarian Party Gears Up for 1976." 28 March 1975, p. 2.

Moneyhun, George. "Third Parties Gear Up for 1976." 28 August 1975, p. 5.

Henley, David C. "American Prohibition Party Seeks Converts in 1976." 16 October 1976, p. 19.

"Libertarian Party Target: Government." 19 July 1977, p. 22.

Stevens, Mark. "Libertarians Set Realistic '80 Goal." 10 September 1979, p. 6.

Stuart, Peter C. "Three Possible Alternatives to Carter and Reagan." 19 August 1980, p. 6.

"Libertarian Party to Be on Ballot in 50 States." 26 September 1980, p. 2.

"Libertarian Party Picks Presidential Candidate." 6 September 1983, p. 2.

Merry, George B. "Why Those 'Other' Presidential Candidates Make the Effort." 12 October 1984, pp. 3–4.

Ladd, Everett Carl, Jr. "The American Idea of Nation." 30 September 1985, p. 16.

Harsch, Joseph C. "Third Parties: Wild Cards in Politics." 16 January 1986, p. 15.

Walter, David K. "We're a Third Party!" 27 February 1987, p. 15.

Evans, Ernest. "Covering Third Parties." 20 October 1988, p. 14.

LaFranchi, Howard. "Third Party Hopefuls Make Little Headway Toward Nov. 8." 26 October 1988, p. 1.

Los Angeles Times

"Three Minor Parties File Petition for Place on California Ballot." 13 April 1972, Sec. I, p. 2, col. 5.

"Minor Political Parties Sue to Modify Election Law." 11 July 1973, Sec. II, p. 4, col. 6.

"Alternative to Democrats and Republicans Viewed." 20 September 1974, Sec. III, p. 6, col. 4.

"New Libertarian Party Attracts Unlikely Mix of Followers." 11 March 1975, Sec. II, p. 1C, col. 1.

"Two Third Parties Have Toehold in California Politics." 20 April 1976, Sec. I, p. 3, col. 1.

Endicott, William. "Libertarian Event Draws Varied Lot." 15 July 1977, Sec. I, p. 3, cols. 5, 16.

"Petition Filed on Behalf of Libertarian Candidate, Ed Clark." 26 August 1978, Sec. I, p. 21, col. 3.

Martinez, Al. "No Groundswell Yet for Wave of Future." 25 October 1978, Sec. II, pp. 1, 8.

Billiter, Bill. "Libertarian Gets 5% of Vote." 9 November 1978, Sec. I, p. 24, col. 1.

"Libertarian Businessman Enters Presidential Race." 25 January 1979, Sec. I, p. 11, col. 4.

"Libertarian Candidates Split on Budget Balancing." 17 February 1979, Sec. I, p. 25, col. 1.

"Libertarians Map Election Strategy." 18 February 1979, Sec. I, p. 38, col. 1.

"Libertarians Tell Conflict on Abortions." 19 February 1979, Sec. II, p. 5, col. 1.

Wolensky, Leo C. "Vote Suit Lost by Libertarians." 14 March 1979, Sec. I, p. 28, col. 3.

Larsen, David. "Libertarian Party Opens Fire on Larger Rivals." 7 September 1979, Sec. I, pp. 3, 22, cols. 4, 1.

―――――. "Libertarians Hammer Out Traditional Platform." 8 September 1979, Sec. II, pp. 1, 12, cols. 5, 3.

―――――. "Clark Nominated to Head Libertarian Ticket in '80." 9 September 1979, Sec. I, pp. 1, 3, 26, cols. 5, 3.

Bernstein, Sid. "County Checks Libertarian Voter Registration Claims." 15 November 1979, Sec. I, pp. 3, 18, cols. 5, 3.

"Libertarian Party Qualifies as Official Political Group in State." 29 December 1979, Sec. I, p. 23, col. 1.

"Libertarian Party Qualifies for 80's California Ballot." 26 January 1980, Sec. II, p. 1, col. 3.

"Libertarian Enters Race for Cranston's Seat in U.S. Senate." 16 February 1980, Sec. II, p. 12, col. 5.

Larsen, David. "Libertarian Candidate Proposes Military Cuts." 12 June 1980, Sec. I, p. 15, col. 1.

"Libertarian Party Candidate Says U.S. Needs Alternative." 2 July 1980, Sec. I, p. 20, col. 1.

Smith, Roger. "A Credible Third Party Is Goal of Libertarians." 6 September 1980, Sec. I, pp. 1, 32, cols. 1, 1.

Reich, Kenneth. "Libertarians Get Boost from TV Ads." 29 September 1980, Sec. I, p. 5, col. 3.

Scheer, Robert. "Libertarian Clark Vows to Create Third-Party System." 18 October 1980, Sec. I, pp. 30, 31, col. 1.

Reich, Kenneth. "Libertarians to Focus on 1982 Legislative Races in West." 12 November 1980, Sec. I, p. 23, cols. 1, 1.

"Libertarians Lose Court Bid on Ballot Designation." 19 December 1980, Sec. I, p. 22, col. 5.

Getlin, Josh. "Libertarian Enters L.A. Mayoral Race." 8 January 1981, Sec. II, p. 5, col. 1.

―――――. "Second Libertarian Enters Mayor's Race." 14 January 1981, Sec. II, p. 3, col. 1.

"Libertarian Bakersfield Mayor Settles In." 19 January 1981, Sec. III, p. 15, col. 2.

Dolan, Maura. "Libertarians Urged to Attack Reagan's Record." 14 February 1982, Sec. I, p. 3, col. 1.

―――――. "Libertarians Meet Again in Spite of Themselves." 16 February 1982, Sec. I, p. 3, col. 1.

Broder, David. "Libertarians Know How to Cut a Budget." 23 August 1982, Sec. II, p. 7, col. 3.

Stammer, Larry. "Minor Party Candidates Strong on Issues." 2 October 1982, Sec. II, p. 1, col. 3.

Love, Keith. "Major Race Attracts Minor Parties." 28 October 1982, Sec. IB, p. 4, col. 1.

Randolph, Eleanor. "Libertarians Pick Their Presidential Nominee at Chaotic Convention." 4 September 1983, Sec. I, p. 8, col. 1.

Sable, Ronald L. "Libertarians Go After Voters Who Have 'Opted Out'." 20 February 1984, Sec. I, p. 3, col. 5.

Oliver, Myrna. "Libertarians Lose Bid to Get DMV Data for Vote Drive." 28 July 1984, Sec. II, p. 3, col. 3.

Love, Keith. "Libertarian's Bergland Stresses Differences with Traditional Politics." 29 September 1984, Sec. I, p. 14, col. 1.

Boyer, Edward J. "Deukmejian, Bradley Aren't Alone in Race for Governor." 15 May 1986, Sec. I, pp. 3, 37, cols. 1, 1.

Wood, Tracy, and Kenneth Reich. "Anti-Zschau Factions Offered Aid, Libertarian Says." 3 November 1986, Sec. I, pp. 3, 17, cols. 1, 1.

Kennedy, J. Micheal. "Hopeless Presidential Race: Libertarian Plods On — Alone and Unheard." 10 May 1988, Sec. I, p. 12, col. 1.

Morrison, Patt. "Three Minor-Party Hopefuls Aim to Be November Spoilers." 22 October 1988, Sec. I, p. 26, col. 1.

Baker, Ross K. "Women's Splinter Party Would Stymie Friends and Comfort Enemies." 27 July 1989, Sec. II, p. 7, col. 1.

McLain, Melinda. "Third Party Sought by Women to Rescue Those Stuck with 'None of the Above'." 30 July 1989, Sec. V, p. 5, col. 1.

Murphy, Dean. "Third-Party Candidates Trying to Get to First Base with Voters." 22 October 1990, Sec. I, pp. 3, 15, cols. 1, 1.

New York Times

"Libertarian Party in New York City and New York State Elections." 5 July 1972, p. 24, col. 3.

Navaez, Alfonso A. "A Party Is Formed by 'Libertarians'." 6 July 1972, p. 24, col. 3.

"Other Presidential Aspirants Offer Wide Choice." 29 October 1972, Sec. I, p. 46, col. 2.

Charlton, Linda. "Libertarian Candidate Would Burn Federal Check Providing Campaign Aid." 19 April 1976, Sec. I, p. 19, col. 1.

"Libertarian Party Confirms Its Presidential Campaign." 15 June 1976, Sec. L, p. 19, col. 8.

Ronan, Thomas P. "Four Minor-Party Candidates Listed on the Ballot in New York State." 24 October 1976, Sec. I, p. 56, col. 3.

"Coast Lawyer Will Lead 1980 Libertarian Ticket." 9 September 1979, Sec. I, p. 38, col. 5.

Hill, Gladwin. "Libertarians, Foes of Big Government, Nominate Coast Lawyer for President." 10 September 1979, Sec. II, p. 10, col. 1.

Dionne, E. J., Jr. "Libertarian's Candidate for 1980 in New York, Urges Budget Cuts." 26 November 1979, Sec. IV, p. 8, col. 1.

"Dissimilar Political Activists Sue Against Election Campaign Law." 18 December 1979, Sec. II, p. 16, col. 1.

"Mayoral Nominee for Huge Tax Cut." 6 August 1981, Sec. II, p. 3, col. 4.

Turner, Wallace. "Freewheeling Libertarians Bid for Power in Alaska." 25 July 1982, Sec. IV, p. 5, col. 4.

"Minor Parties Join Connecticut Races." 15 September 1982, Sec. II, p. 2, col. 5.

Charles, Eleanor. "A Third Party Runs Full Slate in the Elections." 31 October 1982, Sec. XXlII, p. 19, col. 1.

Lynn, Frank. "Libertarian Party Parley to Pick 1984 Slate." 30 August 1983, Sec. I, p. 14, col. 3.

————. "Libertarians Hear Rallying Cry of 'Freedom'." 2 September 1983, Sec. I, p. 15, col. 1.

Shipp, E. R. "Political Use of Auto Fees Is Challenged in Indiana." 29 May 1984, Sec. I, p. 12, col. 3.

"Conservatives Reject Percy, Back Libertarian for Senate." 22 September 1984, Sec. I, p. 9, col. 1.

Goodman, Walter. "Libertarian Asking Less Government." 28 September 1984, Sec. I, p. 22, col. 3.

"State Ballot Restriction Upheld by High Court." 2 October 1984, Sec.I, p. 22, col. 6.

"Libertarian Party Loses Bid to Be on Connecticut Ballot." 2 November 1984, Sec. II, p. 7, col. 4.

Malcolm, Andrew H. "Two Conservative Extremists Upset Democrats in the Illinois Primary." 20 March 1986, Sec. I, pp. 1, 10, cols. 5, 6.

"16 LaRouche Followers Charged with Securities Fraud in Virginia." 18 February 1987, Sec. I, p. 16, col. 1.

"Russell Means Runs for President as Libertarian." 31 May 1987, Sec. I, p. 11, col. 1.

Turner, Wallace. "Major Libertarian Candidate Opposes Party Stand on Abortion." 4 September 1987, Sec. I, p. 10, col. 1.

————. "Libertarians Pick Ex-Congressman in '88 Bid." 6 September 1987, Sec. I, p. 35, col. 1.

King, Wayne. "Some Republicans Back Foe of Bush." 10 August 1988, Sec. I, p. 14, col. 6.

Rosenthal, Andrew. "Now for a Real Underdog: Ron Paul, Libertarian, for President." 17 October 1988, Sec. I, p. 16, col. 2.

Sullivan, Joseph F. "4 Who Say They Are New Jersey Alternatives." 5 November 1989, Sec I, p. 56, col. 1.

Washington Post

Scott, Austin. "What's Fair is Laissez-Faire, 5-Year-Old Party Contends." 25 September 1976, Sec. A, p. 4.

Bumiller, Elisabeth. "Third Partying." 22 January 1980, Sec. B, pp. 1, 2, cols. 5, 1.

"What About That Third Party?" 29 March 1980, Sec. A, p. 12.

"What About That Third Party (II)?" 30 March 1980, Sec. C, p. 6.

Kotkin, Joel. "Libertarian Party." 31 March 1980, Sec. A, p. 4, col. 1.

"Campaign Notes: Clark on Ballot." 9 May 1980, Sec. A, p. 3, col. 1.

Peterson, Bill. "Libertarian Clark Says He's the Real Alternative." 1 July 1980, Sec. A, p. 2, col. 1.

Reid, T. R. "A Rare-Ideas Night as Two Candidates for President Debate." 4 August 1980, Sec. A, p. 5, col. 1.

McCarthy, Coleman. "Successfully Establishing a Libertarian Presence." 21 September 1980, Sec. K, p. 2, col. 1.

"Libertarian Candidate Gains 50 State Ballots." 26 September 1980, Sec. A, p. 3, col. 5.

Broder, David S. "If You Vote Outside the Mainstream." 29 October 1980, Sec. A, p. 23, col. 1C.

Rosenfeld, Megan. "Candidate Clark—Carrying His Banner High." 2 November 1980, Sec. H, p. 1, col. 1.

Reid, T. R. "Libertarian Party Shifts Sights to State and Local Elections." 11 December 1980, Sec. A, p. 10, col. 2.

Shapiro, Margaret. "Judge Orders Another Name Placed on 5th District Ballot." 17 April 1981, Sec. B, p. 3, col. 1.

_____. "Maryland Told to Add Libertarian to Fifth District Ballot." 7 May 1981, Sec. C, p. 2, col. 2.

Reid, T. R. "Libertarians, with Eye on Voters, Debate Need to Be More Radical." 30 August 1981, Sec. A, p. 8, col. 1.

_____. "Libertarians Elect Alicia Clark as National Chair." 31 August 1981, Sec. A, p. 2, col. 1.

Mathews, Jay. "From Fringe to the Mainstream." 7 November 1981, Sec. A, p. 2, col. 1.

"Political Notes: Libertarian Party Runs Candidates for Governor." 22 August 1982, Sec. A, p. 3b.

Reid, T. R. "Libertarians Pick Candidate for President." 4 September 1983, Sec. A, p. 17, 18.

Balz, Dan. "NOW Calls for Expanded Bill of Rights, New Party." 24 July 1989, Sec. A, p. 6, col. 1.

"NOW's Flirtation with Suicide." 26 July 1989, Sec. B, p. 3, col. 1.

Balz, Dan. "NOW's Talk of New Party Attacked as Self-Defeating." 28 July 1989, Sec. A, p. 5, col. 1.

Broder, David S. "NOW's Fantasy." 30 July 1989, Sec. C, p. 7, col. 1.

Balz, Dan. "Rx for Apathy Among Voters: More Parties?" 23 May 1990, Sec. A, p. 21.

"NOW Panel Will Explore Formation of Third Party." 24 June 1990, Sec. A, p. 6, col. 1.

Knoxville News-Sentinel

Kilpatrick, James J. "Extremism Always Repels, Eventually." 30 July 1983, Sec. A, p. 6.

Brown, Peter. "Third-Party Anderson to Run Again." 17 October 1983, Sec. B, p. 4.

Klein, David. "Would-Be President Plans X-Rated Ads." 28 October 1983, Sec. B, p. 4.

"Ban on Pornographic Political Advertisements Proposed." 14 December 1983, Sec. B, p. 12.

Walters, Robert. "John Anderson's Petty Crusade." 23 January 1984, Sec. B, p. 6.

Tiede, Tom. "Communist Seeks U.S. Presidency." 26 March 1984, Sec.B, p. 4.

"Canine Candidate Howls for Presidential Ballot Slot." 12 May 1984, Sec. A, p. 1.

"Sonia Johnson Seeks Place in TV Debates." 16 August 1984, Sec. A, p. 2.

Lyons, David. "Populists in Music City." 16 August 1984, Sec. B, p. 2.

"Populists Plan Comeback Effort for First Election in 88 Years." 18 August 1984, Sec. A, p. 11.

"600 Gather as Populists Convene After 88 Years." 19 August 1984, Sec. B, p. 7.

Ashford, Philip. "Populist Party Nominee Vows Campaign to 'Educate' Voters." 20 August 1984, Sec. B, p. 3.

Kilpatrick, James J. "The Importance of Political Parties." 1 November 1984, Sec. B, p. 6.

Anyone Can Grow Up to Be President — and Many Try." 6 November 1984, Sec. B, p. 2.
"Stevenson Pledges to Dump Extremists." 20 March 1986, Sec. A, p. 4.
"Cop-Turned-Call Girl Seeks Political Office." 21 March 1986, Sec. A, p. 9.
"LaRouche Followers Linked to Fraud Probe." 30 March 1986, Sec. A, p. 5.
Royko, Mike. "Debt Is No Big Deal for Lyndon's Crowd." 4 April 1986, Sec. A, p. 14.
"Jury Findings Credit LaRouche Firms with Fraud." 13 April 1986, Sec. A, p. 10.
"Private, High-Speed Toll Road Proposed." 16 July 1986, Sec. A, p. 1.

Other Newspapers

Wermiel, Stephen. "Libertarian Ed Clark Has One Main Idea: Cut Big Government; As President, He Would Slash Taxes, End Foreign Aid." *Wall Street Journal*, 26 September 1980, pp. 1ff.
Mintz, John. "Lyndon LaRouche: From Marxist Left to Well-Connected Right." *Washington Post National Weekly Edition*, 25 February 1985, pp. 8–10.
Remmick, David. "Nurturing Unorthodox Views at a 'Think Tank for Yuppies'." *Washington Post National Weekly Edition*, 9 September 1985, pp. 14–15.
"Conservative Blasts 'Idiots' of the World." *Knoxville Journal*, 10 April 1986, Sec. A, p. 7.
Farney, Dennis. "Prohibitionists Try to Avoid Hearing Their Last Hurrah." *Wall Street Journal*, 7 August 1986, Sec. A, pp. 10.
Mintz, John. "LaRouche Asked for Attention and Got It." *Washington Post National Weekly Edition*, 29 September 1986, pp. 12, 13.
Shenon, Philip. "Ten Close Associates of LaRouche Charged with Fraud, Conspiracy." *Chattanooga Times*, 7 October 1986, Sec. A, p. 7.
"LaRouche Says He Is Innocent, Warns Against Arrest." *Chattanooga Times*, 8 October 1986, Sec. A, p. 9.
Mintz, John. "The FBI Is in Strange Company in the LaRouche Case." *Washington Post National Weekly Edition*, 10 November 1986, pp. 31, 32.
"LaRouche Indicted by U.S. for Obstruction of Justice." *Chattanooga Times*, 3 July 1987, Sec. A, pp. 1, 7.
Ferguson, Tom W. "Libertarians Look to Restart the Engine." *Wall Street Journal*, 27 August 1987, Sec. A, p. 22.
Levine, Susan. "At LaRouche Trial, Defense Points Finger at U.S. Intelligence." *Philadelphia Inquirer*, 21 March 1988, Sec. A, p. 5.
King, John. "Judge Denies LaRouche Use of CIA as His Defense." *Philadelphia Inquirer*, 12 April 1988, Sec. A, p. 10.
Seelye, Katherine. "Touting Third Party, McCarthy Enters White House Race." *Philadelphia Inquirer*, 2 June 1988, Sec. A, p. 8.
Kenner, Randy. "Falani Out to Crash 2-Party Presidential Race." *Clarion-Ledger*, 8 August 1988, Sec. A, pp. 1, 8.
Winger, Richard. "Why Voters' Options Seem So Few." *Wall Street Journal*, 2 November 1988, Sec. A, p. 20.
Davis, Bob. "Libertarian Party's Ron Paul Offers Platform Based on Polite Anarchism." *Wall Street Journal*, 4 November 1988, Sec. A, p. 16.
"LaRouche Gets 15-Year Prison Sentence." *Clarion-Ledger*, 28 January 1989, Sec. A, p. 3.
"NOW Talks of Forming Political Party." *Clarion-Ledger*, 23 July 1989, Sec. A, p. 3.
"NOW Delegates Vote to Explore Forming Political Party." *Clarion-Ledger*, 24 July 1989, Sec. A., p. 4.

Shribman, David. "NOW Chief's Crusade for Women's Party Favored by Republican Who Prays It Will Ruin Democrats." *Wall Street Journal*, 5 September 1989, Sec. A, p. 20, col. 1.

"National Organization for Women Delegates Vow to Continue Push for Third Political Party." *Clarion- Ledger*, 1 July 1990, Sec. A, p. 11.

Dionne, E. J., Jr. "Voter Beware: Americans Tired of Politics as Usual." *Commercial Appeal*, 26 May 1991, Sec. B., p. 4.

Brown, Peter A. "Study Says Voters Feel Powerless to Change Things." *Commercial Appeal*, 5 June 1991, Sec. A, p. 2.

Libertarian Party News

"Campaign '82." January/February 1982, pp. 1, 4.

DeLiso, Steve. "Randolph Campaign: All Systems Go." January/February 1982, p. 4.

Sanders, Sylvia, and Ben Olson. "Why You Should Run in '82 as a Candidate." January/February, 1982, pp. 8, 9.

Clark, Alicia G. "From the Chair." March/April 1982, p. 2.

"LP Groups Planning April 15 Tax Protests." March/April 1982, pp. 1, 16.

Clark, Alicia G. "Issue Campaigns Can Keep Libertarians Active in 1983." January/February 1983, p. 2.

"National Committee Sets 1983 Goals." January/February 1983, p. 12.

Richman, Sheldon. "An Indecent Agenda: Rebuilding America Neo-Liberal Style." January/February 1983, p. 17.

"Major Victory in Colorado Ballot Case." January/February 1984, pp. 1, 12.

"NatCom Passes Record Budget, Dues Rise." January/February 1984, pp. 1, 25, 27.

Bergland, David. "Voluntary Compliance 1984 Style." March/April 1984, pp. 12, 13.

"Five Win in Wisconsin Primaries." March/April 1984, pp. 1, 23.

"Presidential Campaign Targets Media." March/April 1984, pp. 1, 3.

Winger, Richard. "Ballot Status Faces Obstacles." March/April 1984, pp. 8, 9.

Bergland, David. "Bergland Committee Report." November 1984/February 1985, pp. 9, 10.

"Libertarian Party Gets Good Press." November 1984/February 1985, pp. 11, 12.

"Marrou Gains State House." November 1984/February 1985, pp. 1, 4–6.

"Membership Form." November 1984/February 1985, p. 29.

"NatCom Adopts Party Goals." November 1984/February 1985, p. 3.

"NatCom Meets in Salt Lake." November 1984/February 1985, pp. 1, 2.

"1984 LP Vote Totals." November 1984/February 1985, pp. 13–14.

"Presidential Results Analyzed." November 1984/February 1985, pp. 7–9.

Rothbard, Murray N. "The Consolidation Election." November 1984/February 1985, pp. 22–23, 32–33.

"1984 LP Financial Results." March/April 1985, pp. 3–5.

Thies, Clifford F. "Montana Voter Survey Shows LP Potential." March/April 1985, p. 6.

"Federal Ballot Bill Pushed." November/December 1985, p. 10.

"Randolph Defects." November/December 1985, pp. 1, 8–9.

"Ballot Access—Separate Fund Fights for the Ticket." Spring 1986, p. 8.

Fritz, Marshall. "A True Political Spectrum." Spring 1986, pp. 6–8.

"Party Membership: What's in It for Me?" Spring 1986, p. 3.

"Why You Should Join the Libertarian Party." Spring 1986, p. 1.

"California—Member Drive Hits New High." March/April 1986, pp. 1, 5.

Harris, Louie. "Institutions Losing Ground." March/April 1986, pp. 1, 3.

Hess, Karl. "Why Me?" March/April 1986, pp. 6–7.
Marrou, Andre. "Alaska Party Is Growing." March/April 1986, pp. 1, 3.
Scholl, Dave. "Running to Rouse, Running to Win." March/April 1986, pp. 8–9.
Sturzenacker, Ken. "Roads: Hot, New LP Arena." March/April 1986, p. 5.
"Ballot Access—Disenfranchising the Franchise." May/June 1986, p. 5.
"Financial Status." May/June 1986, p. 9.
Lisheron, Mark. "Ballot Access Dominates NatCom Meeting." May/June 1986, p. 8.
"State Party Rejuvenation." May/June 1986, p. 9.
Winger, Richard."Court Disservice, Socialist Dissent." May/June 1986, p. 4.
Franzi, Emil. "Loss of Ballot Access." July/August 1986, p. 12.
"Libertarian Candidates." July/August 1986, p. 13.
Peron, Jim. "Zschau's Campaign Shows LP Influence." July/August 1986, p. 16.
Bergland, David. "Your Life, Your Way." Autumn 1986, p. 1.
"The Libertarian Party Platform in Brief." Autumn 1986, pp. 12–13.
"The Libertarian Party Platform in Brief." (Special Research Edition) 1988, pp. 6–7.
Dasbach, Steve. "Campaign '88 Highlights." November/December 1988, pp. 6–7.
Dehn, Jospeh W., III. "LP Membership Figures Reveal Distorted Growth." January/
        February 1989, p. 3.
Blumert, Burton S. "A Special Report on Ballot Access." March/April 1989, p. 1.
Jocab, Paul. "Ballot Access Work and Party Building." March/April 1989, pp. 8–9.
"LP Program to Be Debated in Philadelphia." July/August 1989, pp. 1–3.
Nolan, David F., and Steven Alexander. "Matching Funds—Clashing Opinions:
        Take the Money [or] Just Run." July/August 1989, p. 14.
Langhenry, Randy. "The Eighties: A Time for Growing Up." January 1990, p. 7.
"LP Membership." March 1991, p. 1.
Walter, Dave. "The War: LP Stands on Its Principles." March 1991, p. 2.
"1990 Vote Increase." May 1991, p. 2.
Boddie, Dick. "Boddie Outlines Campaign Goals, Tactics." June 1991, p. 8.
"Campaign Ad." June 1991, pp. 3, 8.
Dunbar, Nick. "Coalition Formed, Dunbar on Steering Committee." June 1991, p. 4.
Marrou, Andre. "Why Don't You Join the Republican Party?" June 1991, p. 8.
Hankey, Jim. "It's Marrou/Lord in 1992." October 1991, pp. 1, 4.
Langhenry, Randy. "Paul Testing GOP Waters." October 1991, pp. 1, 4.

American Libertarian

Holmes, Mike. "Is the Libertarian Party in Trouble? Part I." September 1986, 1:6.
"LP Ballot Status Update." September 1986, 1:2.
"LP Natcom Faced with $ Woes." September 1986, 1:1, 3.
"Randolph Loses in GOP Primary Bid." September 1986, 1:1–2.
Holmes, Mike. "Is the LP in Trouble? Part II." October 1986, 1:6.
"Libertarians Run in Major Party Races." October 1986, 1:1–2.
"LP Fields Candidates in 22 States." October 1986, 1:3.
"LROC Stirs Interest Controversy." October 1986, 1:1–2.

Law Review Articles

Esch, M. D. "Minor Political Parties and Campaign Disclosure Laws." *Harvard Civil
        Rights/Liberties Law Review* 13 (1978): 475–520.

Wisehart, Malcolm B., Jr. "Constitutional Law: Third Political Parties as Second Class Citizens." *University of Florida Law Review* 21 (Spring-Summer 1969): 701–68.

Court Cases

American Party of Texas v. Bob Bullock, Secretary of State of Texas (409 U.S. 803, 34 L.Ed.2d 63 1972).
American Party of Texas v. White ((39 L.Ed.2d 744 1974).
Brown v. Socialist Workers 1974 Campaign Committee (74 L.Ed.2d 250 1983).
Buckley v. Valeo (424 U .S. 1 1976).
Communist Party of Indiana v. Whitcomb (38 L.Ed.2d 635 1974).
Jenness v. Fortson (403 U.S. 431, 438 1971).
Munro v. Socialist Workers Party (107 S.Ct.533 1986).
West Virginia Libertarian Party v. Manchin (270 S.E.2d W. Va. 1980).
Williams v. Rhodes (393 U.S. 23 1968).

Index